# MORE HEART and SOUL

## The Character of Welsh Rugby

# MORE HEART and SOUL

## the character of Welsh rugby

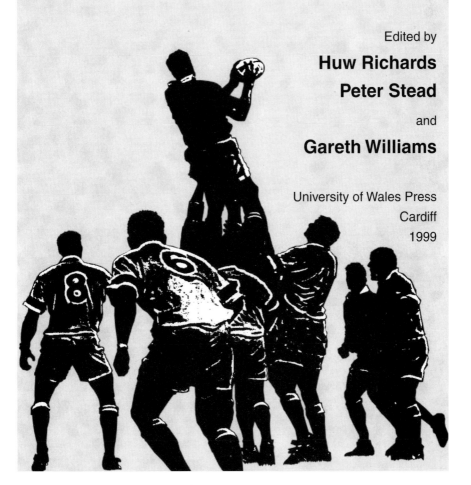

Edited by

**Huw Richards**

**Peter Stead**

and

**Gareth Williams**

University of Wales Press

Cardiff

1999

**British Library Cataloguing-in-Publication Data**
A catalogue record for this book is available from the British Library.

ISBN 0-7083-1557-7

Typeset at University of Wales Press, Cardiff
Printed in England by Bookcraft, Midsomer Norton, Avon

# CONTENTS

# ACKNOWLEDGEMENTS

All photographs by courtesy of the Western Mail and Echo Ltd, except for Lewis Jones (courtesy of Robert Gate), Alun Pask (courtesy of Richard Pask), J. P. R. Williams and Gerald Davies (courtesy of Colorsport), Phil Bennett, Terry Holmes, Chris Wyatt (courtesy of John Harris). The image on the title page and chapter openings is based on a photograph by John Harris.

The editors wish to thank the staff of the University of Wales Press, particularly Susan Jenkins, for their attention to detail and their enthusiasm.

# PREFACE

The publication of *Heart and Soul* in the autumn of 1998 seems to have had an immediately beneficial effect on the character of Welsh rugby. Of course there had to be a sequel. Once again our aim is to celebrate the sheer diversity and the range of personality to be found in Welsh rugby. Individual authors engage with players who helped to shape their sense of the game. In a concluding essay Dai Smith and Gareth Williams update the story they told so memorably in *Fields of Praise*, their classic history of the Welsh Rugby Union which was first published by the University of Wales Press in 1980.

# CONTRIBUTORS

COLIN BABER   Senior research fellow, Cardiff Business School. Author (with D. W. Howell) of the section on Wales in the *Cambridge Economic History of Britain*, vol 1.

HYWEL TEIFI EDWARDS   Research professor, Department of Welsh, University of Wales, Swansea. Broadcaster, literary critic and cultural historian.

ALAN EVANS   A Garw native who taught in England for thirty years. Free-lance journalist and media officer for Cardiff RFC. Author of *Images of Sport: Cardiff RFC*.

ROBERT GATE   Born in Halifax and a historian of rugby league. His publications include *Gone North: Welshmen in Rugby League* (2 vols).

TREVOR HERBERT   A Rhondda man who was formerly a professional brass player with London orchestras. Now professor of music at the Open University. An authority on British music history.

JOHN HOLLYMAN   A native of Barry and now principal lecturer in Spanish at the University of the West of England. Writes on regionalism and nationalism in Spain and is researching the story of Spanish rugby.

SIÂN NICHOLAS   Lecturer in history, University of Wales, Aberystwyth, and the author of *The Echo of War: Home Front Propaganda and the Wartime BBC 1939–45*.

DAVID PARRY-JONES   Television and radio commentator and journalist. Author of many volumes on rugby including most recently a biography of Gwyn Nicholls.

HUW RICHARDS   Free-lance journalist and historian. Rugby correspondent of the *Financial Times*.

DAI SMITH   Head of broadcasting (English Language) at BBC Wales. Author (with Gareth Williams) of *Fields of Praise: The Official History of the Welsh Rugby Union* and more recently of *Wales: A Question of History*.

PETER STEAD   Formerly senior lecturer in history at University of Wales, Swansea, and now a free-lance writer and broadcaster. Author (with David Farmer) of *Ivor Allchurch*.

CHRIS WILLIAMS   Lecturer in history, University of Wales, Cardiff. Author of *Democratic Rhondda* and *Capitalism, Community and Conflict: The South Wales Coalfield 1898–1947*.

GARETH WILLIAMS   Professor of history, University of Wales, Aberystwyth, and associate editor of the *International Journal of the History of Sport*. His most recent book is *Valleys of Song: Music and Society in Wales 1840–1914*.

# AT THE MILLENNIUM

Peter Stead and Huw Richards

The Millennium Stadium was officially opened on Saturday 26 July 1999 when Wales, playing in Cardiff for the first time in over two years, took on South Africa. After ten or so tense minutes there was a slight hold-up during which a section of the crowd in the new North Stand began to sing 'Bread of Heaven – Feed me 'til I want no more'. Other parts of the crowd joined in and soon all 27,000 of us were re-establishing our membership of the newly reconvened choir. Almost everything about the day had hitherto been surreal: a deconstructed Cardiff station, the tropical humidity (as the warm sun gave way to dark clouds we all expected an apocalyptic storm), an Atlantic City boardwalk along the river, computerized turnstiles that were quite obviously designed to malfunction, and an international rugby game that was being played at a building site. Only slowly did we get our bearings and a delayed kick-off helped in that respect. The stadium was clearly magnificent: all the best features of the National Stadium had been retained; mercifully we were near the play, the sight-lines were perfect. What is more we were surrounded by old friends: there were familiar and in some cases much-missed faces in all directions. We had time for firm handshakes and warm embraces before laughing at the Neil Jenkins impersonator and then lustily singing the anthem.

But it was that impromptu rendering of Pantycelyn's hymn that was the first real confirmation that both we and Welsh rugby had come home. There was nothing defiant, audacious or challenging about its rendition: the singing was informal, discreet, cautious, very much *pianissimo*. We were still anxious for there was everything to play for, but already we knew that this was not a Welsh team that would lie down and die. Gently, and almost a little apologetically, we were simply letting the boys know that they were playing in front of their real supporters and that we were there to help them and to carry them through. Not for the first time that afternoon I fought back a tear and experienced a slight shudder. For a moment the atmosphere had been that of a prayer meeting; the spontaneous chorus had owed nothing to an order of service. This was the mood that Evan Roberts had generated in the religious revival of 1904–5, and this was the kind of singing that the congregation at Harlem's Abyssinia Baptist Church engage in every Sunday as they wait for the morning service. As the game restarted and the chorus faded I realized that the Millennium Stadium had experienced a moment of benediction.

The Welsh team that made history that day by beating South Africa was very obviously one that had been skilfully coached and meticulously prepared. It was a game lacking great flourishes, and one that perfectly illustrated and highlighted all the basic ingredients of the modern game. One could easily imagine the Welsh coach saying 'never give or kick the ball away, stand firm in the scrums, time the line-outs to perfection, tackle everything that moves, kick all your penalties and always support the ball-holder trying to punch a hole in the middle of the field'. It was evidently all as simple as that. Rarely can there have been an international match when what was required of the players was so apparent, and certainly it had been many decades since a Welsh team delivered what was asked of it so dutifully.

That June afternoon Welsh supporters were given a text-book demonstration of the elements that had made possible a dramatic recovery in the nation's rugby fortunes. Clearly, Graham Henry was a coach capable of establishing game-plans that boldly defined priorities and minimized error. And, obviously, he was supported by a staff whose sole aim was to convince a group of athletes that they were physically and psychologically strong enough to carry out the coach's instructions. From the kick-off we knew that these were the men for the job. When Craig Quinnell went off in the eighteenth minute we had a moment of doubt, but within minutes it was apparent that Mike Voyle had not missed a single briefing or training session. The whole team looked as if it had been playing together for years. Again we experienced that warm feeling of satisfaction that comes when we know that the selection process is in the hands of somebody who knows more than we do. When Wales is playing badly we all know better than the selectors. But now suddenly control had passed to a man who could conjure up talent not only from amongst the usual suspects but from worlds unknown. With some bemusement and considerable pride we delighted in an Auckland-born full-back, in two flankers born respectively in Rotorua and Sutton Coldfield, neither of whom could stop tackling, and in a Maidstone-born prop whose contribution to almost every aspect of the game was so immense that his discovery could only be attributed to the answering of a nation's collective prayers. Little had we realized that our rugby salvation had been determined by men and women who had left Wales in the years of the depression. The Land of my Fathers was now represented by a team which owed much of its character to a clutch of migrant grandfathers.

More than anything that day it was apparent that Welsh rugby was back in the hands of experts. As ever we were reliant on one man's goal-kicking, but now alongside the flawless technique and total concentration of Neil Jenkins we could place the sheer professionalism of our coaching team, the strength of our front row, the physical commitment of our back row and the impudent choreography of our line-out techniques. Once again there were dimensions to our game, we were aware of riches, we were back in clover. And to cap it all, we obviously knew something about architecture as well. The Millennium Stadium had been built to suit precisely our requirements. Clearly they had consulted musical experts to test the acoustic, and evidently they had learnt from the mistakes made in the rebuilding of Twickenham. At what used to be called 'HQ' the main concerns had appeared to be ensuring enough room for military march pasts around the touch-line and to achieve sufficient height for the stadium to be seen from every part of London. Conversely, the Millennium Stadium had been designed to ensure that the crowd was totally involved in the game.

Not surprisingly, it was the involvement of the crowd that Graham Henry highlighted in his post-match comments. Commentators in general had divided their fulsome praise between the stadium and the team, but for the coach it was both the degree and nature of the support that seemed remarkable. The former Auckland headmaster had come to Wales after a tremendously successful coaching career in his native land, and yet he was to confess that even a country so passionate about its national sport as New Zealand had not prepared him for what he was to encounter in his new job. It had not occurred to him that 'the crowd would regard itself as part of the team' and would react to either defeat or victory in such an immediate and intensely personal way. Naturally, we lifelong supporters had always known that to be the nature of the Welsh dispensation, but even we had to confess that Mr Henry's first year in Welsh rugby had been a highly exceptional one not least because the phenomenal enthusiasm associated with a revival in playing fortunes had been generated in an altogether new cultural and political context. Little did Graham Henry think as he stepped off the plane that within a year he would be the darling of chat-show hosts and the tabloids and that together with a clutch of rock stars, actors, opera singers and television presenters he would be identified as one of the shapers of a national renaissance and one of the arbiters of a new cultural style. No wonder the national rugby coach is fully aware of his public.

There are cynics who suggest that the current emphasis on popular culture and in particular its identification with 'Cool Cymru' is mere media hype. And, indeed, one is aware of the extent to which there are institutional and commercial interests promoting the notion of Welsh identity. It was BBC Wales who let it be known that their news was coming 'from the nation's capital' and who sharpened their presentation of both general and rugby news to such an extent as to suggest that these things were important and therefore required viewing. As never before popular culture and sport were being used to sell newspapers and magazines printed in Wales and a lot else besides. In this volume Dai Smith and Gareth Williams splendidly evoke the incredible reaction to the victory over England at Wembley in April 1999. Fans were subsequently given every chance to sustain the feelings of joy that they had experienced that day. 'Pride of Wales' was the title of the team poster that the *South Wales Echo* immediately made available whilst 'A Day to Remember' was the headline that *The Western Mail* used to advertise commemorative polo shirts and T-shirts, the latter emblazoned 'Return of the Dragon', and the 'Glory Day' video was selling like hot cakes. There were reports that the Sports Council for Wales was capitalizing on the victory as it launched new blueprints of young Welsh athletes, while the *Evening Post* thought it quite remarkable that the lord mayor of Swansea was to give a reception at the Guildhall to honour the five Swansea players who had been in the team at Wembley. Later it emerged that Scott Gibbs had been a vital member of the management team that had secured a £20 million Cable & Wireless call centre for Swansea. Meanwhile, the *Echo* launched a campaign to ensure that Neil Jenkins's remarkable efforts did not go unrewarded at Buckingham Palace and No. 10: the public was invited to write in supporting the 'Give Jenkins a Gong' appeal.

There is no doubt that the support of which Graham Henry had become so aware was institutionally and commercially mediated, but it was nevertheless genuine, spontaneous and freshly minted. By the time of Wembley we were aware of an enormous craving for success; rarely can a victory have been so willed. The vastly improved performance against South Africa in the same stadium the previous November and then the totally surprising and exhilarating victory in the thrilling game in Paris in March had not only whetted the appetite but effectively suppressed elements of despair. The joy of April 1999 was in part a purging of the guilt of all those who had often declared that 'Welsh rugby is finished' and those who in their hearts had felt that it was only Neil Jenkins and Scott Gibbs who were saving the nation from total anonymity. As a people we are easily daunted, and daunted most of us had been. Above all else we wanted to be good at rugby, and once we sensed elements of self-belief amongst the management and the team we wanted victories. And what could be more timely and appropriate than a victory over an over-confident England to mark the end of the Wembley exile?

Many things combined to make Wembley special that day but that craving for success was but one strand in a new cultural dispensation that was now defining Wales. Outsiders had mistakenly thought that the narrowness of the devolution vote and the low turnout in the Assembly elections were signs of a lack of interest in matters Welsh. The establishment of a National Assembly for Wales in 1999 was truly a moment of enormous historic significance, but it is possible to exaggerate the purely political nature of devolution as well as the role of politicians in the life of the nation. Of far more significance is the cultural devolution that has enabled many talented Welsh men and women to think of Wales, and in particular Cardiff, as providing the arena in which they want to develop their careers. Suddenly we were aware of a new generation of musicians, actors, film directors, writers, academics and even entrepreneurs who were filling out our sense of Wales: they were fulfilling their own lives and also ours. Every culture has its iconic figures but what was new in Wales was the emphasis on quality. The nation that had so desperately wanted to win at Wembley also craves a Hollywood Oscar, the Nobel Prize for Literature, the Cardiff Singer of the World award, BAFTA trophies and any other prize that betokens truly international achievement. The nation that proudly rejoiced in the opening of its new Millennium Stadium in June 1999 was one which was establishing excellence as the yardstick of all its collective efforts.

Yet, while the international season was so encouraging, the same could not be said of the club scene in 1998–9. It is doomed to be remembered as the season of the great schism, when Swansea and Cardiff foresook the Welsh domestic game to play friendly matches against teams from the English Premiership amid much undignified name-calling on both sides. As the secessionists, the remaining topflight clubs and the WRU sniped at each other the temptation to call a plague on all their houses was irresistible.

That there was a settlement of sorts for the 1999–2000 season owed much to the insistence of Graham Henry, cashing in much of the political credit accumulated by his revival of the national squad. Henry is to be thanked for that, as for much else, but there is still much to be uneasy about. One need not feel nostalgia for an age when clubs knew fixtures five years ahead – dampening the ambitious and cushioning the moribund – to worry that the structures of the domestic game, let alone specific fixtures, are habitually in doubt only weeks before seasons begin. The 1999–2000 season will, in any case, have a provisional feel, and not only because of the World Cup. The settlement of the schism was predicated on the creation of a British League in 2000–1. Provided that it is fully linked to the national structures by promotion and relegation and does not become a self-perpetuating élite, the case for a British League remains overwhelming. Its major problem is that it is dependent on the support of the English clubs, modern rugby's monsters of greed and inflated self-regard. Their recent accomplishments include the spectacle of Bristol, fearing that it would not be good enough to win promotion on the field, buying itself an insurance scheme by purchasing London Scottish. It is occasionally said of teams that they have bought success, but other sports still generally require them to win matches to do so. This was followed by the folding of London Scottish and Richmond into London Irish. The reaction of the English Premiership clubs to the loss at top level of two identities with a combined history of 259 years was that this was excellent news as it facilitated their restructuring. The restructuring was, incidentally, a reversal of the ill-advised expansion the clubs insisted on only a season ago.

That clubs would crash was inevitable, the conseqence of supposedly shrewd businessmen who came charging into the game in the mid-1990s assuming that the mere act of going professional would make it attractive to a wider public. Thirty seconds contemplation of how rugby league has been trying to make this dream reality for more than a hundred years might have shown them the flaw in this argument. Such criticism will automatically attract the label of 'whingeing Celt' from some quarters. Old enmities certainly exist, but an alien from Alpha Centauri who had found himself by some malign cosmic fluke embroiled in British rugby from 1995 onwards might have ended up regarding the behaviour of some of the English clubs and the Rugby Union with fear and loathing.

It is a mark of the desperation which had overtaken Swansea, whose reluctance to secede was in marked contrast to Cardiff's apparent disinterest in Wales, that it should have thrown in its lot with the English game. The benefits from the friendlies were uncertain after the initial surge of excitement and public interest. Swansea played well enough, particularly in a memorable SWALEC Cup Final display, to induce serious regret that the club was only in contention for this one trophy, as it must have been a serious candidate for European honours. Cardiff's miserable collapse in their most important match of the season, the semi-final against Llanelli at Bridgend, yet again cast doubt on the policy of development by cheque-book. The tendency to hoover up talent would have been destabilizing enough even if it could be argued that playing for Cardiff improved players for the national team. Instead the Arms Park has become club rugby's Moloch, devouring its annual tribute of youthful promise.

The prodigals are unlikely to get a friendly welcome on their return. The 1998–9 season was one where Welsh clubs forgot that point-scoring is only profitable as an on-field activity. Neath traded insults with Cardiff. Scott Gibbs, in the season when public affection finally caught up with his status as a player, offered an unwelcome reminder of reasons for that lag by his ungraciously patronizing 'men against boys' comments after the SWALEC Cup Final. Pontypridd were unhappy with just about everything. Ebbw Vale, to be fair, were entitled to feel ill-used when the post-schism settlement handed their European Cup place to a Cardiff team that had done nothing to merit it. Given that, as we write in July, little else is in place for 1999–2000, would it not have made sense to settle the issue through a play-off? If Cardiff are as greatly superior to Ebbw Vale as is alleged – on the basis of their semi-final form one might hesitate to back them against Pyle – then the play-off would have been no obstacle.

At least the competition to which Swansea and Cardiff return should be stronger than the one they left, since both the financial lunacy of the English clubs and Graham Henry's promptings have contributed to a reverse migration across the Severn Bridge. How competitive it will be is unclear. The WRU handled the 'Super Club' issue with the incoherence we have come to expect. Should the British League not come to pass, it will have to think again. A competition in which the top four clubs are funded by the Union, but others are not, will hardly be tenable. Insistence on having precisely four left the alternatives either of excluding one of the clubs who have proved themselves superior to the rest over recent years or of no representation from Monmouthshire. The 'Super Club' concept is an attempt to legislate the world into the shape the marketing men think it should have. One of the pleasures of sport is that it refuses to conform to their logic – that Glamorgan's cricketers win county championships, that Wales has beaten England more times than vice versa at rugby, that the Neath club continues to regenerate when all seems lost, that clubs like Caerphilly and Dunvant refuse to respect the boundaries of magic circles.

In spite of the absence of Swansea and Cardiff, and a bizarrely structured season, there were some things to be pleased about. Llanelli recovered from European misadventures, Neath managed yet another Lazarus act and there were welcome signs of a Gwent revival – Newport made something of the top flight reprieve offered by the secession, Pontypool challenged for promotion and Ebbw Vale, in spite of financial troubles, stayed in the top half of the league. Pontypridd fell from their recent high standards and clearly feel that the WRU is out to get them. They can, however, take comfort in the success of Dunvant, another club with every reason for paranoia. But if the WRU has been out to get Dunvant – and its handling of league restructuring in recent seasons lends itself to this theory – it has been as successful in this as in just about every other enterprise of late. Dunvant once again bounced out of the Second, with a homegrown squad playing freeflowing rugby. Their success sits alongside that of Caerphilly. When Caerphilly was promoted, one club was heard to protest that no league with Caerphilly in it could possibly be good enough. Rugby clubs have still to learn one of the rules of professionalism – that only amateurs get to choose their own fixtures. Professionals have to play the teams who have qualified to play at their level. Caerphilly showed themselves good enough not only by the standards of the Welsh League, where they finished a creditable fifth, but by the rather more demanding ones of European competition, winning two matches against French clubs and qualifying for the quarter-final of the European Shield.

If modern sport were truly concerned with excellence, clubs like Dunvant and Caerphilly, like Castleford in rugby league and Wimbledon in football, would be admired for making the best of their limited resources. Instead, by some demented logic, they are treated as an embarassment, as obstacles to progress, depriving alleged betters of top-flight status and forcing the élite into matches that are less financially profitable than is desirable. Marketability is deemed more important than merit. Clearly, however, Welsh rugby needs more clubs like Dunvant and Caerphilly who make the most of limited resources. It also needs as a matter of urgency a policy and an attitude that show that the Welsh Rugby Union is dealing openly, honestly, fairly and sympathetically with clubs at all levels.

Meanwhile in the summer of 1999 it was apparent that everything was militating in favour of 'Super Clubs'. Geography, history, ground capacity, commercial structures and cash were predicating the emergence of Newport, Cardiff, Swansea and Llanelli as 'flagship clubs' with realistic aspirations. But at a time when Manchester United could withdraw from the FA Cup, thereby denying the Swans, Cardiff City and others the prospect of a lucrative tie, there is obviously a need for us all to contemplate the implications of planned super clubs. If the heart and soul of Welsh rugby is to be preserved, we must certainly apply logic at the top but as far as the rank and file are concerned what is required is loyalty, empathy and, perhaps, above all, imagination.

# JACK AND BLEDDYN

Alan Evans

It could be any one of the last thirty or forty winters but it just happens to be that of 1998–9. One Saturday afternoon, they sit together in the front row of the committee box of the Arms Park with mixed feelings, pleased that their beloved Cardiff club is playing against the English clubs just as they had done when they themselves were in their prime, but also worrying as to where the so-called rebellion within Welsh rugby might end. The next Saturday they have decamped to London and are tucked away at the back of the spacious Wembley press box, the one browsing through the glossy match programme but hidden behind the smoke of the ever-present cigar, the other reflecting, if only momentarily, on the pre-match interview with Sky TV that had been preambled with the young researcher's request not only to spell his name but also to explain exactly what his claim to fame was in the great game. Soon they would be flying off to Dublin, this time as the guests of Karl Mullen their old Lions' skipper and the Irish Rugby Football Union: another international and another seat in a committee box, sandwiched between an appetizing lunch and a sumptuous dinner. In between they would think nothing of a drive up the valley into the heart of Ponty n' Pop country on a dark, damp November night for a grassy bank view of the magic of the cup as Cilfynydd anticipated their moment of glory against the city slickers of Cardiff. And wherever they went and whenever they were seen they were, quite simply, Jack and Bleddyn.

Fifty years ago, Jack Matthews and Bleddyn Williams seemed as inseparable on the rugby fields of the world as they are today as friends in life in general. Then they were regarded as the perfect centre combination by which all others were judged; now they are universally accepted as comrades with a built-in mutual support mechanism to whom friends and confidants, administrators and admirers from near and far can turn for the most sensible of advice or just an hour or so of pleasant conversation and reminiscence. They are welcome wherever they go in the world of rugby, partly because of what they achieved as players in their heyday, partly because of what they contributed to the game in their different ways in the years that followed, and partly because of what their friendship is seen to represent in these days of shifting values.

Jack Matthews arrived on the stage of senior rugby first, in 1939, and Bleddyn Williams lasted three years longer as a player, until 1955, but in the years that their careers overlapped every team that they played for, whether Cardiff, the Barbarians, Wales, the British Lions or the many charity XVs that they never hesitated to support long into the twilight of their days, benefited from their complementary skills and unfailing commitment. Born within twenty miles and three years of one another, their paths did not cross for the best part of two decades. Jack received his early education at the Oldcastle Primary School in Bridgend before proceeding to the local County School for Boys where he was the star player on the Saturday-morning pitches of Glamorgan and west Wales and the head prefect in the weekday corridors of learning. By 1934 he had made his first appearance at Cardiff Arms Park, an automatic choice for the Bridgend Schools district side that beat Newport and took the Dewar Shield. Meanwhile, Bleddyn was being brought up with his seven brothers and four sisters in Taff's Well and becoming equally prominent in schools' rugby so that by March 1937, at the tender age of fourteen years and three weeks, he was selected for the Wales Schools team that beat England 29–0 at Gloucester. That his position was full-back never ceases to amaze him, as he had never played there before, had been good enough as a schoolboy centre to see the wings outside him grab a handful of tries in the final trial the previous week, and was never to play at full-back again. Six months later he was heading north to Rydal School, on the recommendation of Wilfred Wooller, for the next stage of his secondary education.

Both Bleddyn and Jack remain hazy about when they first met or, indeed, when they first played with or against each other. Wooller, though, came into contact with both of them and there are parallels in the early careers of all three. In January 1933 the precocious Wooller had gone straight from Rydal School to a Welsh final trial in Swansea and from there a fortnight later into the first Wales XV to win at Twickenham. The 18-year-old Jack Matthews almost repeated the feat in 1939 as he, too, went from school to a trial at Swansea – where his opposite number was the giant Wilf. But Jack's rise to the top was halted as he failed to get into the national team and was to wait eight years for his first cap. Instead, he dipped his toes into senior club rugby not with Cardiff but with a couple of games for Bridgend and then

Aberavon and Neath. As luck would have it, no sooner had he gone to the Gnoll than Cardiff turned up for a game and Jack spent the afternoon tackling Wooller – 'low and hard' as he proudly recalls – in a stalemate 0–0 draw.

The outbreak of war in September 1939 effectively put an end to Wilfred Wooller's rugby career, but not before Jack Matthews had played alongside him for Wales in a Red Cross international against England at Gloucester in April 1940. Jack admired his partner's long stride and phenomenal kicks ahead, which he was instructed to chase! chase! chase! By then, he was already a medical student who would spend the war years at home. A meeting with Douglas Bader had strengthened Jack's appetite for action as a fighter pilot. He had joined up in Penarth at the earliest opportunity, but his medical ambitions decreed that he would be sent back from his RAF camp in Oxfordshire to Cardiff and nearly six years of study at the Welsh School of Medicine. The only action he saw was on the rugby field as he captained the Meds against local teams including a Cardiff XV in an unofficial match at the Arms Park. He was soon to play there again and with Bleddyn Williams for the first time.

Bleddyn had also impressed Wooller in the early months of war. Still only sixteen, he had played with Wooller for a Cardiff team at Chepstow and had shown 'all the power and strength of a future international but not yet the speed'. Years later, whilst rather quirkily likening him to 'the chubby consistency of a teddy bear', Wooller extolled Bleddyn's copy-book, orthodox style, his superbly controlled side-step and his uncanny knack of timing. He concluded, 'If I were forced to choose one player from the long line of centres who made the ball do the maximum of attacking work by simply giving a pass from the right position at the right moment, I would certainly choose Bleddyn Williams as my prototype'. And ideally at the end of the pass would be Jack Matthews and his 'torpedo projection', who Wooller believed was at his most effective when the ball was put in front of him and he could run into it at top speed and crash his way past any defence.

Three years after Jack had gone back to Cardiff to pursue his medical studies, Bleddyn left Rydal and immediately joined the RAF. In the fifteen months before he was sent overseas on active service he resumed his contacts with the Cardiff club. He had already played four times for

Cardiff Athletic when still at school but now he found himself in the first team and in a series of other wartime scratch sides. Whatever the uncertainty of their first meeting, there is no doubt that Jack Matthews and Bleddyn Williams appeared in the same East Wales XV that took on the British Army at Cardiff Arms Park on 9 January 1943. Bleddyn was at fly-half and the pack included such stalwarts as Stan Bowes, W. E. N. Davies (who really was known as 'Wendy'), Bill Tamplin and Eddie Watkins. Though not together in the centre, a start had been made on the road towards their great days ahead.

By 1945 Bleddyn was already a famous name in rugby, with the closing years of war littered with games for Wales in the Services Internationals, guest appearances for clubs like Rosslyn Park and the Barbarians, and deadly serious matches for the RAF against the Army, the French Services, the Scottish Services and just about anyone else who could raise a team. Then came peace and, although Bleddyn saw out his service days at St Athan in the Vale of Glamorgan and the newly qualified Dr Jack was finally allowed to join the RAMC and go off to camp in Crookham and the occasional games for Hampshire, they did not begin their mid-field partnership in the Cardiff team until the season of 1945–6. Both agree that their friendship blossomed over many years, though Bleddyn has no doubts that they were kindred spirits from that first full season with Cardiff. For him, it was something that overflowed from his admiration for Matthews the skipper and mid-field dynamo. As Bleddyn recalls, 'Attack! That was the operative word. That was the only instruction Dr Jack gave his teams in 1945–6. You had to attack to win in rugby, and we found every man in our team imbued with the attacking spirit.'

That spirit took the club to seventeen straight wins, before the renowned New Zealand Kiwis, in the middle of a 33-match post-war tour of Europe that earned them admirers wherever they went, scraped past them 3–0 in front of a capacity crowd on Boxing Day 1945. The sport-starved fans of south Wales were flocking to both Swansea and Cardiff for the representative games that came thick and fast. Jack and Bleddyn had already made their first appearance together in Welsh colours in the Victory International against France. Jack had been captain that day, and when his niggling rib injury forced him to drop out of the next Welsh game against the Kiwis in January it was Bleddyn who assumed the captaincy. They were to partner each other in three more Victory Internationals in the spring of 1946 and the effectiveness of their combined play was already very apparent.

From the outset they had decided to play as right and left centres, rather than inside and out. Much as they had admired the play of the New Zealand mid-field, with Fred Allen at first five-eighth, Proctor or Kearney at second five-eighth or inside centre, and the impressive Johnny Smith at centre – which meant he was permanently on the outside – Jack and Bleddyn felt that their destiny lay with the more traditional left and right formations. They realized that Bleddyn was a left-footed kicker, and as the years went by and the fame of his passing and jinking grew and grew the lethal nature of his little chip kicks tended to be taken for granted, and that Jack's equally overlooked speed off the mark honed by his background as a track sprinter made him just as likely to break the defence out wide as next to the fly-half, and that between them they would prefer to keep their options open, allowing the sheer variety of their play to test the tightest of opposition defences. So Jack was always right centre and Bleddyn always left.

For Cardiff and for the Matthews–Williams duo 1945–6 had been a roller-coaster of a season. The club had scored 149 tries in forty matches, with Jack and Bleddyn getting forty-two between them and their two regular wings another forty-seven. Marshalled by the two Billys, Cleaver and Darch, at half-back the mid-field had purred along in a manner not seen for generations. Cardiff were box-office wherever they went, with the kick-off delayed at Rodney Parade to allow the queueing Newport throng to pack the ground, and a record crowd at Coundon Road to see the club smash Coventry's five-year unbeaten home record. And off the field the club had a nucleus of officials and players who had stayed in contact through the long years of war. It was in this atmosphere of stability and success that great friendships were born and further cemented by the gruelling tours then and later to France. Chastened by their recent hardships and personal losses, the young players were quick to realize how fortunate they were still to be part of a sporting culture that allowed them to travel freely and play rugby. No one quibbled over an itinerary in the last days of 1945 that had them travelling by train to Bristol in the early afternoon of Saturday, 29 December, playing a game there before continuing by train again to Paddington and then by boat train from Victoria to Paris and a further day's rail travel to arrive in Nantes in the early hours of Monday morning for a game against Stade Nantais later that afternoon. The reception during the final hours of that New Year's Eve would allow Jack Matthews to give his captain's thanks for the no doubt generous hospitality received before another journey due south as 1946 dawned and another game against US Cognacaise – and another banquet and speech. The return journey would be just as arduous before the weary party arrived back in Cardiff late in the evening of Thursday, 3 January, in readiness for their next game at Leicester thirty-six hours later.

It was rugby of another age, but one of which Jack and Bleddyn and the rest of the team felt privileged to be part. To their great credit, the Cardiff officials of the time left no one in doubt of their responsibilities: 'Each one of us is a member of the Cardiff Club; this is an honour in itself' was the printed reminder to every player and committeeman before they set off. It continued, 'Each one of us represents the Club . . . We are confident that the name and traditions of the Cardiff Club will be enhanced on this tour . . . We shall be honoured guests in France and our French Allies in common with Great Britain have suffered much during the War . . . The manner in which we play and conduct ourselves on the soil of France can be a token of our Club's contribution to that supreme camaraderie between sportsmen of the two nations.' Subsequent trips across the channel were to involve ambitious and elaborate air expeditions, with Bleddyn on one memorable occasion in the flight deck assisting an errant French navigator as he mistook Arromanches for Cherbourg, whilst further back Dr Jack administered in his own inimitable way to the first-time fliers as they swore that they would never leave *terra firma* again. What remained constant was the expectation of high standards whilst allowing for just a little bit of fun, and what grew stronger was the comradeship and trust amongst what today would be called a first-team squad and what was then a hardly changing group of amateur sportsmen.

When the Wales team did eventually play its first official post-war international against England in January 1947, Haydn Tanner was scrum-half and captain and his Cardiff clubmates Cleaver, Williams and Matthews formed the mid-field triangle. The match programme notes urged the forwards to 'heel and leave the rest to the backs'! Mistakenly, perhaps, Bleddyn was flirting with a return to the fly-half position in which he had been so successful at Rydal, and the national selectors duly switched Billy Cleaver to team up with Jack in the centre. All three were winning their first caps, but Bleddyn pulled a thigh muscle in the opening minutes and, in those days before replacements, was handicapped throughout the match. Wales lost and for the next match, against Scotland at Murrayfield, Bleddyn was moved back to centre and Jack was dropped. They were not to start their international partnership for another two years. By then they were playing in the warm afterglow of the Cardiff club's greatest modern season.

Cardiff had swept all before them in 1947–8 with thirty-nine wins in forty-one matches and two unlikely away defeats at Pontypool and Penarth. The Barbarians and the touring Australians had been beaten and Newport went down four times in their battles with the old enemy, but the season is remembered more than anything for Bleddyn's four tries in the final match against Gloucester, giving him a record forty-one in thirty-one games. Inevitably, Jack was at his side as he rounded off a great season in front of 20,000 on a Wednesday evening at the Arms Park. The following year the club lost only three games in forty-five, and so it was hardly surprising that Cardiff players formed the nucleus of Welsh XVs at the time, with no fewer than eleven being capped in 1948. Jack was one of them but was disappointed to be picked for three games on the wing, a selection that baffled Bleddyn who regarded his great friend as an out-and-out centre – 'Jack never let Wales down on the wing but he was not at ease in the position because his style was never suited to the flank.'

One way or another, their efforts to establish a consistent pairing on the international stage were frustrated. They did finally appear together in three championship matches in 1949, before Bleddyn missed the final game against France in circumstances that say much for the integrity and values that he and others took for granted. He had made a long-standing promise to appear in a charity match on the Sunday before the game in Paris and, whatever the risks of injury before the big game, a promise was a promise. The fates conspired against him in that he strained a muscle in the final moments of the charity game and was forced to pull out of the international. So the Matthews–Williams international roadshow was halted and did not appear for another fifteen months, and when it did it was 12,000 miles away with the 1950 Lions in New Zealand.

The only doubt about whether they would both go with the Lions centred around Bleddyn's fitness, for he had missed most of that season with a serious knee ligament injury. While Jack was helping Wales complete a Grand Slam over France in Cardiff, Bleddyn proved his match fitness in a club game at Bath the same day and was, as they say, on the boat. The long sea voyage to New Zealand brought them even closer together as the two of them shared a cabin with the English flanker Vic Roberts, another great friend over the decades since and who is now a vice-president of the Barbarians. Such tours, lasting as they did over six months, saw many players become friends for life and that of 1950 was no exception with differing combinations billeted together at the numerous stopovers. As it happens, Bleddyn and Jack rarely roomed together on the trip once they were off the *SS Ceramic*, but for the first time away from the club environment they played together regularly on the big stage.

With the tour captain Karl Mullen struggling with fitness and form, Bleddyn led the Lions seven times, including three Tests, and Jack also captained them three times. More significantly, their centre combination took the field in twelve games and impressed all who saw them. There were, as on any tour, moments of controversy and some bordering on pantomime. Bleddyn laughs now, as he almost did then, when recalling a bizarre moment in the mid-week match at Palmerston North against a combined team. By his own admission the Lions were struggling and for the captain of the day the prospects of victory did not look promising when Billy Cleaver retrieved a dead ball for a drop-out, and whilst Bleddyn and the Lions waited on the 25 for the restart, the ball thrown to them was intercepted by an opposing player who galloped over unopposed and claimed a try. In the best traditions of local referees, Mr L. K. Murray duly awarded the score and at 8–3 down the Lions faced defeat. These days such a home-town decision would provoke all manner of protestations if not tantrums. For Bleddyn and the Lions it was simply a case of shrugging their shoulders and getting on with it. And not being afraid to make tough decisions he soon moved himself to fly-half at the expense of Ivor Preece, who was having the unhappiest of games, and an injury-time try by Roy John snatched victory.

The great disappointment of the tour was the failure to win the Fourth Test against the All Blacks. Lewis Jones's break from the shadow of his own posts and Ken Jones's try at the other end is well documented, but it all resulted from a missed call by Bleddyn and Jack. As he now readily admits, Bleddyn fancied his chances against his opposite number Roy Roper, and as the Lions' scrummage formed on their own line, Bleddyn and Jack decided to go for the most daring of outside breaks. Instead, as Jack Kyle moved the ball towards them Lewis Jones sliced through at an angle and set up one of the great tries in Test history. Victory, though, eluded them despite two scintillating breaks by Bleddyn in the dying moments.

When talking about their playing days now, it is clear that people were and are more important to Jack and Bleddyn than mere matches. Ask them about the greatest fly-half they encountered and they both unhesitatingly nominate Ireland's Jack Kyle because he was deceptively fast over ten yards, a faultless handler and a mature link who controlled the game. Both, of course, retain the deepest affection and admiration for Cliff Morgan who enjoyed so many great days with them at Cardiff after the ropiest of debuts at Cambridge for which Jack gave him a rollicking and 'Cliffie thanked us for teaching him more in one afternoon than he'd learnt in his entire career up to then!' Cliff runs Kyle close as their favourite fly-half, but after them it is interesting that Jack speaks highly of Ivor Preece of Coventry, another 1950 Lion and a typically dependable English fly-half, whilst Bleddyn talks effusively of W. T. H. Davies, a darting, unpredictable product of the west Wales fly-half factory whom he played with and against in war-time services' rugby.

If pressed to talk about a special club game they will always relive the day that Cardiff took on the Springboks at the Arms Park in October 1951. It was a match that Jack, even though he was club captain again that season, almost missed. Both were recovering from injuries and there was much drama on the Monday before the game when word leaked out to the players that their captain might not be selected. In went Bleddyn, Cliff Morgan and Rex Willis to the committee room with the clear message that if Jack did not play then neither did they. The club's selectors relented and Jack and Bleddyn had particular cause to relish the game ahead. Their opposite numbers were Tjol Lategan and Ryk van Schoor, two Springboks who were popularly regarded as their mirror-image. Lategan was the dazzling runner and van Schoor the crash tackler, but they met their match at the Arms Park as Jack had a try disallowed and Bleddyn scored from a brilliant effort made for him by Cliff Morgan and Jack and which he finished off with a spectacular dive over the covering van Schoor. To this day they believe Cardiff threw away the game with inaccurate kicking and an over-cautious approach as a try by Chum Ochse four minutes from the end was the vital score in the desperately close 9–11 defeat.

But friends for life were made even in high profile games such as those. When Jack took a break in South Africa early in 1999, two of his hosts were Lategan and van Schoor and, almost inevitably, he also found himself as a guest at a dinner given by the South African Rugby Football Union. Look through the guest lists of rugby dinners around the world over the decades and sooner or later the names of J. Matthews and B. L. Williams will feature, and look further down the lists and the names of their contemporaries – Willis and Morgan, O'Brien and Mullen, Steele-Bodger and Roberts – will be there, too, and more often than not seated close by. Their conversation will be rich in reminiscence and realistic in diagnosis of the current strengths and weakness of the game.

For Jack and Bleddyn, though, the most vivid tales still revolve around their exploits for Cardiff. Meet them as a pair and ask them to recall their favourite Cardiff story and sooner or later Bleddyn, with a wicked glint in his eye, will talk of the day he was walking into The Reddings, Moseley, long after he had retired and was covering a game for *The People*. A complete stranger came up to him and asked if he remembered *that* try at the ground twenty-five years before. 'Before he had finished, I knew exactly what he was talking about', says Bleddyn, and each of them in turn takes the listener step-by-step through an elaborate scissor move they tried twice in the first half and each time Jack, taking the pass from Bleddyn, was flattened. 'But we fooled them the third time', says Jack. The third time was the dummy scissors and this time not two but three tacklers were waiting for him. Down he went in a heap and, as he got up, he protested to his puzzled demolition trio that he did not have the ball. Instead, Bleddyn, who had not parted with it as the scissors was offered, was touching down under the distant posts. 'You see,' says Bleddyn, 'Jack was my fall-guy.'

Four months later, Jack Matthews retired from regular rugby, though he still turned out from time to time for various invitation and charity teams and even the Barbarians. In his parting message to the Cardiff faithful he wrote, 'This good old rugby game teaches a lot: it teaches us to play the game under all manner of conditions and circumstances and be a good loser as well as a good winner. The memories will remain, real living memories; and the friendships cemented will endure for a long time.' When Bleddyn Williams followed Jack into retirement at the end of the 1954–5 season, he had long since reached a similar conclusion. 'Rugby football is a great game to play,' he wrote, 'and I treasure every moment of it and I value pricelessly the friendships I have made.'

If we didn't believe them at the time, we certainly do now: the game is a game, but friendship is for life.

# LEWIS JONES

## Robert Gate

If, around 1897, anyone in the English or Welsh Rugby Union establishments had shown the courage of their convictions, or even the merest scrap of decency, things would have been quite different. Wales would have followed the path of the Northern Unionists, probably drawing the clubs of the West Country along with them and the resultant domino effect may well have marginalized English rugby union in exactly the way that rugby league would be marginalized in the succeeding century. That none of this happened was the result of the fudge over the infamous 'Gould Affair'. Arthur Gould, captain of Newport and Wales, the Welsh nation's greatest centre and contemporary sporting icon, had been presented with the deeds of his house as a testimonial. The Welsh Rugby Union backed the testimonial and, for its troubles, was ostracized by the International Board which regarded the testimonial as an act of professionalism. To the Victorian rugby union establishment this was a grave matter, although not grave enough for principles to be upheld.

Scotland and Ireland refused to play Wales in 1897 and the Rugby Football Union bellowed loud and long about the heinous act perpetrated by the Welsh. When it came to the crunch, however, the estimable Gould simply retired from playing, thus enabling the RFU to forget that it had driven a coach and horses through all its own laws on professionalism. For their part, the Welsh authorities fell back into the embraces of the men who a little earlier would have been prepared to cast them adrift. Result: a defeat for Principles by Expediency. There were beneficial side-effects, of course. The north of England got to love and cherish a lot of entrancing Welshmen upon whom they might never have clapped eyes had the decent thing been done back in 1897 for, without such expediency, rugby league would not have become a mecca for the many disaffected, penurious, curious or simply sportingly ambitious Welsh rugby players, who would enrich themselves and that alien northern game. Certainly, rugby league would have been deprived of the joy of nurturing arguably the most devastating attacking back Wales has ever produced – Lewis Jones, the archetypal 'golden boy'.

Lewis Jones was, however, just one in a long and distinguished series of golden boys lured to rugby league in the years since the Northern Union cocked its snook at the RFU in 1895. Yet he may well have been the best of the lot, even allowing for such competition as William 'Buller' Stadden, Owen Badger and the James brothers (the 'curly-haired marmosets') from the Victorian era, Dickie Ralph, W. T. H. Davies, Keith Jarrett, Terry Price, David Watkins and Jonathan Davies, to mention but a few. Irrespective of whether Lewis Jones was the greatest of them all, there is no doubt that he was touched with genius. He had the power to beguile, to mesmerize, to put bums on seats and, conversely, to draw criticism whenever his virtuosity failed to reach the towering heights expected of him. Genius can be a charm and a curse, as Jones would learn in both codes of rugby.

Rugby union was Benjamin Lewis Jones's stage until he was twenty-one, and the blinding light of his talent illuminated Welsh rugby all too briefly. Blessed were those who saw him and retain the memory. He was born in Gorseinon near Swansea on 11 April 1931 and was a schoolboy prodigy. His preferred sport was soccer, but while at Gowerton Grammar School he won Welsh caps at both cricket and rugby union. The latter cap, as full-back, was awarded against France in 1947–8 when his fly-half and captain was Carwyn James. From the local club at Gorseinon, he graduated to first-class rugby at Neath before being called up for the Royal Navy. He won his first full caps for Wales whilst playing with Devonport Services and ended his union career with Llanelli. Lewis was only eighteen when he earned his first cap against England at Twickenham on 21 January 1950. There was a record crowd of 75,000 in the ground that day and thousands were locked out, yet Jones was not overawed by the occasion. Playing at full-back, he was the star of the game, audaciously creating the first Welsh try with a bewildering run from the back and then sealing the match with a conversion and a penalty. He was chaired from the field as Wales won 11–5, their first victory at Twickenham since 1933.

In his second game for Wales he was not as prominent, but he did land a penalty in a 12–0 win over the Scots at Swansea. For the Irish game in Belfast on 11 March 1950 he was moved to centre. With three minutes remaining, the scores were tied at 3–3, and Wales's dreams of a first Triple Crown in thirty-nine years were fast receding. The Irish won a scrum near their own 25, but fearsome Ray Cale harassed poor Jackie Kyle so much that the ball went loose and like a flash Billy Cleaver was on to it. Cleaver passed out to Lewis Jones and once more hope sprang eternal as Jones drew in George Norton and slung a long pass to winger Malcolm Thomas. Everything and everybody arrived at the corner-flag at once – the daring, diving Thomas, the welter of green shirts and the touch-judge. The corner-flag went down and the touch-judge's flag stayed down. Try and Triple Crown to Wales. That was not all, either. In the final match of the tournament against France at Cardiff on 25 March 1950, Jones displayed an undreamed-of brilliance in the Welsh centre, sending the home crowd into transports of delight and plunging the French into the depths of despair. His nine points with the boot were mere top dressing to his virtuosity as Wales won 12–0 to take the championship outright for the first time since 1936 and their first Grand Slam since 1911.

The summer of 1950 had a British Lions tour of New Zealand and Australia scheduled. Lewis Jones, the toast of Welsh rugby, was surely the find of the season. It could not have been a lack of talent or potential which impelled the selectors to leave him out of the touring party. His omission had to be down to his extreme youth unless, perish the thought, the selectors really were numbskulls. Unfortunately, problems with selectors would dog his career for years to come. However, in this instance, there was a belated call to represent the Lions. The Irish full-back George Norton suffered a broken arm in a game against Southland, and Lewis was summoned with the tour half-finished. This was not too late for him to take New Zealand by storm. In only seven games he bagged sixty-three points and, even more impressively, captured the admiration of the locals with his daring and unpredictable attacking ploys. The Lions had already lost the Test series when Lewis was drafted into the team for the Fourth and final Test at Auckland's Eden Park. They did not win this game either, but the match went down in history as one of the finest ever played on the ground. Yet again, no player shone more brightly than the precocious boy from Gorseinon. He tackled well and kicked an early penalty goal, but late in the proceedings the Lions had slipped further behind at 3–11. At this point Jones created what must be one of the most magnificent tries in Test history. The Lions took a scrum on their own goal-line. Scrum-half

Rex Willis fed Jackie Kyle, who aimed a pass to Bleddyn Williams but it never reached him . Lewis Jones pounced onto the ball and bolted into open territory. Perhaps any other full-back would have kicked, but this was not any other full-back. The bemused All Blacks back-pedalled desperately as Jones flew to half-way. There he was confronted by the formidable full-back Bob Scott, while Empire Games sprinter Peter Henderson hared back to cut him off. Scott made the tackle but not before Lewis had lobbed the ball over Henderson and into the arms of winger Ken Jones, the Olympic sprinter, who raced fifty yards for a stupendous try, converted by Lewis. It was not enough to win the game, but it did mean that Lewis Jones's place was marked indelibly in New Zealand folklore. Moving on to Australia he played in both Tests, which the Lions won 19–6 at Brisbane and 24–3 at Sydney. In the first of those games Jones added to his laurels by scoring sixteen points, then a Test record for a Lion. He came home a hero.

He was still a hero on 20 January 1951 when he converted four of Wales's five tries in a 23–5 rout of England at Swansea. Two weeks later, however, his status changed to that of scapegoat as Wales went down 0–19 at Murrayfield. It was a national disaster and heads had to roll. It did not seem to matter that backs could do precious little when packs caved in as abjectly as the Welsh forwards did on that day. Lewis Jones was dropped for the remaining internationals of 1951, neither of which was won. The words sacrificial and lamb sprang to many minds. The 1951–2 season saw normal service restored. Lewis was reinstated in the Welsh XV, playing on the wing against the Springboks, the English and the Irish and at centre against France. Although the game against South Africa was lost 3–6, Wales won another Grand Slam and Lewis Jones was again the nation's darling. It was not to go on for much longer, however.

Prowess on the Lewis Jones scale could not be hidden under a bushel. The men from the North could tell a good thing when they saw it, and Lewis made their eyes bulge. Rugby league scouts were shrewd judges, and they quickly recognized greatness in him. He had the hand-and-eye co-ordination of all natural ball-players, he had pace and balance, he played with his brain and on instinct, he knew what he was doing, even if others did not, and he most certainly had crowd appeal, whatever that meant. They had also heard the other side of the story. He could be inconsistent, he had quiet periods and, most damaging of all, he was tackle-shy. Llanelli's chairman probably put his finger on the truth when he said, 'They come to Llanelli in their thousands, some to cheer him, some to deride him – but they all come to make the turnstiles click.'

The fact that, in November 1952, Leeds reputedly paid a fee of £6,000 for his services – more than any previous fee for either a league or a union player – was eloquent testimony to the club's view on the subject. He was given a nine-year contract, a staggering endorsement of the regard in which Leeds held him. Economic circumstances, as always, were a major factor in inducing Welsh players to trek north. Lewis was shortly to be married and, lionized though he was in his own country, adulation did not pay the bills. There was not much future in playing as an amateur and driving lorries. For Jones, as for generations of rugby players from south Wales, the future was brighter in the north of England. However, Leeds and Lewis were taking big risks. Financially, Leeds could have come a real cropper if their capture proved to be a dud. Lewis, for his part, was putting his reputation on the line to play a game that was merciless to those who could not reach the required standards. He would have to train harder than he had ever done, he would face more implacable tackling than union could offer, his opponents and team-mates would be fitter, faster and more unforgiving than in the amateur code and in defence it would be impossible to hide. On the other hand, his new game would allow him to run, to handle and to indulge his creativity as never before. It would test his abilities to the full and reward him in equal measure if he fulfilled his true potential. If he failed, there would be no shortage of flak.

The capture of Lewis Jones ranks with the most significant in league's history. It was big news. If it had happened in today's sporting climate the hype would have been unprecedented. On 8 November 1952, 17,000 fans gathered at Headingley for Lewis's debut – a fairly nondescript league fixture against Keighley. He played at full-back, landed seven goals (but missed nine) as Leeds cruised to a win by 56–7. A fortnight later the critics were in their element as the touring Kangaroos crushed Leeds 45–4 before 20,000 chastened Loiners. Lewis scored all the Leeds points, but he failed to impress and spent much of the game limping on the wing with an injured ankle. Things got even worse. On 24 February 1953, Leeds won 10–5 at Batley but an innocuous tackle resulted in Lewis breaking an arm. His first season in his new game was already over. By the start of the 1953–4 season his arm had healed, but his form was poor and Leeds decided that a spell in the reserves was the answer. Naturally enough, the carpers had a field day. If Lewis Jones was going to fail in rugby league this was surely the critical time. His resolve must have been severely tested, his confidence rudely shaken. In almost a year as a league player he had made only ten first-team appearances. It was now or never. Suddenly, in November 1953, everything clicked. In three games against Hull KR, Wakefield Trinity and Castleford he piled up sixty points and a record-shattering career was back on the rails. By the season's close he had racked up 302 points (18 tries, 124 goals) in all games. Leeds supporters were now in no doubt about Jones, who was operating at centre – they simply adored him. They realized that he was the man who might turn their underachieving team of stars into trophy-winners. They were right, but they would have to wait a while.

As a union player Jones had won ten Welsh caps. He would represent his country only once at rugby league, against France at Marseilles on 13 December 1953. He kicked five goals in a splendid game which France won 23–22. At that point the Rugby Football League decided that there were not enough Welshmen in the game and disbanded the Welsh international XIII. It was not revived until 1968, by which time Lewis Jones was resident in Australia. As it happened, it was Australia which exercised most rugby league people's minds in 1954 when a Great Britain tour was set for the summer. Lewis's form made him a prime candidate for the trip and he was selected for the first tour trial on his home ground at Headingley on 24 February. There may have been nothing in it, but fertile minds saw his selection at centre for a Red XIII as a special test set to see how he would cope with extreme pressure. Directly opposite him in the White XIII was Duggie Greenall of St Helens, a centre who made up for a lack of weight with frightening bellicosity. If he could survive this ordeal even the doubters would be satisfied. Lewis was to sail through that examination, running incisively, landing four goals and avoiding or surviving Duggie's closest attentions. He was duly selected to tour as one of four centres in the Great Britain squad, along with Greenall, Ernie Ashcroft (Wigan) and Phil Jackson (Barrow).

There were four other Welshmen in the tour party – skipper Dickie Williams, Billy Boston, Ray Price and Tommy Harris. Billy and Lewis were to be the sensations of the enterprise. Boston, aged only nineteen, proved unstoppable on the Lions right wing to run up a tour record of thirty-six tries. At the same time Lewis, now a veteran of twenty-three, was creating his own records. Although selected at centre, injuries to both full-backs, Ted Cahill and Jack Cunliffe, meant that he spent most of the tour playing in that position. He was a revelation. In only twenty-one games he scored 278 points (127 goals, eight tries) to set a record which still stands today. He made his debut in the First Test against Australia at the Sydney Cricket Ground on 12 June 1954 on the wing. Despite his three goals, the game was a disaster for Great Britain who lost 12–37. Noel Pidding, the prolific Australian wing, notched up nineteen points (eight goals and a try), a new record for an Ashes Test. The Second Test in Brisbane on 3 July was a different story. By now Lewis was playing at full-back and the form book was shredded as Britain ran riot to win 38–21 despite a treacherous pitch. Lewis was at his magnificent best, especially with the boot. His ten goals and twenty points eclipsed Pidding's record in the previous Test. Even now no British player has exceeded Jones's ten goals in a Test, although Bernard Ganley, John Holmes, Jonathan Davies and Bobby Goulding have matched him. Two of Lewis's goals were dropped, one of which probably only he could have put over the bar. It was landed from thirty yards after he turned and slipped on the greasy surface but managed to hook the ball over with the side of his foot instead of his toes. One scribe described it as 'a classic example of concentration under difficulties'. Others may have called it a stroke of genius or a fluke. Whatever – only Jones knows. Amazingly, he had set Test records for both codes of rugby on the same ground, as Brisbane was the scene of his triumph for the rugby union Lions back in 1950.

In the years between 1954 and 1957 Lewis Jones dazzled the world of rugby league. He became a match-winner *par excellence*, his sleight of foot and hand bewitched opponents and spectators alike, his hitch-kick and God-given acceleration off the mark punctured the most obdurate of defences, the game's hit-men rarely got near him and he became arguably the biggest box-office attraction of his time. He went on an orgy of points-scoring and record-breaking in those golden years, culminating in the 1956–7 season with an all-time record of 496 points, equalling the goal-kicking record of 194 set in 1933–4 by his immortal compatriot Jim Sullivan. Jones though added thirty-six tries for good measure. Perversely, one game in which he did not trouble the scorers that season was the Challenge Cup Final. Leeds beat Barrow 9–7 to take their first Challenge Cup since 1942. Leeds has also taken the Yorkshire League Championship in 1956–7, a trophy they had already lifted in 1954–5 and which they would win again in 1960–1, after grabbing the Yorkshire Cup in 1958–9. Lewis Jones had indeed proved a talisman for the Leeds faithful.

At the very highest level Lewis had repeatedly proved his mettle – in home Tests for Great Britain against New Zealand and France, in internationals for the celebrated Other Nationalities XIII and in various representative XIIIs against Kangaroos, Kiwis and the French. It was therefore no surprise when he was selected for the Great Britain squad for the World Cup in Australia in June 1957, a tournament for which Britain were firm favourites. However, things were about to go badly wrong both for Lewis Jones and for Great Britain.

Lewis had been chosen as a centre in the eighteen-man party for a tournament which pitted Great Britain against France (17 June), Australia (19 June) and New Zealand (25 June), all at the Sydney Cricket Ground. If those three matches had been the sum total of the expedition, in an age of no substitutions, remember, it would have been hard enough. These eighteen men, however, were faced with a warm-up game in Perth (9 June), a fixture against Queensland at Brisbane (1 July), a game against the French in Auckland and another three games against the French on a promotional tour of South Africa on the way home. Things immediately turned nasty as stand-off Ray Price was injured at Perth and played no further games. Billy Boston and Alan Davies were flown home injured after only three games, leaving only fifteen fit men. In Billy's case it at least avoided the probability of an international scandal, as South Africa's apartheid laws would have had to be confronted. Lewis, and several of his colleagues, played in all nine games. Moreover, he played for the Rest against Australia on 29 June – ten games in seven weeks, in Australia, New Zealand and South Africa, and all for a measly £125. Great Britain beat the French but lost heavily to Australia and abjectly to the Kiwis, and to all intents and purposes

Lewis got the blame. At least that is how history seemed to judge matters. He never played in another Test match or in a full international after 1957 despite maintaining his standards of excellence. He had played fifteen times for Great Britain in three years, scored in every game (sixty-six goals, five tries, 147 points) and played at full-back, wing, centre and stand-off. Even today, only Neil Fox has kicked more goals for Britain and only Fox and Garry Schofield have scored more points.

Clearly, Jones had been scapegoated again – shades of 1951. True enough, Great Britain had blown the World Cup. No one had a glorious time, but it certainly was not all Lewis Jones's fault. The Australian press laid the blame fairly and squarely on the British forwards, who were too fond of playing out wide and not prepared to work. In their view, there had never been a worse Lions pack. Certainly George Watt, the Australian Test hooker of 1946, who later played with Hull, knew class when he saw it. He declared before the victory over France, 'Lewis Jones is the world's best rugby league player'. Unfortunately, this did not seem to be a view shared by Bill Fallowfield, the British tour-manager, who was also the secretary of the RFL. Although he did not have executive powers, Fallowfield was the most influential man in British league at the time. His official report on the 1957 World Cup tour (never published, incidentally) gives a clear indication that for some reason he did not rate Jones, particularly defensively. Fallowfield, an autocratic figure, was not a selector but after 1957 he continued to manage and to coach all the Great Britain squads on home territory. If he had set his face against Lewis, it was inconceivable that the selectors would oppose him. Lewis was thus cast into the international wilderness. To his credit, Lewis always maintained his dignity and silence, embodying those old-fashioned virtues of sporting heroes – modesty, reticence and fair play. He simply got on with the game and left politics to the politicians. It was international rugby league's loss.

Even after the traumas of 1957 and his effective expulsion from the representative arena, Lewis Jones continued to grace Headingley for another seven years, his career there finally encompassing 385 games, 144 tries, 1,244 goals and 2,920 points. In all games in British rugby league he amassed 3,372 points. Leeds fans could not get enough of him, and in 1960–1 he delivered to them what they had never had before

– the Rugby League Championship. Aristocratic Leeds might have been founder members of the Northern Union back in 1895, but astoundingly they had never been champions. As the 1960s approached Lewis began to play at stand-off rather than centre and he took on the captaincy. Even though Leeds topped the table in 1960–1, many critics felt this was a false position and that St Helens and Warrington were somehow superior. Yet Lewis's team accounted for Saints 11–4 in the Championship semi-final and then in the final at Odsal hammered Warrington 25–10 in front of 52,000 fans. Lewis played one of the games of his life, kicking five goals and scoring the last try of the day. That would have been a fitting end to a fantastic career, but Leeds retained his sublime talents until 1964 when he decamped to Australia where he captain-coached a phenomenally successful Wentworthville in the Sydney Second Division for another half-dozen years, rattling up almost another thousand points.

One of the most intriguing coincidences thrown up by sport links Lewis Jones with another Welsh icon, John Charles. It could easily be argued that this pair represents Wales's very finest exponents of their particular brands of football. It is extraordinary that the two were born within months of each other, and only a few miles apart. Both went on to become national heroes, renowned for their versatility and charisma. Moreover, the two played simultaneously (1952–7 and 1962) in the city of Leeds before pursuing careers in faraway places, only to return to Leeds once their playing days were over. Whilst Leeds and Leeds United struggled to win the hearts, minds and entrance money of Loiners by enticing Wales's most famous sportsmen North, the local newspapers, the *Yorkshire Evening News* and the *Yorkshire Evening Post*, also knew the value of sporting heroes. *The Post* signed up John Charles for a series of ghosted articles which severely dented the sales of *The News*. There was only one possible response. *The News* recruited Lewis Jones and honour was satisfied.

Lewis Jones's ultimate low profile return from Australia to live and teach mathematics in a girls' school in Leeds probably added to the mystique of his legend. His nearest post-war equivalents, David Watkins and Jonathan Davies, returned to Wales and were reintegrated into union, both subsequently being honoured with MBEs. Even Bill Fallow-field received an OBE.

# CLEM THOMAS

Peter Stead

It sometimes happens that writers provide their own epitaphs. Clem Thomas certainly did when in 1989 he set out to salute and publicize what Gareth Jenkins had achieved in his eighteen months as coach of Llanelli. 'Really big men are rare', said Clem who made it that clear that he was not referring to physical stature but rather to 'those who emerge from the pack with a brightness, resolve and an intellectual understanding of their subject'. Such men have the capacity 'to shine like a beam and capture the affection, admiration and respect of those they set out to influence'. As it happens Clem was a big man physically, especially in later life as his 6'-1" frame squared out, but he was far more noticeably big in the way he loved his life and commanded attention. Even thirty years after hanging up his boots he still brought to journalism, politics, business and social life all the enthusiasm, bravery, robustness, directness and flair that had characterized his back-row play. It was as if the teenager who had taken up rugby had discovered not just an identity but a complete lifestyle, as if the former player had wanted all his actions to be described in the same words that the *Evening Post* had used to describe his play in the 1950s. His performance as a whole was 'rip-roaring' and 'all-action', and it was inevitable that his friends and acquaintances would be swept along just as had been the case with the St Helens crowds of old. He truly was a big man whose death in 1996 at the age of sixty-seven not only impoverished many individual lives but suddenly made Wales seem dull and Swansea very provincial.

Clem was above all a Swansea man, as entitled as anybody to be called 'Lord Swansea' although a title was the last thing the person who rejected the opportunity to be high sheriff would have wanted. He was always in evidence whether it was at St Helens, in the pub, talking to shopkeepers, or just jumping in and out of his car to pick up cigarettes and the newspapers. He was always on the go and yet he always allowed time to give off his latest snipe at the authorities or to reveal his enthusiasm for either a new player or more likely a new foreign part to visit. He was always just back from somewhere, but it was that very coming back that was vital, for there were always matters to be settled in Swansea. Those matters related in particular, of course, to meat, for famously Clem was a wholesale butcher often to be seen discussing and analysing his product (and seeming very much the best advert for it) at shops in Mumbles and the Uplands. Occasionally I had dealings with him and this was particularly the case during the years when, as seemed entirely appropriate, he was the proprietor of Swansea's most distinguished, distinctive and famous watering hole, the No Sign Bar in Wind Street. The Luftwaffe had succeeded in destroying most of Swansea's Victorian and Edwardian distinction, but mercifully parts of Wind Street survived not only aerial bombardment but also the inanity of later planners. And so it was that the city could boast of an eighteenth-century business premises long associated with wine-importing. An exterior plaque somewhat arbitrarily identified this as 'the best pub north of Salzburg', but more accurately a visiting American was heard to declare that he felt exactly as if he was drinking in Cheers, Boston's most famous bar. It was a super bar, especially when Clem was there to enthral the lingering lawyers and estate agents who constituted the usual suspects. But even better than the booth-lined bar and dining area was the cellar below, still in those days referred to by its traditional name of 'Munday's wine cellar'. This was the genuine thing: a stone-walled eighteenth-century cellar that looked a little as if it had once been used as a torture chamber but which now served as a jazz venue with a perfect acoustic or as a very baronial dining room. It was the perfect place for me to take the quite demanding University Staff Dining Club of which I was secretary. I discussed the menu with Clem. 'It has to be my new season Welsh lamb', he decided and we proceeded to choose a date that would allow perfection. On the night I was acclaimed as never before or since by thirty totally contented diners and I rejoiced in the way in which my friendship with the proprietor had paid off.

I had first got to know Clem in 1979 when we were both prospective parliamentary candidates. He was once again preparing to fight Carmarthen for the Liberals, I was 'nursing' Barry for Labour, but in our home base of Swansea we were able to come together in the campaign for the Welsh Assembly. We were both enthusiastic supporters of the 'Vote Yes' cause and in the process of realizing that not many people shared our enthusiasm. In the end, after some perfunctory canvassing and half-hearted meetings, what the Swansea campaign amounted to was a wonderful musical evening which probably raised some money but which even more, and largely due to the talents of Delme Bryn Jones and the Pontarddulais Male Voice Choir Glee Club, confirmed all those present in their love of Wales. It was during that evening that I came to realize how deeply attached Clem was to west Wales and how passionately interested he was in its history, literature and above all its art. Until that time I had associated him only with the playing and reporting of rugby. I now came to know a man who from his business base wanted to establish links with academics and politicians in order to shape a new Wales. He wanted to learn, he wanted to note new names, book titles and ideas, but he was also conscious of the practical no-nonsense entrepreneurial dimension which he could almost uniquely bring to the world of Welsh radicalism. It was easy to see why in 1979 he wanted to be associated with a Liberal Party advocating that Wales should be developing management skills and to that end should establish a business school, and why later that year he should seek membership of the European Parliament. His electoral campaigns were never successful and some national pundits found this surprising. Of course, he had chosen to fight in Carmarthen at a time when electors were all too aware of the need to vote tactically in a battle for supremacy between Labour and Plaid Cymru, but in truth Clem was not a natural politician. As one close friend was to put it, 'he was not a man for the cut and thrust'. He was far too big a man for mere party politics. His mind had always moved on to other interests, there were always other fish to fry.

He was better in the pub than on the stump, and he was particularly good when the conversation was open-ended and he could mix a little pontification with anecdotes and enthusiasms. There was always that wonderfully fruity public school voice whose formality was emphasized by the somewhat genteel curl of the lip. He had been born with generous lips but somewhere along the line a few random and some deliberate punches and kicks had given them further character and ensured that their deployment in conversation would be his hallmark. Intriguingly, he was never quite as fluent as he wanted to be: there was always an element of hesitancy and uncertainty in his anecdotes, and often his eyes and rhetorical questions would indicate that he was in need of reassurance or assistance. From other people he wanted precise and definite information. He wanted to learn quickly, but he also wanted to be amused. Those who told him jokes were richly rewarded, for that big face would light up feature by feature and the most marvellous smile ensue. It had become a much-lived-in face and one was always looking into it to see the handsome, curly-haired and rather Italianate young man who had cut a dash in the 1950s, and who had been one of my first rugby heroes.

Clem had been there from the outset of my days as a follower of rugby and he had helped to define my allegiances. My first rugby game at St Helens was Swansea's 12–6 defeat by Australia in January 1958. Already my attention was focused on Swansea's pack in which W. O. (Billy) Williams and R. C. C. (Clem) Thomas were prominent: both were asterisked as Welsh internationals and both were well known to me as stars of the 1955 Lions tour. Three weeks later I saw my first international and, in that 8–3 victory over Scotland at Cardiff, Wales was captained by R. C. C. Thomas of Swansea. In fact, Clem was to captain Wales in the first four matches I saw: his place in my pantheon was guaranteed. We thought of him as absolutely the right man for the job. He had after all been around for quite a while and had first played for Wales as long ago as 1949. Furthermore he was a public schoolboy, a Cambridge blue and a forward who, whilst nearly always in the thick of things, had that ability to stand in a detached way at the back of a line-out, hands in pockets looking as if he had devised a master plan. As we reflected on the career of our natural leader, two particular moments were often highlighted, although it was only much later that we came to see the extent to which they neatly reflected something of the duality that was indicated in the way in which the R.C.C. of the programme always became Clem in local argot.

It had been R. C. C. Thomas who, as he later recalled for radio, had 'hoofed' the ball across the field for Ken Jones to score the try that allowed Wales to beat New Zealand at Cardiff in December 1953. It was in the words of *The Times* 'the most famous cross-kick in post-war rugby'. The Welsh outside-half that day was Cliff Morgan and his rather unkind judgement was that when Clem had gathered the loose ball it seemed as if he 'didn't know quite what to do with it'. What Cliff, a player often troubled by Clem in club matches, chose to highlight was the impulsive nature of the kick and the extreme kindness of the bounce. A more generous G. V. Wynne-Jones, who was commentating on the game, remembered 'an un-expected and intelligent cross-kick'. But it is the player's own characteristically casual recollection that will live on as an expression of his whole attitude to the game and as a reminder of that basic stature that all Welsh players who have helped defeat the All Blacks acquire. Somewhat less gloriously it was Clem Thomas who was dropped by Wales in 1957 after Wales had lost 3–0 to England at Cardiff. Clearly the two players most blamed for that defeat, both of whom were also dropped, were Keith Maddocks, the winger who had stood offside and therefore gave England their three points, and scrum-half Onllwyn Brace who like his partner Cliff Morgan had been 'hounded and harassed' by the English back-row of Robbins, Ashcroft and Higgins. The game had been 'as high and rough a struggle' as any reporter Ron Griffiths had ever seen; the forward battle had been 'a grim affair' with 'no quarter asked and none given'. In that 'forward slog' Clem Thomas had given his all as well as having the energy to worry Bartlett the outside-half. Clem did not play in the next international and only returned, albeit as captain, to play against England at Twickenham a year later.

Throughout his career it was always to be rugby's essential duality which appealed to Clem Thomas, and he was very aware of how his background had prepared him for it. At school at Blundell's in Somerset and then at St John's College Cambridge he had gained admission to that gentlemen's club which at the time constituted the very core of international rugby. He was always at home in that world, it was where he met many of his closest friends and it ensured that the camaraderie offered by both the Barbarians and the British Lions was always recognized by him as the best thing that the game of rugby union had to offer. But the youth who went to Tiverton and then Cambridge had grown up in Brynaman, the son of Davy John Thomas, farmer, butcher and entrepreneur. The moorland frontier that separates the south Wales coalfield from rural mid Wales is as beautiful, dramatic and crucial as other more legendary frontiers in North America and South Africa and Brynaman is one of its most extreme and wildest spots. The young schoolboy whom Swansea RFC was first to encounter playing for his village when they called in to play 'a missionary game', had been brought up in a Huckleberry Finn-like culture in which, as Geoffrey Nicholson recounted, he had trapped rabbits on his father's farm and sold them in Swansea market and where there were plenty of stories of how his short powerfully-built father had been in scraps at Carmarthen mart. Over the years there were to be rumours of scraps that Clem himself had been in, and in any case there was all the evidence of how on the field he was always in the thick of things. 'Violence is a terrible thing but I do love it', he told Geoff Nicholson, and it was his adversary and subsequently friend Peter Robbins who wryly and famously pointed out that as a wholesale butcher Clem was 'the only player to take his profession onto the field with him'.

At various moments Clem was to be associated with calls for the playing of open rugby. That was certainly the case when he was given the captaincy of the All Whites in 1954. Swansea responded, as David Farmer describes, by promptly losing their first ten games. Later operating as a journalist and historian of the game, nobody was more pleased that Welsh rugby was to enjoy another golden era chiefly through the 'breathtaking excellence' of their backs. In the bad days that followed he always argued that Wales needed to redevelop and play its own game rather than attempt to emulate the 'power play' favoured by England. Yet, ironically, circumstances had dictated that Clem had found himself caught up in an era of very physical rugby when 'no prisoners were taken'. Norman Lewis remembered him as being 'as tough a rugby player as any', 'a good man to have on board when the going was tough', whilst Swansea's David Price's abiding memory was 'of a powerful man in a white jersey pounding up field, scattering opponents left and right'. That rugby world now seems very distant. Week in, week out, we watched games that were won by one or two scores. Later my eye caught reports by Ron Griffiths of a 6–6 draw against Newport at St Helens in 1957 in which Clem was 'the outstanding forward in a rampant mobile pack', he was 'disconsolate that he had not been carried over for what would have been a well-deserved winning try', and two weeks later he was 'outstanding' in a 3–3 draw at Coventry. At Twickenham in 1958 there was 'a rip-roaring forward struggle which never abated' and which ended up with another 3–3 scoreline, a great success for 'the tactically-minded skipper Clem' who had 'banked on his rampaging pack'. One television shot seemed to suggest that Clem was up to no good in the maul, but the incident was quickly forgotten: his visits to Twickenham were seldom uncontroversial. Later that season I had looked forward to my first Baa-Baas game: that was certain to provide better entertainment. In the event it was an Easter treat which ended in a mere 6–5 victory for the tourists over a Whites side that had included both Clem and W.O. In 1959 I eventually saw England for the first time. They lost 5–0 to Wales in the mud because Dewi Bebb scored an opportunist try and captain Clem thereafter ordered his pack to wheel the scrum whenever necessary. Clem never forgot the reaction to an earlier and rare Welsh loss in Dublin. On the Sunday morning as the team walked past supporters queuing to board the boat at Dun Laoghaire they 'were booed and catcalled every inch of the way, some but not all of it', recalled Clem, 'was in good humour'. Even now I sometimes yearn for the tension of those low-scoring games. Did rugby have to evolve into a game that resembles basketball?

Captain Clem flourished in those battles of attrition. They were very much games in which natural-born leaders came into their own. Clem had never forgotten his first game for Wales in Paris in 1949. He was a 20-year-old undergraduate yet to win a Blue but his captain Haydn Tanner hardly spoke to him throughout the weekend and 'his team talk was of such brevity', recalled Clem, 'that I was totally unaware of any tactics to be employed: the result was we played like a scratch team and lost'. Clem was far more impressed by his next Welsh captain John Gwilliam, who when things appeared to be going against his pack would 'run up, hit them on the backside, and tell them not to play like silly boys'. When his own time came Clem knew exactly what to do and later confessed that he had often resorted to 'a sly dig to get them going'. In one England game his club colleague and fellow back-row forward John Faull turned round just in time to see Clem 'kicking his bum to get him going'. Clem's recollection was that 'after that he played a blinder'. He had so much to contribute as captain it was a great shame that he was never given the chance to captain the British Lions tour for he always regarded that as British rugby's greatest honour. He had gone to

South Africa with Robin Thompson's 1955 Lions and been forced to undergo an appendix operation which meant missing the first ten games of the tour. But Clem declined the opportunity to come home and was rewarded with a place in the team for the last two Tests and the captaincy in a victory over Natal in Durban. After two seasons leading Wales Clem was, as J. B. G. Thomas pointed out, 'in line for the Lions captaincy' for the 1959 tour of New Zealand and Australia. Nine Welshmen went on that tour including the newly inspired John Faull, but Clem was not amongst them. Once again Wales had been denied the captaincy which went to the Irish hooker Ronnie Dawson. Immediately, it became apparent that the great Welsh hooker Bryn Meredith might be excluded from the Test matches. Later, in his *History of the British Lions*, Clem conceded that Dawson was 'a hard-working captain' but concluded that this had been 'another example of poor selection by those seventeen men in the East India Sports Club in St James's Square': Clem knew that the Establishment was never to be trusted.

When the Lions went to South Africa in 1955 they were accompanied by just two reporters, Vivian Jenkins of *The Sunday Times* and J. B. G. Thomas of the *Western Mail*, although they were joined half-way through the tour by Roy McKelvie of the *Daily Mail*. Within a few years things were to change dramatically, and J.B.G. in particular was somewhat amused by the sudden appearance of so many former players in the press box. Clem was one of the first of a new generation for, having played his last game for the All Whites in 1959, he was immediately asked by his old Cambridge friend Chris Brasher to cover Welsh rugby for *The Observer*. A year or so later, as Geoff Nicholson has explained, he was asked to succeed 'the revered H. B. Toft' as rugby correspondent, a position he was to hold for thirty-five years. Professionally his closest association was to be with Nicholson, who served first as his 'curate' and later as his boss: the friends also co-authored a history of Welsh rugby between 1968 and 1980, a period they described as 'The Crowning Years'. The former Wales captain, as Nicholson readily admits, 'was not a great stylist and never claimed to be' and indeed in the 1960s I remember my Swansea University colleague David Sims explaining that he had been called in to help Clem with his adverbs and adjectives. Very quickly the rookie in the press box realized that to make any report he needed to be as much his own man as he had been on the field of play. There were to be occasional attempts at purple passages: once in the darkest days he suggested before a game that victory would only come if there was 'a dredging from the deep in the Welsh soul for the qualities inherent in the Welsh spirit of a feeling for rugby football'. In the great days of the early 1970s he gloried in the greatness of the four heroes, Barry John, Gareth Edwards, Gerald Davies and J.P.R., and gave thanks for the privilege of having seen them play. They had provided 'exquisite pleasure', they were 'the very best', displaying 'the excellence' more usually 'instinctively and instantly recognised' in 'the form of a Russian gymnast, a Swedish tennis player, an American golfer or a West Indian cricketer'. For Clem 'the immortal Welsh forward from this period was Mervyn Davies' and he was always to appreciate the enormous talents of the Swansea and Wales number 8 whom he saw as being 'deceptively lazy' yet 'like a steel spring, all tensile strength and unbreakable resolve, an absolute hammer of a player'.

It was always worth reading what Clem had to say about particular games, but increasingly one looked forward with rather more eagerness to what he would have to say about things off the field. He was to find his subject in officialdom and, in particular, in the affairs of the Welsh Rugby Union. The game belonged above all to its players and yet it had passed into the hands of the little men in blazers. He had known that to be the case in his playing days, but in those relatively undemanding times the game had more or less run itself and officials could be tolerated. Now the game was changing and there were new demands at every level. In the long term the amateur game would suddenly become professional, but long before 1996 the game was facing the need for professional attitudes towards coaching and management and relations with the press, not to mention marketing and financial administration. In almost every respect Clem found the WRU wanting in these matters, and it became more or less his life's work to spell out the disasters as they occurred. He had identified the appointment of Ray Williams as national coaching organizer in 1967 as 'the best decision made by the WRU in my lifetime' but then noted that Williams 'had no say in the national team in 1967 and 1968'. In 1968 Wales chose to tour Argentina without a coach: the team was led by two administrators. Only under the leadership of Cliff Jones did attitudes to the press change: until his time reporters had been treated 'like something which had crawled out from under a stone'.

The constant theme of his journalism was that Wales had to judge its rugby by the highest standards. However golden the 1970s had been, Wales did not have a good record against southern hemisphere nations and the prospect of the World Cup had made radical changes imperative. He had long ridiculed the so-called 'Big Five' and a system of team selection based 'on whim': in fact the whole squad system 'had become incestuous and ineffectual'. As good players lost interest in playing for Wales he urged the appointment of a team manager, a strong personality to take control in precisely the way Brian Thomas had at Neath and Ray Prosser at Pontypool. Wales could just not afford to lose prematurely players like Mike Watkins, Eddie Butler, Jeff Squire and Graham Price. As games were lost in the 1980s he referred to 'the intransigence and naïvety' of the way in which forwards were selected: the selectors were committing 'almost criminal mistakes'. But it was increasingly the big political issues that were exposing the inadequacy of Welsh administrators. Clem had become a fierce opponent of apartheid, and he was greatly saddened when an extraordinary general meeting of Welsh rugby clubs held in 1984 voted to continue links with South Africa. Delegates had been greatly influenced by a WRU document which had been circulated to the clubs before the meeting and consequently Clem argued that they had been 'misguided and misinformed' as well as 'wrong'. For him the nadir of Welsh fortunes, both on and off the field, came with the turmoil over the South African centenary celebrations in 1989. The poor performances by Welsh players and the subsequent unseemly row between Welsh administrators revealed to the world as a whole that the game in Wales was 'in disarray'. 'No leading rugby nation', declared Clem, 'had lost its way more fundamentally than the Welsh in the last decade.' At every opportunity both in newspapers and in the new spate of rugby journals, one of which, *Rugby Wales*, he edited, he called for the WRU to be 'accountable to Welsh rugby at large': both 'open government and better PR' were essential.

He had campaigned throughout the 1980s, but things had only got worse and his voice of sanity was to be even more necessary in the next decade. The edge in his writing became more pronounced and, as Geoff Nicholson has suggested, it was to be the readers of Clem's new column in Swansea's *Evening Post* who experienced the best of his journalism. In what was to be the last year of his life he yearned for Welsh rugby to 'rise from the slough of despondency' in which it had been 'deeply immersed for the last decade'. Several investigations had called for the reorganization of Welsh rugby and he was concerned that only a fundamental reorganization would 'release the true and abundant energy of Welsh rugby'. But then he sighed: 'if only pigs could fly.' What needed to happen was that power had to revert to the clubs so that they could be in charge of their own destiny. A newly constituted WRU could then take its place within a new, enlightened and democratic framework controlled by 'intelligently concerned rugby men'. The present system in which the WRU was dominated by appointed district representation was one that guaranteed 'mediocrity'. It had brought into play 'those terrible aspects of Welsh politics that saw the cream sinking to the bottom', and it meant that coaches had often 'spent most of their time looking over their shoulders at those who have interfered and conspired against them'. He urged the recently appointed coaches Kevin Bowring and Allan Lewis to be 'their own men', for according to Clem, 'recent team managements have been disgracefully treated by megalomaniac forces in the WRU'. By this time almost everybody in Wales knew what Clem thought about 'the clowns' in charge of Welsh rugby. They also knew that he was opposed to the redevelopment of the National Stadium. In what was his last great campaign he argued for the building of a new stadium at Bridgend: he wanted Millennium funds to be used for a regeneration of south Wales as a whole. When the decisions went Cardiff's way he accepted it graciously but pleaded for Swansea not to be forgotten as everything seemed to be going the capital's way.

Swansea had remained his base; it was a place where he was surrounded by friends and it was the centre of his many business interests. The rest of Wales had come to think of Clem as a rather angry and perhaps obsessive campaigning journalist, but at home in

Swansea it was his love of life in the round that was always more apparent. Geoff Nicholson has commented on how much Clem relished 'the sport of making money'. He had never lost his appetite for 'the haggling in the cattle markets and nothing pleased him more than the pressure of a roll of bank notes in his trousers pocket'. He was first and foremost an entrepreneur, and it was that fact which essentially accounted for his confidence, his courage and especially his independence. I once heard him describe with real enthusiasm how much he had enjoyed the American West and I could see immediately how successful he would have been as a rancher, the owner of a big spread in the classic days of Hollywood's cowboys. He would have run his ranch brilliantly: his beef would have been the best west of the Mississippi, rustlers would have been dealt with summarily and all the petty, corrupt and office-seeking politicians of the nearby town would have been fiercely denounced. And at the heart of things there would be the family, for above all Clem was a family man whose wife, four children and two step-children came first. He was tremendously pleased that his three sons, Chris and Greg and Mark, had played for the All Whites, but was heard to comment that the boys 'were too nice' to have joined him in any all-time back row. I shared this conceit of the western ranch with one friend of Clem's who readily concurred and thought it would be a veritable Ponderosa.

In reality, it was France that became his spiritual home. Both his first game for Wales in 1949 and his last in 1959 were in Paris, and there is no doubt that in his subsequent career as a reporter it was his visits to internationals played in the French capital that he enjoyed most. Clem and Peter Robbins would arrange a magnificent weekend of food and drink, especially champagne, and there would be a fresh round of anecdotes to share with other former players. The two friends, who once when asked on a long-haul flight whether they wanted to start with caviare or *foie gras* had replied 'Both', knew exactly what they wanted when in France. Some people were lucky enough to see the two former back-row men do their famous song-and-dance act. Perhaps it was not really surprising that the first indication of Clem's heart problem had come during a Paris weekend, but he recovered from that serious warning and survived for a few more traditional trips to his favourite venue. 'The Reaper took a swing and he missed', he would comment, quickly placing his cigarette in a friend's fingers if his wife, a doctor, came into the room.

Clem willingly confessed 'to being an unashamed Francophile, who had spent a lifetime visiting and pillaging the riches of this great nation'. He would never admit it but his French was excellent, and this allowed him to derive full benefit from the time he and Joyce spent at their house in St Vivien de Medoc some sixty kilometres from Bordeaux. For a while he was enticed by the idea of developing a hotel and golf course in the Medoc, but chiefly his time in France was an opportunity to entertain both French and British friends. The menu would be irresistible, oysters and crab bought earlier at the stalls in Montalivet, *foie gras* sent by the former forward 'Bambi' Moga from his shop in Bordeaux's market, and of course Clem's own Welsh lamb accompanied by local *grands crus*. Meals were eaten outside under the trees he had planted for shade. Swansea friends Nigel and Marie-France Addinall loved to see Clem relaxing with his friends and family in the Medoc, rarely wanting to talk rugby and very reluctantly responding to praise at a banquet of notables at Lesparre. Occasionally there would be games to see in France, and as he hated to be late he would drive through French lanes 'in much the same style as he had played rugby'. Clem was not a singer but Nigel found that a tape of the Pontarddulais Male Choir would help the frustrated driver to cool down. It is easy to believe that Clem had come into his own as a *proprietaire*. It is not inappropriate that it was the Monaco-based Welsh artist Andrew Vaccari whose leonine portrait did most justice to Clem, or that the former Welsh forward features as a character in a well-received French novel entitled *Adios*.

Clem's funeral in September 1996 was adjudged to be 'the largest in Swansea for many years'. Both on that day at St Paul's Sketty and three months later at a service of celebration held at St Bride's Fleet Street many tributes were paid by friends from the worlds of rugby and journalism. He was particularly missed in Swansea, a town and later a city that Clem had come to represent internationally. The journalist, Alan Watkins, who having established a reputation as a lobby correspondent suddenly decided to write on rugby as well, fully acknowledged the help and encouragement he received from Clem and Geoff Nicholson. As an Ammanford man Watkins was able to identify precisely both his helpful colleagues as members of 'the galère who had originated in the Swansea of the 1950s' and who included Kingsley Amis, Nicholson's wife, Mavis, and the late John Morgan who had been 'a pioneering writer on the game'. This is indeed the company with which we should associate Richard Clement Charles Thomas. The Swansea of Dylan Thomas and Ivor Allchurch was a town still capable of nurturing and sustaining considerable talent. The excellence on display at St Helens was but one strand in a rich local tapestry which gave Swansea Jacks the confidence to take on the world on any terms it chose to offer.

*My considerable pleasure in recalling Clem was greatly enriched in conversation with Chris Thomas, Geoff and Mavis Nicholson, David Price, and Nigel and Marie-France Addinall. I am indebted to them.*

# TERRY DAVIES

## Hywel Teifi Edwards

It was his likeness to the sporting demi-god who first held me in thrall that fixed my attention on Terry Davies. Lew Hoad, the incomparable Australian tennis champion whose death in 1994 aged fifty-nine caused me much heart-ache, has only ever been challenged by the superlative John Charles as the player I would have most liked to be. Hugely talented and handsome, Hoad combined physical power and grace, resolve and captivating insouciance in a way that turned the playing of a game into an affirmation of *joie de vivre*. Lew Hoad and Ken Rosewall were hardly more than schoolboys – my age – when they defeated America's Budge Patty and Vic Seixas in a magnetic doubles match at Wimbledon, and my first Pathé News glimpse of Hoad in action left me permanently aced. I ached to serve and volley just once with his imperious ease. What wonder, then, that I looked twice at the picture of the 18-year-old Hoad look-alike who was to play at full-back for Swansea RFC against the Springboks on 15 December 1951. Could it be that he, too, would bring to his game a presence and range of skills of a superior order. This Terry Davies bore watching. He looked the part and he spoke Welsh.

Around 1950 rugby was just beginning to make inroads into our awareness as soccer-mad Cardiganshire boys in Aberaeron Grammar School. Talk of a Llanelli-playing wizard called Lewis Jones, known to his idolaters as *y gwaredwr* (the saviour), had reached us and we knew that the coming of the 1951–2 Springboks would impact upon their opponents with the force of a panzer division. J. B. G. Thomas in the *Western Mail* had done his best to warn Welsh rugby, players and supporters alike, to prepare for a relentless challenge, but the Springboks were to play a game of a standard which no advance warning could help to counter. They were even intimidating when viewed from the distance of the stand, a bionic pack in which Van Wyk, Muller, Geffin and Koch rampaged tirelessly, complemented by seemingly nerveless backs who frequently released Ochse or Marais to flash down the wings like exocets. I saw them reduce the Barbarians to harmlessness at Cardiff Arms Park on 26 January 1952 and am not surprised that they are still considered one of the greatest touring sides ever to ravage the British Isles. It would take a particularly self-assured 18-year-old full-back to face such opposition without qualms.

Talking about that game almost forty-eight years later – Terry Davies lives just over the hill from me in a splendid, unostentatious house within a stone's throw of his birthplace in Bynea on the outskirts of Llanelli – I quickly realized how much he had relished the encounter. A mere stripling who had been denied a Welsh Youth cap by stolid selectors who thought he was too small, he insists that Swansea would not have succumbed to a late try if his wing had stayed out, as commanded, with the opposing wing. Instead, anxious lest the oncoming ball-carrier power past the youthful full-back, he came protectively infield, the pass was given and the Springboks' wing ran in the clinching score. Swansea lost 11–3 and the reminiscing 67-year-old was still quietly aggrieved that his tenacity at eighteen should have been cause for concern.

Listening to him good humouredly mulling over the past, I remembered the dozen or so occasions on which I had seen him play and I knew him to have been steadfastness personified. He admitted to a quiver of apprehension on lining up opposite the Springboks on that December day in 1951, *Roen nhw'n ddiawled mowr* (They were big buggers), but once the game started they were there to be stopped. No Welsh full-back ever committed himself with greater intensity to the task of repelling the opposition until J. P. R. Williams came along and in giving J.P.R. his vote as the very best of full-backs Terry Davies is quite properly saluting a kindred spirit. To see the two in play was to see resolution incarnate and having made their mark in their day, time's charge is powerless to dislodge them from memory.

Terry Davies naturally played for his local club side, Bynea RFC, before progressing to the first-class game with Swansea and then Llanelli, and he was to finish his career with Bynea when he decided to ease his way into retirement in 1961 after winning twenty-one caps for Wales and playing in two Tests against the All Blacks during the British Lions tour of Australasia in 1959. Today he can name no local 'star' who acted as a spur to his boyhood ambition but inspiration aplenty came in the form of his father, Edwin (Ted) Davies, a centre-forward with a 'Roy-of-the-Rovers' cannonball shot reputed to have broken a goalpost at least once, and a champion Loughor estuary swimmer who nowadays would surely make his fortune promoting the sale of Guinness.

Ted Davies played for Llanelli AFC and was good enough to be offered a trial by Middlesbrough. But he was too deeply rooted in his community – the Davies family goes back in Bynea some two hundred years – even to contemplate such a move. A 'behinder' in St David's tinworks for years, he was a redoubtable character whose three sons – Roy who played a few games on the wing for the 'Scarlets', Len who died a cruelly untimely death aged twenty-six after winning three caps as a wing-forward for Wales, and Terry – inherited his athleticism. Even more significant in Terry's case, he inherited from his father a furnace-tested toughness, an unyielding determination to face down the opposition that was the hallmark of his prowess as a player. The 'hard stuff' never unnerved him and his still powerful frame prompts the thought that any intruder rash enough to risk a confrontation with the man who built 'The Sycamores' for his wife, Gill, and their three children, could have little care for his person. He recalls brutal trials of body and will with the chuckle of the fearless, noting that he survived the hardest tackle he ever suffered when no more than a youth playing his third or fourth game for Swansea. Rashly attempting to run the ball out of defence against Cardiff, Jack Matthews hit him with a merciless intent that left him disorientated and somewhat dismantled. *Fe ges i berlad ond es i ddim bant* (I was hit for six but I didn't go off.) 'Dr Jack' enjoys reminding him of their first brief encounter whenever they meet.

It was a small schoolboy who entered Stradey Secondary School where his potential was quickly spotted by two of the teachers, the long-serving D. T. (Toy) Henton and Hywel Thomas who was briefly in charge of PE. In those coupon-cramped austerity days, soccer and rugby boots were wondrous things you prayed for. A pair of ordinary boots, reinforced with strips of leather attached to their soles by his father, had to do for Terry until his selection to play at outside-half for Llanelli Schoolboys was rewarded with a pair of Cotton Oxford's – the footwear of the gods. But imperfectly shod as he was, nothing could disguise the fact that this slight boy could already kick a rugby ball a fair distance. And he could field it from all angles and heights with a grasp as firm as a behinder's hold on his tongs.

To say that Terry Davies excelled during the 1950s when a full-back was selected to tackle, catch and kick is to state the obvious. 'Toy' Henton, who imparted the Llanelli passion for rugby to his boys, and Hywel Thomas set about developing Terry's skills. He remembers with affection how 'Mr Henton' would urge his charges to 'tackle me! tackle me!' until one day Jones *bach* of Llangennech, smaller even than Terry but a tackler of kamikaze volition, took him at his word and put a permanent stop to his goading with a lethal ankle-high hit. As Terry recalls, 'Toy' Henton was a scourge of smokers, constantly complaining that there were 'too many Woodbine chests' around, and as the owner of the most Woodbine of chests Jones *bach* had a point to make. In his triumphant words, *Fe ges i'r diawl!* (I got the bugger!)

Hywel Thomas would put a gym shoe on Terry's right foot and make him punt with his booted left until he came to think of himself as a 'natural' two-footed kicker of a kind all too rare nowadays, as he pointedly remarked when talking about angled counter-attacking kicking. No one who saw him play can forget the power and beauty of his place-kicking and punting in those days when both rugby and soccer balls weighed a leathered ton. To see Terry Davies kick 40- and 50-yard penalties on an Arms Park pitch resembling Tregaron Bog was to enjoy eye-rubbing wonder.

His career was studded with magnificent kicks – a 55-yard penalty from the touch-line to clinch victory against France in Paris in 1957, a 45-yard penalty into the wind at Twickenham in 1958 to secure a 3–3 draw (not to mention the 55-yarder which bounced back from the crossbar prompting outraged Welsh fans to remove the offending piece of woodwork afterwards), a 90-yard relieving(!) punt against Northern Transvaal during the Barbarians tour of South Africa in 1958, a touch-line conversion on a foul Arms Park surface of Dewi Bebb's historic match-winning try against England in 1959, his five penalties and four conversions in a haul of twenty-three points for the Lions against North Auckland at Whangarei in September 1959, and his two stupendous drop-goals from the half-way line against Aberavon on 10 October 1959 within a few days of his return from New Zealand which brought a legion of his exultant admirers pouring on to Stradey Park to chair him from the field. All these and many more came from the boot of the schoolboy who in practice matched Hywel Thomas, then a centre for

Llanelli, kick for kick and catch for catch before he left at fifteen years of age to make his way in the world.

By now he had set his heart on winning a Welsh Youth cap and aware that the Bynea team was not strong enough to help realize his ambition, he tried his fortune with neighbouring Llangennech for a season – but to no avail. That he should have 'risked' such a move is proof enough of his desire to play for Wales. The rivalry between the two villages went back a long way – certainly as far as 1908–9 when Llangennech took Bynea Village Boys' ground record – and is best illustrated by the story that tells of a primordial struggle in Bynea when the home side had Llangennech defending 'in the trenches'. A demented maul on the try-line ended when the referee awarded Bynea a try. As the players emerged from the slough an enraged Llangennech number 8 was seen to have the ball secured under his capacious stomach and would not release it for the conversion. His reply to the referee's threat of a sending off was instantaneous: 'Listen wus, they scored without the ball let 'em bloody convert without it.' Like all players in that part of the world Terry learnt early that it was one thing to lose but another thing entirely to concede defeat.

Denied a Youth cap, it gave him much satisfaction as a 17-year-old to make his debut for Swansea in an away game against Ebbw Vale in January 1951. At that time Gerwyn Williams, first choice for Wales at full-back, was a Llanelli player, which accounts for Terry's move to Swansea. The bus journey to Ebbw Vale left him sick as a dog, but his play prompted talk of a future international in the making. Eleven months later, following the game against the Springboks, his credentials elicited widespread commendation and it could only be a matter of time before he won a senior Welsh cap.

In February 1952 he began his National Service with the Royal Marines and the next two years saw him playing for Devonport Services, the Royal Navy, Swansea and Wales. On 17 January 1953 the 20-year-old Terry Davies made the first of his twenty-one appearances for Wales against England at Cardiff Arms Park. Wales lost 8–3, their only score a penalty, a 'beauty' kicked by the new full-back who, despite being overshadowed that day by England's Nim Hall, gave notice that he intended to make the position his own.

It was for me a moving experience to listen to him recount how he was plucked without warning or explanation from the snowy wastes of the training range on Dartmoor, where he was being instructed in the priming of grenades, and whisked to see his CO at Bickligh to be told, finally, not that he was 'on a charge' but that he had been selected to play for his country. There he was, a young Welshman walking on air, and there was no one to share his exhilaration. *Doen nhw ddim yn deall beth oedd e'n olygu i Gymro* (They didn't understand what it meant to a Welshman.). Forty-six years on his memory unfailingly traced the events of the leave – all of two days – he was given to play for Wales. And as he talked, the train journey to Cardiff clamorous with well-wishers, the streets leading to the Arms Park flowing with flat-capped anticipation, the dressing-room heady with embrocation, the roar of a nation's hymns for its team, assailed the senses and we were both young again – he in deeds and I in acclamation.

The Sunday morning after his third cap against Ireland at Swansea in March 1953 – he had converted Gareth Griffiths's try to secure a 5–3 victory – as he lay abed in his council-house home in Pen-y-graig, Llwynhendy, his mother roused him with the news that two strangers with a large briefcase wanted to talk to him. They were Wigan representatives intent on persuading him to follow in Lewis Jones's footsteps and 'go North'. They felt sure that they had found another Jim Sullivan. It got to the point where sums ranging between £5,000 and £9,000 were being discussed, and £5,000 in notes were actually piled up on the kitchen table. Terry heard his mother's gasp as she glimpsed the fortune through the dividing curtain: *Arglwydd mowr, drycha ar yr arian 'na, Ted!* (Lord God, look at that money, Ted!). Such a sum in 1953, so Terry the businessman reckons, would have bought sixteen houses in Llanelli or three local farms! He rejected his would-be Wigan captors as he would later reject Leeds and Bradford. Like his father before him his roots went deep, and more to the point his newly acquired status as a Welsh international had even conferred a certain distinction on his mother as a faithful member of Soar Baptist chapel! With so much to savour at home it was no time to 'go North'. As for the fortune he spurned he would, as he said phlegmatically, most probably have misspent it. For him, the truly rewarding aspect of the affair was that he had been headhunted by Wigan. He was rated as a front-rank international player with enormous potential yet unfulfilled

The 18-year-old who joined the Marines at 5'8" and 11st. 8lbs was built up to 5'11" and 13st. 3lbs. His experience of first-class rugby was enriched and one can only guess what priming grenades, which allowed no more than three to seven seconds to make good his escape should things go wrong, did for his fielding. His hands hardly ever failed him. But an accident when on a commando assault course in Cornwall badly injured his right shoulder and when on tour to Romania with Swansea in 1954 a tackle sent him crashing onto a concrete perimeter, putting the same shoulder horribly out of joint, his rugby career seemed finished. As he told me of the excruciating pain he endured in two hospitals in Bucharest – in one of which patients lay dying in the corridors – as doctors made a hash of putting his shoulder back, I admit to feeling queasy. Like J. P. R. Williams here was another full-back with a seemingly superhuman capacity for resisting pain and standing fast.

Terry Davies did not play again until 1956, his recovery having been effected by the skills of Gordon Rowley, a Swansea surgeon, during an eight-hour pioneering operation and expedited by his own determination to come back. During his recuperation he laid the foundations of a profitable business as a timber merchant, building sheds and garages, felling trees and at one stage manhandling up to forty tons of railway sleepers a day to toughen himself anew. Playing for Bynea he appeared in three Welsh trials and on 19 January 1957 he returned for Wales, winning his fifth cap against England at the Arms Park. Wales lost 3–0, but for Terry Davies it was a day of triumph and his greatest achievement as a player. It is no exaggeration to describe as heroic his two-year struggle to reclaim his place in the Welsh team, his one lasting regret the fact that his injury deprived him of the huge satisfaction of playing for Wales alongside his brother, Len, who won his three caps in 1954–5.

Terry played his first game for the 'Scarlets' away against Bath on 17 March 1956, and by the time he retired from first-class rugby in 1961 his place in the forefront of the Stradey Park pantheon as a great full-back was secure. His talents made more formidable a Llanelli side that provided six players for the Welsh team which defeated Australia 9–3 in January 1958, the other five being Ray Williams, Cyril Davies, Carwyn James, Wynne Evans and R. H. Williams, and with the indestructible 'R.H.' who played in all four Tests for the 1959 Lions, Terry Davies was to enhance the reputation of Welsh rugby in New Zealand. He was subsequently to captain his country on three occasions, including the ludicrous encounter with Avril Malan's Springboks, lost 3–0, on an Arms Park pitch better suited that day in December 1960 for aquatic sports. With true obduracy he still insists that he was right to play against the wind in the first half and that the referee, Jack Taylor, was wrong to deny Danny Harris an equalizing try for Wales. Confronted with such issues he tackles them in characteristic fashion – head on.

In his prime when the full-back was expected above all else to defend his line, it is inevitable that Terry Davies rides high in the estimation of those who saw him play by virtue of his inspiring defensive qualities. But it should be remembered, too, that the schoolboy outside-half played some first-class matches in that position, and the Welsh selectors in 1956 had him playing as a centre in their trials – a position he occupied in a number of games for Llanelli. He treasures the memory of one game for the Royal Navy when his play at outside-half was monitored by Carwyn James at full-back – surely the most diverting example in the history of rugby of a dove covering a hawk. He would have revelled in the adventurousness of the 1970s for he had the physique and the temperament to excel at the running game as he proved when starring for England and Wales against Scotland and Ireland in the Jubilee match played on 17 October 1959 to celebrate Twickenham's fiftieth anniversary. Of the twenty-three Lions who played that day none shone brighter than the irrepressible full-back who kicked four conversions in a refulgent game won 26–17 by England and Wales. Terry Davies would have been a superior player at any stage of rugby's evolution.

Welsh poets when eulogizing a leader who defended his people against the incursions of foes would sometimes liken him to an oak door, *derwin ddôr*, and it is an apposite image for Terry Davies. Like 'J.P.R.' he closed the door on even the thought of giving way and made it his business early on in a game to impress on opposing backs the wisdom of passing the ball before they got within range of his tackle. Welsh players of his day, he assured me, were never in awe of the opposition. Often the physical and mental products of communities battle-hardened in the service of heavy industry, no opponents, no matter how forbidding, held any terrors for them, especially those forwards with Charles Atlas torsos and spindly legs of steel he joyfully calls to mind with much admiration. Inured to the trials of coal-face and furnace, All Blacks and Springboks amounted to no more than another hard shift.

Terry Davies's toughness was bred in the bone. In his first game for Wales he suffered a broken rib when stopping Woodward, the shire-horse England wing, but he played on. In the Second Test against the All Blacks at Wellington on 15 August 1959 he was savagely kicked on the thigh but still outplayed his opposite number, none other than Don Clarke, kicking a penalty and converting John Young's try in a game the Lions lost, 11–8. New Zealand recognized from the moment he fielded the first box-kick meant to 'skin' him, the spirit and skill of a competitor totally committed to winning. In the monstrous brawl with the New Zealand Maoris on 5 September 1959 which left J. B. G. Thomas outraged, Terry Davies, by then a 14-stone deterrent, gave no less than he got. In thirteen appearances for the Lions he scored 104 points from twenty-eight conversions and sixteen penalties and how the selectors saw fit to play him in only two Tests is another of rugby's mysteries. In the Fourth Test, which the Lions won 9–6, his play won universal acclaim and he was the Lion the All Blacks coveted above all others.

It is still a joy to recall his kicking, the way his magnificent punts would send the ball soaring like some fledgling condor afloat on an Andes thermal. But it is the memory of one particular tackle that for me crystallizes the power, the timing and lethal focus which made Terry Davies a choice warrior full-back fit for the storyteller's art. Those who saw it can be relied upon to relate how the famous Davies shoulder shook François Roux, the scalp-hunting, late-tackling Springbok wing to the very core of his malevolence when Llanelli lost 21–0 to Avril Malan's team on 13 December 1960. I was not there to witness that feat of retribution, but I was at Cardiff Arms Park in April 1957 when Wales defeated an International XV 17–16 in a game to drum up funds for the 1958 Empire Games.

The crowd was electrified by the running and elusiveness of Arthur Smith and Tony O'Reilly, Gareth Griffiths and Gordon Wells, Cyril Davies, Jeff Butterfield and Phil Davies, Cliff Morgan and Carwyn James, but what I still marvel at when I relive the game is Terry Davies's second-half tackle on Phil Davies. From the half-way line the mighty England centre came thundering down towards the river end with only the full-back, some fifteen yards in from touch, body angled like a stake driven into the ground to repel a cavalry charge, to beat. He feinted to come infield, but Terry knowing, as he told me, that Phil Davies rarely side-stepped off his left foot, held his ground. As the centre went to pass him on his right side, Terry seemed to uncoil into a length of Trostre steel and brought him down with as conclusive a tackle as one could wish to see. The stadium resounded with a huge roar in recognition of the high endeavour of a player who exerted himself to the utmost each time he played for Wales.

Terry Davies won his last cap against France in Paris on 25 March 1961. He was a full-back for all seasons, for all encounters. When asked what Terry's presence on the field meant to him, the highly regarded winger Ray Williams, a team-mate for the 'Scarlets' and Wales, said simply: 'When Terry played you could fully commit yourself to attack. You never needed to worry about what was happening behind you.' Nowadays, could he but return in all his 18-year-old glory, as captured by Andrew Vaccari's oil painting of him in Bynea's colours, the Welsh Assembly would seriously have to consider cloning him.

# ALUN PASK

John Hollyman

The Arms Park, 26 September 1964, Wales versus Fiji in an unofficial international. From a set scrum mid-field in the Fijian half, Wales win the ball against the strike and number 8 Alun Pask, 6'3", head-banded and imperious, picks up and starts a looping run out to his left. Gaining speed as he charges through the first line of defence, he straightens up his run with first a two-handed dummy to his left, then beats two more defenders with a couple of one-handed dummies in the air, before bouncing away a tackle from the covering second-row forward and diving over the line right in the corner. This was a sensational solo try in an emotionally charged game which produced thirteen tries in a 28–22 win for Wales. For the 50,000 spectators and for John Billot it was 'a revival meeting rather than a rugby spectacle . . . a step into the past, to the days of the Golden Era when everyone ran and attacked and rugby was a handling game'.

In the 1960s, Wales managed to win only twenty-one of their fifty-nine games, and in the early sixties in particular the national team struggled to rise above the mediocre and achieve any sort of consistency or coherent strategy. The 1963–4 season brought a share in the championship with Scotland and there were two outright champion-ships in the following two seasons, the second under Alun Pask's captaincy. In those years the Welsh game clung to the conformist belief in the value and effectiveness of tight forward play, which when successful established a platform from which the backs could attack. Unfortunately, when unsuccessful, there was little left to offer, and the fans were left hungry in a famine of tries and low-scoring games. Later, Alun Pask was often asked who had been the model for his style and approach to the game. He replied that his style was his own, the way he felt the game should be played. When he started his senior rugby career at twenty years of age, France was the team that captured the imagination for the way they transformed the European game. The French had been defeated by Wales in 1957, but they were not to be beaten again in Paris until 1971. Inspired by Lucien Mias, the French used the forwards as handlers and runners with the ball, peeling off the line-out to set up momentum and drive, picking up the ball from the back of the set scrum to initiate attacks, and using speed and fitness to attack defensive gaps and finish off with tries. This was a style that appealed to Alun Pask and he threw himself into playing a fast, running rugby that involved forwards and backs, linked together by their back row. No one was better equipped to show how mobility and fitness, speed and strength were qualities that forwards needed in order to play beyond the confines of the ball-winning set piece and liberate themselves into a ball-using role. The French press regularly made appreciative references to 'le grand Alun Pask', sentiments echoed even further afield by South Africans, New Zealanders and Australians who saw in him the world-class back-row player so prized by their own rugby cultures. Alun Pask's individual play shattered the tactical conformity of the Welsh game, opening up new areas of attacking play and adding to the winning instinct the spice of enterprise and innovation.

Alun Edward Islwyn Pask was born on 10 September 1937, at Blackwood, in the Sirhowy Valley, Gwent, the second son of Winifred and Gwyn Pask. In a valley where most employment was provided by the Oakdale colliery, level and drift mines around the town and the steel works of Ebbw Vale to the north, Alun's father was a civil servant educated at Newbridge Grammar School. He established the rugby pedigree in the family, playing as a second-row forward and later becoming president of the Blackwood club. From the Libanus Primary School in Blackwood, Alun moved to Pontllanfraith Grammar School in 1948; pitched into rugby straight away, he was a successful scrum-half for his own school and Rhymney Valley Schools at thirteen, and it was this experience as a scrum-half that gave him the taste for handling, tackling and kicking that was to stay with him through his senior career. His rapid physical growth from the age of fourteen onwards meant that as soon as he went into the sixth form at Pontllanfraith he was put into the pack, and in his first school game as a forward he made such an impression that he was immediately selected as number 8 for the Monmouthshire Secondary Schools against the Eastern Transvaal touring side. This performance catapulted him into the first of three appearances for the Welsh Secondary Schools.

In 1955, Alun was called up for National Service and after a spell with the South Wales Borderers he volunteered for the Parachute Regiment, which led to active service in Cyprus and on the ill-conceived

Suez expedition; while off duty on the island he met Haydn Morgan, who persuaded him to join his own team, Abertillery, once his two years' service was completed. The Army wanted to use him as a shot-putter and discus-thrower in the inter-services tournament, but after athletics trials the selectors could not fail to recognize his speed on the track, and switched him to the 220- and 440-yards events.

It was the end of 1956 before he played his first game for Abertillery at Bridgend, thus beginning a back-row partnership with Haydn Morgan that was to be repeated at international and Lions level. He had always intended to train as a teacher in physical education and geography at Loughborough College, and he began his studies in 1957. During that first year he played for the College XV, Leicestershire, Abertillery, Monmouthshire and the UAU, going on in his second year to captain the College and win the Middlesex Sevens in 1959. His physical presence, at 6'3" and nearly fifteen stone, plus his natural speed, added up to a big man by the standards of rugby in the 1960s. During his second year at college and while playing regular games for his club he was given the first of thirteen Welsh trials and thirteen trips as reserve before winning his first cap.

Alun Pask's rise to prominence in Welsh rugby was helped by his selection, while still at college, at number 8 for the combined Abertillery/Ebbw Vale team that beat the touring Australians in January 1958, with Haydn Morgan playing alongside him in such devastating form that he won the first of his twenty-seven caps nine days later against England. In November 1960, however, it was the Springboks who were held to a bare 3–0 victory by the combined side whose Abertillery back row of Morgan, Pask and John Lewis gave a tough defensive display. Wales selected David Nash of Ebbw Vale as number 8 against the Springboks, but in the last game of the 1960–1 home championship Alun Pask, in his first year of captaincy with Abertillery, was selected against France, out of position on the blind side as a replacement for the injured Glyn Davidge. This was to be the first of Pask's twenty-six consecutive caps, and he marked his debut with a try opportunely snatched from a long French throw-in on their own line.

His partnership with Haydn Morgan was an important element in his success for both Abertillery and Wales. Morgan was a destroyer with the speed of the converted centre three-quarter, and was the perfect foil to Pask, the constructive, sure-handed number 8 who had the height to win line-out ball, strength in the tight scrums and mauls, and a calm tactician's appraisal of the course of a game which enabled him to materialize in unsuspected corners of the field to set up counter-attacks and bring off tackles. Given that the conventional view of the nature and role of a forward at this time was that he should fight for the ball in close encounters that seemed destined to end in the referee blowing for a set scrum to restart the process yet again, Pask was sometimes darkly referred to as a 'seagull', supposedly hanging off the heavy-duty mauling and waiting for developments elsewhere. In truth, having ensured that his team won its own ball in the set-piece scrums, Pask believed that the back-row player's role was a dynamic one. Against convention, he would take a long ball from the end of the line-out and flick it on direct to the outside-half, at the time a totally un-orthodox move which allowed a fast number 10 to exploit the space created.

Pask's selection for the England game at Twickenham in 1962 was once again as a replacement, this time at number 8, after David Nash's late withdrawal on the morning of the game. Lloyd Williams at scrum-half was the captain, a player whose reputation as a 'ninth forward' was in tune with the orientation of the tactical thinking of the era. Pask's speed, mobility and tackling made him a class player on the blind side, as his first game for Wales had already demonstrated, and the view of Pask as a mobile flanker was to continue into the summer in South Africa. The Twickenham game was a scoreless stalemate, as the two back rows cancelled each other out. A patternless forward display against Scotland in February, the Welsh unable to ruck the ball effectively, led to Scotland's first victory in Cardiff for twenty-five years; but the French game saw a victory inspired by the Welsh forwards, who drove a wedge into the French line-out, held them in the tight and took them on in the mauls with a muscular display. The decisive score was the early penalty goal from Kelvin Coslett, to compensate for his five missed penalty attempts at Twickenham, but the most vivid memory of the day was a brilliant defensive effort from Alun Pask, who according to *The Times* played the 'all-round game of his life'. Late in the game, the French winger Henri Rancoule broke clear of the Welsh defence on a run down the right-hand touch-line from outside his own 25. Pask, on a corner-flagging run from the other side of the field, had the fitness and speed to turn, overhaul the winger and drag him down, saving a certain score and preventing a French win. The Lions' selectors watched, and his selection for the South African tour was beyond doubt.

The Lions' selectors had taken note of the Welsh forwards' domination of the French. They had already seen the Barbarians beat the Springboks by matching and dominating them in the tight in the last game of their British tour in 1961, and on this evidence they concluded that it was essential to take on the formidable South African pack with a heavy-weight pack of forwards who would win the bulk of the possession. Unfortunately the corollary of this argument, that the backs should use the dry conditions to run the ball at the opposition, could not be confidently maintained. The Lions' backs of 1962 were nothing like their predecessors of 1955. No Morgan, Butterfield, Davies or O'Reilly. Instead, they had the more prosaic virtues of Waddell and Weston, and the burden of injuries to Richard Sharp and David Hewitt. But it was the decision to take on the Springboks by playing the static forward-dominated game that was the true tactical source of the tour's problems. The Lions had a fine pack of big, heavy forwards, and early on it was decided to select Alun Pask as a blind-side flanker. Thus he made only two appearances at number 8, where Campbell-Lamerton, the huge Scottish second row, was played out of position. Injuries and loss of form compounded this tactical error, leaving three number 8s and two specialist open-side flankers to fill both flanks. The South African officials and press were no less perplexed than the Welsh public at Pask's selection on the blind side instead of at number 8. Selection in his normal position could have brought mobility, tactical awareness at the fringes of scrum and line-out and the understanding he had with his club partner, Haydn Morgan, to balance the extra stone or two of weight lost.

Pask had already confirmed his presence on tour when he scored in the first game against Rhodesia, supporting at speed a fifty-yard break from Sharp. Long-legged and with a straight-backed upright stance, his pace in support play brought him tries against Boland, Eastern Province and Western Province, the latter with a one-handed try in the right corner, famously captured in a photo showing him apparently suspended before the tackler bundled him into touch. His support play, positional sense and assured handling were enhanced by the firm conditions and such was his mobility and confident all-round skills that when injuries occurred, in the era before replacements, Pask filled in for Niall Brophy on the wing in the First Test and and for Dewi Bebb in the Third, looking 'good enough to stand in almost anywhere' as Reg Sweet commented. The qualities that the Lions missed by playing him out of position were amply revealed in the game against Transvaal, when his tackling and attacking in a range of back-row moves were irresistible, and he set up the moves that led to three tries, one by Bill Mulcahy and two by captain Arthur Smith. For the last of these tries, Pask broke free of the defence to race up the touch-line with the ball in one hand, eluding the full-back's tackle to pass inside for Smith to score. For the Third Test, he was selected once again at blind-side flanker, and his fitness and reading of the game took him everywhere on the field, but yet again the Springboks won, if only by a narrow margin. Alun Pask's tour ended when he was tackled into a crowd of schoolboys on the touch-line and his tacklers landed on top of him, breaking a rib. He scored four tries in his fourteen appearances on tour, and was the back-row forward most admired by the South Africans for his outstanding abilities. The South Africans were not his only admirers. In the autumn of 1962 rugby league took an interest in both him and Haydn Morgan. Yet Pask's loyalty to the amateur game and its qualities was as unwavering as his loyalty to Abertillery, despite the attractions of more fashionable clubs. He had settled into his work as a teacher at Tredegar Grammar (later Comprehensive) School where he taught physical education until he took early retirement in 1987.

The Welsh team began the 1962–3 season with a new captain and scrum-half. Clive Rowlands proved a controversial partner for the quick-silver new outside-half David Watkins and the dynamic Pask at number 8. His preference for the kicking game and his short pass probably prevented colleagues from achieving their full potential. In that season, Wales lost to England at Cardiff but restored confidence against Scotland with a game dominated by the kicking of Rowlands to set up driving mauls from the lines-out. Led by Pask, the Welsh forwards denied the Scots any chance of possession, the ball reaching David Watkins from his captain on only two occasions. Pask's outstanding form at number 8 showed what a waste his selection at blind side in South Africa had been. In the following games against Ireland and France that year the Welsh forwards were well beaten by the Irish but succeeded in subduing the French eight. Nevertheless, Wales lost that game by failing to release the backs. The French regarded the Welsh back row as the best in the home countries, and their plan was to draw them into mauls with long throws at the line-out and then try to release their own backs down the narrow side. By obsessively kicking into touch, Wales fell into their trap and there were calls for a change of captaincy as Wales slid to the bottom of the championship, having scored only seven tries in their last thirteen matches. Rowlands's skills as a motivating leader could not outweigh his preference for the kick over the pass, and for tight forward play over the speedy break or the release of the backs.

The start of the 1963–4 season was dominated in Wales by the visit of Whineray's All Blacks. On three occasions, Pask played against them at number 8: for the Abertillery/Ebbw Vale Combined side, Wales and the Barbarians. It is significant that New Zealand's travelling correspondent wrote in *The Times* that Pask 'would certainly go straight into any world scrummage chosen by a New Zealander'. Wales lost 0–6 against the All Blacks, but in a drab home championship won two and drew two games to become undefeated joint champions. After this modest achievement there was much worse to come: on a short tour to South Africa, the Welsh team succumbed to its biggest defeat in forty years. They lost by 24–3 in the Test, wilting in the heat and fading dramatically in the last quarter. Once again there was a reluctance to use the backs, and the team was worn down by the fitness and speed of the ball-handling Springbok forwards, who were better used to the high temperatures. Immediately before this tour, Pask's South African admirers had made clear their high regard for him by inviting him and David Watkins to be Welsh representatives at their Jubilee celebration games. Mixing and matching South African forwards with the invited team's backs and vice versa, Pask was named alongside the illustrious Wilson Whineray and Colin Meads as the men of the match in the last of the three games played.

As joint champions, grimly determined to hold on to their revival of the previous season and gain their first Triple Crown since 1952, Wales opened the 1964–5 season playing England in Cardiff in conditions that would have halted a club game. The golden glow of the early season victory against Fiji soon disappeared in the rain-lashed gloom. Yet the pack under Pask's leadership controlled the line-out and won the exchanges on the fringe of the scrum; despite the conditions, Wales scored three tries, the second after Pask had chipped over the heads of the forwards, scrum-half style, for his flanker to score. At Murrayfield an intoxicating game saw the lead change hands four times, before Wales snatched victory by 14–12, with Pask again stamping his leadership qualities on the forward effort. Unstoppable against Ireland, Wales won the Triple Crown, but not before John Dawes spent twenty minutes off the field injured. At this point, Terry Price went to centre and Pask was asked to fill in as emergency full-back by Rowlands. With the Triple Crown at stake, Pask's fielding and positioning in defence were faultless, as he fired the remaining seven forwards with confidence and kept the Irish at bay. But the French game at Colombes upset all hopes. On the firm surface, the Welsh forwards could not match the French in mesmeric running mood; they were 22–0 down by just after half time, although they fought back to 22–13 with three tries and a conversion. The Welsh forwards, brought up on the wet-weather game, could not adapt their game in response to the multi-skilled French forwards. Despite winning the Triple Crown and the Championship, Rowlands fell victim to this defeat, and the selectors ended his run of fourteen games in the search for a fresh captain and a new scrum-half.

After twenty consecutive caps Pask became captain for the 11–6 victory over England in January 1966, only the fourth to lead Wales to a win at Twickenham. Allan Lewis, by now Pask's club scrum-half at Abertillery and a longer and more fluent passer of the ball than Rowlands, won his first cap in that game. It was Pask who scored the single Welsh try, supporting a fast D. Ken Jones run to take a difficult pass five yards out and dive into the left corner. The three tries in the win against Scotland were achieved despite the pools of water on the Cardiff quagmire and would have been impressive even on a dry day. A second successive Triple Crown looked a near certainty in the game against Ireland and, in press interviews, Pask gave the impression that he thought as much. Where a Rowlands might have raised the heart rate and nagged his team to a win, Pask's quieter expectation that his team would play to their full potential was let down against a resolute Irish side. No Triple Crown then, but an exciting Championship decider against France. Wales's 9–8 win could not have been more dramatic, not just for a memorable interception and 75-yard run by Stuart Watkins, but also for the last penalty kick of the match by Claude Lacaze which could have won the game for France but which faded at the last, as did French hopes of sharing the Championship spoils.

As captain of the Championship winners, Pask must have been confident that his name would be among the first to be considered for the captaincy of the British Lions tour to Australia, New Zealand and Canada that summer. But if the 1962 tour had come to grief on a tactical misjudgement, the 1966 tour fell victim to mismanagement and amateurish complacency. The selectors took what seemed to be a political decision to exclude Wales from providing a tour captain out of the ten Welsh players originally selected, and surprised Scotland's Mike Campbell-Lamerton with the task. Campbell-Lamerton showed whole-hearted commitment to the job and a good deal of courage in leaving himself out of two Tests, but his tactical limitations were exposed, despite the loyal support given by Alun Pask and other senior players. The firm leadership and guiding hand that the tour needed were fragmented, and discipline and direction were lost. Although they won three out of seven Test matches played, and although they had exciting three-quarters and forwards who earned the highest praise from the New Zealanders, the Lions lost all four New Zealand Tests, an un-precedented record, and the captaincy was passed around haphazardly, devaluing and undermining the leadership on and off the field. New Zealand's use of the then innovative idea of second-phase attacks derived from the inside centre deliberately taking the ball into the tackle required a tactician's response on the field, but the Lions' play was naïve and allowed scrum-half Laidlaw and the back row of Waka Nathan, Lochore and Tremain to dominate.

At twenty-nine years of age, Pask must have been disappointed at the captaincy decision, but he accepted it like the gentleman he was. It must have been of some consolation that he was able to play in his natural position at number 8 for most of the tour, despite a repetition of the 1962 tour's injuries to the first-choice flankers. He was made acting captain on only four occasions and was dropped for the Second Test against New Zealand after the heavy 20–3 defeat in the previous Test. The Australian leg of the tour had brought victories in both Tests, the first by 8–3 and the second, by 31–0, as well as a perfect exhibition from Pask, who in the view of the Australian press 'lived up to his reputation as the world's greatest number 8'. As captain in the NZ Universities game ten days later he scored a try after a classic close inter-passing back-row move and an optimistic mood was set that the rest of the tour could be equally as free-scoring. However, this proved to be one of only three games in New Zealand when the Lions scored more than twenty points and played fluently. They could match Meads, Nathan, Tremain and Lochore but chose not to play to their strength, their outstanding backs. As Terry McLean wrote, in the clash between 'the classic style of the Lions and the powerful workaday method of the All Blacks . . . method . . . triumphed but style at its best . . . is superior to method'. The Lions lost the First Test, complaining about poor refereeing and dirty play after the Canterbury game. The disarray was evident when the tour captain dropped both himself and Pask for the Second Test, and without a link man between forwards and backs the game slipped away yet again. Restored for the Third Test Pask was back at number 8, in a game lost through errors. He was then pushed back to blind-side flanker for the Final Test and overlooked for the captaincy in favour of David Watkins, with Campbell-Lamerton again standing down. The politics of the original captaincy issue had become part of the shambles of the tour management. For Pask it was to be his last game of the tour, as he broke his left collar-bone before half-time.

Alun Pask would play just three more games for Wales. In December 1966, the touring Australians gained their first victory over Wales by 14–11 in an exciting attacking game, but the running style manifested in that game was not maintained for the first home championship game in February 1967, a defeat against Scotland, and there was criticism that tactics had not been changed to encourage the new half-backs to run at the Scots instead of kicking. The defeat meant a demotion for Pask, and David Watkins was appointed captain against Ireland, having earlier lost his place against Australia and Scotland to Barry John. The selectors used twenty-three players in just three games, and their confusion mirrored the bewilderment of the team, who failed to score for the first time in sixteen games in a 0–3 gale-blown defeat by Ireland. Alun Pask was dropped against France, and Wales went down to their fourth defeat in a row, a sequence that had not happened in over forty years. It was not until seven games later, in 1969, that Wales found in Mervyn Davies a player as consistent and reliable as Alun Pask to form the centre of a settled back row. The end of Pask's international career was shortly followed by the announcement of his retirement from club rugby in June 1967, a decision made when his enthusiasm for playing the game was at a low ebb following his brother David's death from leukaemia. Pask was involved with the WRU's early coaching panels following the Lions tour, and his expertise and knowledge of the game continued to be appreciated for many years in his role behind the scenes, and occasionally in front of the cameras as a part-time producer with BBC Wales, when he devised a method of visually logging on paper the details of an 80-minute game so that the video tape could be expertly and rapidly edited for showing during weekly rugby programmes. Tragically, in November 1995 he died in a fire at his home in Blackwood.

Alun Pask was a gifted rugby player and accomplished athlete who gave consistent, loyal and magnificent service to the national game, a physically impressive forward with pace and imagination whose handling, tactical awareness and positional sense enabled him to think and react like a three-quarter. He defended and tackled tirelessly in the traditionally assigned role of the back row, he had strength and power in tight forward play, but his individual style broke out of the dour conformities of the 1960s to create moments of inspirational artistry. In many ways, he was the precursor of the great Welsh era of the 1970s when the national team produced the adventurous and risk-taking rugby that was at the heart of his own brilliant play.

# BRIAN PRICE

## David Parry-Jones

Asking a man who lives between the Usk and the Wye where he hails from is like putting a question by telephone to someone in another hemisphere: a short pause always ensues before you hear anything back. The delay in this south-east corner of Wales, however, is not down to distance. It usually means that the latest geopolitically correct reply is being groped for.

Nomenclature has certainly been confusing here even without Siluria, a beautiful name dimly recalled now and then through the mists of time. During the twentieth century alone this unique amalgam of mineral-rich valleys and rolling pastureland has been known as 'Monmouthshire' (a part of 'Wales and Monmouthshire'), 'Gwent', a throwback to Roman *Venta Silurum*, and now, again, 'Monmouthshire'. Its chief town Newport, however, though in it is not of it. Hm.

So far, so intriguing. Let us stir the pot further with a sidelong glance at Newport Rugby Football Club. Becalmed, not to say beached, in these last years of the twentieth century, it was once a capital ship in Welsh rugby's battle fleet. In post-war decades men like Ken Jones, Malcolm Thomas, Roy Burnett and the two Watkins, David and Stuart, were stars who drew big crowds to Rodney Parade and many far-flung venues. Complementing such backs was a heavily armoured breed of forwards which included R. T. Evans, John Gwilliam and the great Bryn Meredith. And – there were men who played for England too: Newport enjoys a unique status in the game through its affiliation to two Unions. Soon after being formed in 1875 it joined the Rugby Football Union, before also figuring a few years later among the founding-members of the Welsh ruling body.

For all these reasons, therefore, do the good people of Gwent experience on-going identity crises? A provocative, challenging way, methought, of beginning an essay on one of the county's great rugby men.

Yet, as he held off hairy-arsed (not a term applied to any player behind the scrum) opponents bent on doing him a mischief, so Brian Price can stop in its tracks a thesis that is apparently progressing plausibly. Having heard me out patiently, his polite response was, 'Well, I couldn't say. Remember – I wasn't born in Gwent'.

On 30 October 1937 the mining village of Deri, nowadays part of Caerphilly, lay just inside the old county of Glamorgan. A tiny place; yet its small grammar school tutored not just Brian Price but rugby luminaries such as one-time Wales hooker Billy Thomas and Dick Uzzell, a mid-field player destined to achieve immortality in 1963. Like almost all valleys communities of the time Deri had sprouted around a pithead; but Tom and Mavis Price were adamant that young Brian would not earn a living underground. The genes did the trick: as he moved into his teens, the offspring they produced was already far too tall to contemplate mining meaningfully in a four-foot seam. Schoolmastering: now there was a good career.

When a major rugby talent-in-the-making is identified in Wales green lights show, doors glide open and the product is handled with this-side-up care and concern (all of which remains true in the new professional era). With the glittering influence of former student Bryn Meredith behind him it was a formality for Brian Price to be admitted to St Luke's College, Exeter. His mother, who escorted her tender 17-year-old to Devon for his admission bid, felt faint when, after other applicants had spent twenty minutes being exhaustively interviewed, her son emerged from the principal's office in a tenth of that time. He had only been asked one vital question: if St Luke's took him, would he abandon ambitions to play his rugby at number 8 in favour of the second row? The answer was given swiftly: the young man had already privately decided that the lock position held more appeal for him.

Newport RFC selected him during vacations (his first major game was against Leicester) and had been tracking his ambitions and potential. His career progress was next influenced when, at the club's bidding, he accepted a first post at Tredegar Technical School attached to the physical education department. Introducing three recruits at the start of a new school year the headmaster told members of staff, 'This is Mr Jameson, who will teach physics. On my left, Mr Evans, our new chemistry master. And this is Mr Brian Price who plays rugby for Newport.' That was something that 'Big Ben' continued to do throughout his lustrous career – 'In those days Newport was the club everyone in our part of the world wanted to play for.' Travel to and from Rodney Parade was facilitated when he applied for a post at Caldicot's recently built comprehensive school. The headmaster, Bill Silk, wanted to develop rugby football; his campaign to secure the services of this particular recruit included the arranging of local digs and a job for his wife-to-be, Dorothy (Matthews).

The move went through, and Price was integrated into a school with distinct targets and ambitions. He was soon in charge of PE, and coached boys with a positive desire to excel at rugby. Off duty he greatly enjoyed spending lunchtimes in the new school's well-equipped gymnasium where he could practise basketball, thereby (like Allan Martin and Mervyn Davies after him) cultivating skills which stood him in good stead at rugby football's lines-out.

Twin factors, then, have conspired to cause Brian Price to be perceived, willy-nilly, as 'Monmouthshire man' throughout his adulthood. One was the long, loyal teaching career located in what Fred Hando referred to as 'The Pleasant Land of Gwent' (and where he coached the grown-ups of Caldicot RFC for a decade). Secondly there has been devotion, mainly unswerving, to Newport RFC. Price is quick to acknowledge early outings with Bargoed RFC and Cross Keys; he confesses to a single game for Llanelli; and during his absence abroad on National Service an over-enthusiastic uncle's offer of his nephew's services to Pontypool RFC had to be unscrambled on his return home. But the launch-pad which projected him to the highest level of the game was Rodney Parade and the eleven seasons he spent there, two of them as skipper. His accumulation of thirty-two international caps climaxed with the captaincy of his country. He became a British Lion and he was a member of sides that beat the three great southern hemisphere nations. Always, he would play for the county when picked.

And, no, he will tell you. Monmouthshire does not have any identity crisis. With one or two exceptions, like Colin Smart and Stuart Barnes who were transient elements in Welsh society and understandably opted to play Test rugby for their country of birth, its players passionately want to represent Wales. In Price's time, Bill Clement was the WRU secretary who sent out invitations to players selected for the National XV. The first acceptances to reach his desk were invariably from Monmouthshire.

By July 1963 Brian Price had completed most of life's essential apprenticeships and some trials and tribulations were in the past. These included formal education, though a knee-cap shattered at the wrong time robbed him of schoolboy international rugby. That most socially valuable experience, National Service, had taken him to exotic, faraway climes but was now finished. A career in teaching was blossoming to his satisfaction. He was about to become a happily married man. Even a weight problem – how to put it on – had disappeared: a sudden spurt to fifteen and a half stones meant that he could now look after himself on any rugby field, against any opposition.

According to Newport RFC's historian Jack Davis, 'The great freeze-up of 1963 which made Rugby impossible through January and February came as a merciful release for Newport . . . already defeated eleven times.' It was also a precious moratorium in which the Black-and-Amber think-tank, which contained wise administrators like Bill Everson, Vince Griffiths and Nick Carter, could plot policies and a way ahead. Undoubtedly, one of their preoccupations would have been leadership. The days of Bryn Meredith, Brian Jones and Glyn Davidge, if not done, were numbered. Martin Webber was not yet in the frame. David Watkins, though an international stand-off half, was still a lad. All the signs pointed towards a certain 25-year-old lock forward.

Price had scarcely been hanging around waiting for captaincies to be conferred upon him. In his first few seasons at Rodney Parade he had gained a Welsh trial, played in the Newport team which lost to South Africa 0–3 and was in the Barbarians XV which relieved Avril Malan's tourists of an unbeaten record. After progressing to a first international cap (against Ireland in 1961 after Danny Harris failed a fitness test) he had made six further appearances. His influence in Newport's championship side of 1962 had been considerable. Moreover, he was a schoolmaster, accustomed to unbuttoning his lip when necessary. Such men, like lecturers and (in bygone days) parsons, are communicators who can convey urgency, criticism, perception, wisdom, cunning, encouragement, hope and other positive messages to their followers at exactly the right time. In the heat of battle, the calm voice counts; when the initiative is drifting away towards opponents a great leader's words must act like a whiplash. As a spectator at international or club level I often cringe at the sight of a captain, or pack leader, who seems to have nothing to say to the troops.

The one thing which could have given Newport's decision-makers pause for thought that summer was the autumn engagement awaiting the club with the Fifth All Blacks, due at Rodney Parade for the third fixture of a 36-match tour. It was possible that tourists might be vulnerable at this early juncture: but then so might Newport under a new untried skipper. In the event the committee's decision went, boldly, in favour of Price. He proved unable to inspire his men to instant success, and by the morning of 30 October Newport had won six games, drawn two and lost four.

These days international rugby teams hop the hemispheres as casually and as regularly as catching a bus. The motivation is profit; and visits from the southern giants have become so regular that the autumn of 1997, for example, saw England take on Australia, New Zealand (twice) and South Africa in the space of one hectic month. Such frequency brings in its train, if not indifference, then a cooling of ardour. It is hard for today's fan to comprehend the frenzied enthusiasm and huge anticipation that motivated spectators in the first three-quarters of the twentieth century, when not only was television coverage of big sport very limited but, in addition, major overseas visitors would pay only one visit to the United Kingdom per decade. Their appearance at Rodney Parade in 1963 would be the first by an All Blacks side in Wales since 1954. It might turn out to be no contest; but 25,000 fans would squeeze into Rodney Parade to see it.

For Newport's players too, the day was sure to be special. The careers of rugby's star performers move steadily along at altitudes that are beyond the rank and file. But even to seasoned first-class players, some of the challenges which have to be met from time to time are out of the ordinary. These can only be overcome by unstinting commitment allied to out-of-the-ordinary skill. Temperament will play a part: the great performers are those able to remain equable under pressure. And there is appetite: all other things being equal, the hungrier side will win the day.

Maybe that last consideration dominated Brian Price's frame of mind as he led his men along the forbidding 200-yard walk that once lay between Rodney Parade's changing rooms and the pitch. Newport teams of past years had defeated touring sides from South Africa and Australia. The scalp of a New Zealand XV had so far eluded them.

Certainly during the next eighty minutes the pragmatic side of the club captain was laid bare. His broad vision of rugby football was positive; his approach to match-play had been fine-tuned in Exeter, at one of the game's great finishing schools. He may have been a tight forward but Price liked to run and handle with the best of them (and was an expert Sevens player). His swift delivery of quality line-out ball embodied his belief that the principal role of forwards was to secure and provide the possession that would lead to tries, usually by backs but often by the forwards themselves. Dead balls were without appeal for spectators – and useless to players.

Except – that is, if they could tilt the balance away from a world-class team in favour of fifteen less talented but more determined opponents.

Price is on record as admitting that he ordered his pack, above all Glyn Davidge at number 8, to lie on and kill any ruck ball which there seemed the remotest possibility that the tourists might win. The laws of the game today mean that such tactics would attract a series of yellow cards, penalty tries and perhaps even a sending-off. As it was, Don Clarke, one of the two or three greatest goalkickers in New Zealand's history, was not allowed a single penalty opportunity from inside 60-yards range (in addition to which his 30-year-old legs were tormented by the teasingly placed tactical kicks of stand-off half David Watkins). Everything conspired to make the All Blacks hopping mad; in the post-match showerbath their frustration was writ large on Davidge's back in criss-cross tramlines of blood.

But his bravery paid off, and Price led his team into history, thanks to the goal dropped by Dick Uzzell after fifteen minutes. Scotland would subsequently play out a 0–0 draw with the All Blacks, but Newport's victory was the New Zealanders' only reverse of the 1963–4 tour. It was certainly one of the pinnacles of their captain's career, thrown into stark relief by the eight subsequent matches he played against New Zealand which all ended in defeat.

At this time, Brian Price's playing career entered a rollercoaster period which, in retrospect, can be seen to have lasted until his retirement. The 'Big Five' (a term for the selectors who chose Welsh teams in rugby's Middle Ages) picked and dropped him more than once before settling upon him as their first-choice mid-line jumper for the Five Nations tournaments from 1964 to 1967. This meant that he was in title-winning sides and contributed to the 1965 Triple Crown. But there were massive disappointments, too, notably in South Africa where a

Welsh side of which he was vice-captain lost the single Test by the then huge margin of 24–3. His 1966 tour with the British Lions ought to have been a triumph, but as Clem Thomas was to note in his *History of the British Lions*, poor captaincy and maladroit selection led to a 4–0 whitewash in the Tests.

Apart from a thrilling victory over England in the 'Jarrett game' of 1967 Welsh rugby was lacking in direction and conviction as the end of the 1960s approached. But, nevertheless, whether fit or carrying an injury, whether in the selectors' good books or out of them, whether teaching small boys or training with Black-and-Amber squads, Price continued to work on his game, improving and polishing it. When historians come to chart the technical development of rugby in Wales, they will name the Newport man as the first of Wales's 'modern' lock forwards.

If you are someone who played (or spectated) in the 1940s or 1950s, try to remember the signals which preceded throwing in to a line-out. Signals? What signals? Top-flight forwards of that era will tell you that the destination of a throw from touch was a secret closely guarded by the man with the ball, who at that time would be the near-side wing – not necessarily someone in sympathy with the problems and aspirations of the eight donkeys in front of him. One famous Welsh player, when asked who was to be his target jumper at the game's first line-out, told his scrum-half, 'Mind your own business; just watch'. Both packs of forwards, at any given line-out, were to be taken by surprise.

Then there were the characteristics of throwers-in. At Newport in the Price era, Stuart Watkins's throw was conventional and right-handed; Peter Rees's left-handed delivery differed both in angle and trajectory – and the man they were aiming at had to work it all out. These confusions continued through the 1960s, and when Gerald Davies was chosen on a wing for the first time in a 1969 Test against New Zealand, what troubled the pack was not his capacity for scoring tries but whether he could throw in accurately. At least a measure of consistency was achieved when hookers assumed regular responsibility for the task.

Brian Price was well equipped to set new standards for Welsh line-out play. On entering international rugby he was probably the loftiest forward ever to represent Wales (just taller than Neath's Roy John). A standing jump could take his fingertips eight and a half feet off the ground; given a couple of strides' momentum that might rise to nine feet; while by using a single hand only – a technique through which, clearly, the height of a shoulder and hence a hand can be increased – he could reach nine feet three inches. Photographs of him in action sometimes show superb one-handed leaps – but usually the second hand is ready to exert instant control upon the ball.

Occasionally, Price allowed himself the luxury of providing possession by downward deflections: a risky ploy but one which could lead to tries like that snapped up for Wales at Murrayfield on one occasion by an alert hooker, Norman Gale, operating close to the corner flag. As for opponents, it is clear that once he had reached maturity he could out-manoeuvre and out-jump the vast majority. Against a select few, he knew that he would need to be in peak form: the All Black Stan Meads, for example, Frik du Preez of South Africa, France's Benoit Dauga and, mainly because he stood 6′10″, Peter Stagg of Scotland.

It was during this era that lifting at the line-out plus double-banking by support forwards was legalized, only to be banned very soon after-wards. Specialist line-out forwards regretted its quick demise since, no matter which side won the ball, lifting led to clean possession, which instantly restored momentum to the game. It is for this kind of reason that Brian Price appears to have no hide-bound objection to the out-and-out lifting of the 1990s, which many onlookers and critics find both regrettable and grotesque. His reservations are less about the operation itself than about its height, and the possibility of a man being badly injured in an awkward fall.

During the 1960s, before the laws of the game decreed an obligatory gap between forwards at the line-out and touch-judges were empowered to point out miscreants to referees, Price and his contemporaries owed much to support players who gave vital protection. At Newport there was Ian Ford, mild-mannered and soft-spoken off the field; on it, a commanding figure bristling with menace. A lock for Ebbw Vale but used as a prop by Wales, Denzil Williams would momentarily stabilize his jumper at the top of his leap, so that the ball could be sighted and seized. Brian Thomas was a trusty 'minder' in Test Rugby (and has remained a very close friend of Price), but not someone on whom you turned your back if Neath were Newport's opponents.

The help such men gave was essential to the securing of good-quality possession, for in those days the line-out was a bear garden of skullduggery. This included barging, shoving, jersey-tugging, elbows-on-shoulders – plus the kind of mischief once done to Price by an Irishman at Cardiff in 1969. It drew a retaliatory flail – hardly a punch – from its victim, beneath the Prince of Wales's gaze. For a line-out forward, looking after himself was a priority like winning the ball; but all assistance was gladly accepted.

Forwards of those days testify that Price gave his all at rucks, mauls and scrummages. Such close-range evidence is invaluable. Backs activate game-plans whose skill and efficacy is plain to see. Loose forwards enjoy a high profile and win plaudits when the performance of a pack is under discussion. But compared with what happens out in the open, cause and effect in tight exchanges are hard to discern from the fringe (ask any referee). Almost the only way to discover which player(s) exercised a decisive influence on the convulsions at the heart of a scrummage or in a maul is to button-hole an opponent afterwards. A rugby team's 'powerhouse' – the front five – may not be a sporting hi-tech area, but its oft-hidden moving parts are expertly engineered. When not airborne at lines-out Brian Price was happy to be one of these.

Many people, including his own team-mates, thought that a distinguished career might be over, certainly at Test level, when the big fellow dropped out of international contention in the autumn of 1967. Wales were fortunate that the up-and-coming Delme Thomas of Llanelli could plug a gap in the second row when inconsistent form and a bout of appendicitis broke up the Newport man's season. Then, in summer 1968 came Price's unexpected acceptance, at the age of thirty-one, of a second stint as captain of his club. The declaration that followed, of a renewed appetite for Test rugby, brought a feeling of expectation to the Welsh camp and its followers.

The rugby scenario which Price was re-entering contained numerous new features. Kicking to touch on the full had been restricted to the 25-yard (as it then was) area. Replacements could be used for injured men. Wales's coach was now Clive Rowlands, an impressario who unashamedly let his heart rule his head. A brilliant back division was fast maturing, and promising new forwards were about to join the fray. To be named captain of a national XV with such enormous potential must have struck one who was now a veteran as a huge privilege.

The season came good. After leading Wales to Five Nations victories against Scotland and Ireland plus a draw in Paris, Price was forced by injury to spectate as his men ran up a 30–9 victory over the English to clinch a seven-point Championship title with a Triple Crown. The success must have been another career pinnacle for the skipper, bracketed in his memories with Newport's defeat of New Zealand six years earlier. Incidentally, in his last season as captain at Rodney Parade the club won thirty-eight of its forty-five fixtures, losing a mere four games.

With hindsight it can safely be said that Price, in harness with the national coach, had played a major role in laying foundations for Wales's third golden era. Before the Dragons ran amok in the 1970s, however, there were two painful lessons to be learned in New Zealand. As champions of the northern hemisphere, the Welsh had gone to Australasia full of confidence, only to lose their two Tests against the All Blacks by 19–0 and 33–12. Rumours percolated to a shell-shocked Welsh public of loose living and under-commitment; a comment typical of those made about the tour by pressmen was John Billot's: 'Mostly the Welsh forwards disappointed . . . [they] could and should have provided more wholehearted endeavour.'

Victories in Sydney and Suva could not expunge the captain's bitter memories of maulings in Christchurch and Auckland. He had decided to retire from the game on his return (the announcement was made on July 4) and had high hopes of going out as a winner. Responding to critics he allowed himself a sniping comment about the Welsh itinerary and pointed to the draw and two wins secured against New Zealand provinces. But he added the opinion which he still holds – that the All Blacks of 1969, having played together for six years, were one of the strongest sides of the twentieth century. They were, simply, much better than his team.

Later that year came the event that effectively shaped his future relationship with rugby football. In the autumn, Price disclosed that he had accepted payment for three fairly bland articles in the *Sunday Express*. He was immediately professionalized by the Welsh Rugby Union, which was at this time paranoid over the defection of amateur stars like Keith Jarrett, David Watkins and others to rugby league and felt impelled to make an example of their immediate-past captain. Today's reader may need reminding that professionalization kicked a player into territory beyond rugby union's ethical touchlines. It meant that one of Monmouthshire's ablest and noblest sons could not serve the amateur game at senior level *in any capacity whatsoever*.

It is tempting, three decades on, to conclude that his club was more upset than the player. Determined to bring their man into the Rodney Parade coaching system Newport appealed, unsuccessfully. From Price came a – figurative – shrug of the shoulders. As a teacher, whose job actually included and would continue to include the teaching of rugby, he was disappointed that he could no longer assist Newport but, soon, together with newly retired Denzil Williams, he accepted an offer from RC Vichy to play weekend games in the heart of France's rugby country. Although the weekly commuting was tedious, there were many compensations. *Haute cuisine* and *premiers crus* featured at post-match functions; there were generous expenses, and life and rugby could be viewed from a French point of view: 'I thought I knew it all, but Vichy's coach Gerard Dufau had a few eye-openers for me.' Price loved every minute of the experience and still treasures his French connections.

Since he had been professionalized anyway, he now decided that having gone in for a penny, it might as well be for a pound; and when BBC Radio Wales offered him paid weekend work as a 'second voice' – analysing what match commentators had just described – he happily accepted. Despite being balanced and perceptive, his comments on individual performances have occasionally drawn retaliation bordering on the hysterical. Later, though, people who inveighed against him have often proved big enough to admit that it was just *possible* that they deserved his criticisms.

Few forwards win medals. Like strong, loyal, dutiful shire horses they are normally rewarded with bright blue rosettes for their ability to push, pull, rip, rob and exert other forms of dynamic, paralysing pressure. Their one skill with polish all over it, as opposed to spit, is the line-out jump. It belongs in the same category as the jinks, side-steps and outside breaks that happen in back divisions – and is, for a split second, more spectacular than any of those. Just as Bennett's side-step, Edwards's hand-off, or John's spectral running are forever in minds' eyes, so Price at full stretch is a fixture on the retina.

Heart and soul went into his game. As did that third, vital ingredient: a spring-heeled athleticism that, literally, elevated him to the heights.

# GERALD DAVIES

Huw Richards

Some time in the mid-1970s a Welsh rugby fan was introduced to an international referee. He asked the referee which player he found hardest to deal with, fully expecting to be filled in on close-up details of front-row villainy. He was flabbergasted to be told 'Gerald Davies'. 'Why?' he asked. 'I'd always thought he was an absolute model of how a rugby player should behave.' 'He is,' replied the referee, 'but the trouble is when he gets the ball, you can't follow where he is going. He seems to disappear and there's nothing worse for a referee than not knowing where the ball is.' Gerald himself wrote in *Gerald Davies: An Autobiography* (1979) – the exception to the general rule that memoirs so baldly labelled will be no more interesting than their title: 'For me the players who have given the greatest pleasure are those who have been able to run and to pass accurately to create space, who use their hands, eyes and minds to create time and their bodies to deceive and manoeuvre.'

A clear case of like appealing to like. Nobody ever epitomized the traditional appeal of Welsh back play at its best more than Gerald Davies. We all have our own mental images of the second golden age of the 1970s, but some are surely common to all. Gareth's kick, chase and instant mud pack at the Arms Park in 1972 and J.P.R.'s concussive *frappe* of the flying Gourdon for instance. Just as vivid is the recall of a diminutive moustachioed figure – if Cliff Morgan's facial contortions summoned up thoughts of Italian opera for Dai Smith and Gareth Williams, then Gerald's features and reserve would look perfectly at home in Seville or Madrid, making him modern exhibit number one for the concept of the Iberian Welsh – running improbable patterns close to the touch-line. The sheer wonderment he induced was beautifully summed up in a cartoon by Gren in the *Western Mail*. Seizing the opportunity provided by an international preceded by several days of snow he pictured a couple of groundsmen standing by the posts and looking at a pattern of footprints in the snow incorporating several sharp changes of direction, an improbable gap and finishing under the posts. One is saying to the other, 'I see Gerald's been out for a run'.

Gerald clearly also enjoyed this image of himself – it is reproduced both in the *Autobiography* and in *Side-Steps*(1985), a two-handed diary of the 1984–5 season written with the journalist John Morgan. Gareth Williams rates him 'one of the two greatest players ever to wear the Welsh jersey'. To David Duckham, the other Test wing for the 1971 British Lions and an opponent for Coventry and England, he was 'the ultimate example of artistic wizardry'. For sheer, instantaneous excitement there is nothing in rugby to match the moment when a great winger receives the ball in half a yard of space. For spectators there is the anticipation of a likely score, for opponents the fear not only of conceding points, but of being made to look slow-witted and inept. In recent years the bison-like Jonah Lomu, diametric opposite of Gerald in style and approach although with a decidedly useful side-step, and rugby league's Martin Offiah, combining a top-class sprinter's pace with a Gerald-like capacity for apparent disappearance, have been the great crowd-pleasers and marker-terrorizers.

David Parry-Jones, in a memorable passage, described the effect Gerald had on a game and its spectators: 'The bald recitation of the Davies repertoire fails utterly to meter the electric shock experienced by a game of rugby when the ball finally reaches his hand at his outpost close to the touch-line. For a few moments the afternoon is super-charged with amps and volts. Crowds jerk to tip-toe with expectancy; the antennae of team-mates vibrate with tension; in the twinkling of an eye a defence can shrivel, blacken and blow a fuse.' The particular nightmare for those defenders was the same experienced by the later generation who had to cope with Lomu or Offiah. You know what your opponent is going to do, but have almost no chance of stopping them. Duckham's description of Gerald's side-step conveys the near-impossibility of defending against it: 'He left it late, coming right up to the defender, then murmuring the side-step without noticeable loss of speed or line.'

Even Gareth Edwards, rarely confounded by anything on a rugby field, had to concede defeat on a rare occasion when they were opponents: 'Halfway through the first half he got loose on the wing and I cut back to intercept him. I steadied myself just in time to meet him face to face. I anticipated the famous side-step off the right foot. I lurked just outside to wait for it and also to drive him out towards touch. I was confident of stopping him. I got my geometry exactly right. In he came, but a split second later I was grasping thin air. It was not the angle that beat me, but the sheer speed. He could change direction by almost ninety degrees. I knew that, but at ninety miles per hour! Nobody told me that.'

Like his great contemporary, Mervyn Davies, Gerald was known by his second christian name – a coincidence averting the need for them to be known as T.M. and T.G.R. Given the number of Tom Davieses there are in Wales it is extraordinary that none has ever been capped, but no more remarkable than the coincidence that cast Thomas Gerald Reames Davies and Thomas Mervyn Davies, neither using their first name, as key members of great teams over the best part of a decade. Gerald explains: 'I was given the name Thomas because of my mother's brother Tom Reames who was killed in a mining accident at a very early age. My mother decided I should carry the name on, but I was never called Tom.' There is something appropriate in that gesture to family and mining heritage. Gerald Davies was an instinctive rugby player, one who readily confessed to John Morgan that 'the worst thing that could happen to me was to have a lot of time to think about something on the rugby field'. But no player was ever more aware of his cultural roots. Gareth Williams and Dai Smith were writing in 1980 when they commented that 'he was, perhaps more than any Welsh International since 1945, deeply contemplative about his reasons for playing rugby far beyond his thinking about the technicalities of his own game'. Two decades on, there is little reason to differ from that conclusion.

The extraordinary efflorescence of rugby talent among the sons of west Wales miners born in the mid-1940s looks like sport's answer to turn-of-the-century Budapest's output of mathematicians. Barry John (6 January 1945), Gerald Davies (7 February 1945) and Gareth Edwards (12 July 1947) were born into mining families in the space of two-and-a-half years. The Wales team of the early 1970s was not the best ever – if it were, it would have beaten New Zealand. But it is unlikely that any other team has deployed a back division with quite so many all-time greats. There is perhaps an element of fortune in quite so much innate talent being showered on a single district. But there is nothing fortuitous about the chances of it being nurtured. Gerald recalls: 'I was lucky that at every stage I had someone who could give me good advice about my next step.' His luck was no coincidence, but is what happens in a deep-rooted, highly-sophisticated sporting culture. And, while the individual is inescapably the product of his times and social context, his relationship with them is anything but passive. Gerald's rugby career intersects with many of the most important social and sporting forces of the time, but this is no *Candide*-type progress, wholly at the mercy of the external. He was fortunate in his family background, schooling and college education, and even in the club rugby context provided by London Welsh, but the truly great player is always *sui generis*. However ideal the context, greatness requires unusual natural talent harnessed by an inner drive.

He was not hothoused from an early age. Gerald's recall of his first years in Llansaint, lovingly evoked in the *Autobiography*, is that rugby ran behind football and cricket as a street game, not least because of the painful consequences of tackling. Nor was he coached at primary school: 'There was very little serious rugby until I got to secondary school.' But the sense of rugby as a game to be enjoyed was inculcated by those early street games, while listening to his father and other men discussing sport was an indication that excellence at it was highly valued – even if at the same time his father was wary of his enthusiasm for sport, fearing that it would detract from his education. When he returns to Llansaint now, the main contrast that strikes him is the absence of children from streets once filled by them. 'It is as if some Pied Piper has passed through.'

He and his contemporaries had opportunities denied to their fathers. 'My father was determined that I should not follow him down the mine. He had had no alternative. But a new attitude and new opportunities came out of the end of the war years. There was a sense of idealism and a belief that there could be something better. A grammar school education became available and my parents were insistent on the importance of making the most of my education and passing exams.' He, Gareth Edwards and Barry John all started their working lives as teachers, post-war Wales's route out for working-class men and women, leading to such phenomena as the annual train from Swansea High Street chartered by Birmingham City Council to bring back its teachers at the end of the summer, and the school in Bristol where a pupil stole the 'S' from the staff-room door.

When the West Indian intellectual C. L. R. James talked of 'welfare state cricketers' in the 1960s, he was deriding a safety-first culture.

Gerald, Gareth, Barry and their contemporaries played their rugby with the mixture of audacity and discipline James so admired in the best West Indian cricketers – Gerald wrote that 'rugby is a game of calculated risks'. Yet they were 'welfare state rugby players', their sense of the possibilities of life transformed by post-war social change. Their on-field existence also offered a wider range of possibilities than was offered to their predecessors. Their formative years were spent amid the sterility of the 1950s game, with back divisions standing toe-to-toe in mid-field and double-figure scores a rarity in international matches. In rugby's continuous dialectic, with rule-makers seeking ways of opening the game and defenders progressively learning to negate them, defence was clearly ascendant.

The next shift came in the 1960s, as Gerald and his contemporaries were entering the first-class game. He was an international before the liberating rule changes – the separation of opposing mid-fields, touch-kicking dispensation and the liberalized knock-on rule – were completed. But he and the others had learnt to play, and to create space and time, in conditions offering about as much freedom of movement as a crowded commuter train. It was little wonder that the wide open spaces of the new dispensation generated play of unprecedented brilliance. There was also a better analytical understanding of rugby, with the growth of coaching. As a journalist Gerald has been highly critical of coaches who try to control every aspect of play, robbing players of initiative and spontaneity. He argues: 'A coach can tell you how to do something, but not when to do it. Players have to accept responsibility for the way that they play and the coach's main objective has to be to allow talent to blossom.' There were no such problems in the mid-1960s when Gerald was one of the students to benefit from the coaching of John Robins at Loughborough University: 'John argued that we should follow the New Zealand example of "getting fit in order to play rugby, rather than playing rugby to get fit". Because coaching was still relatively new, coaches were less sure of themselves and felt they needed the help of their players in understanding the game. They were much more humble in their approach and there was much more co-operation.' He has no doubt that the Loughborough experience played a vital part in his development as a player. His going there was a consequence both of wider opportunities and of the good advice which he received:

'People who went to college normally went locally – to Carmarthen, Swansea or Cardiff. But the PE master at my school, who had been at Loughborough himself, suggested I should go there.'

The next step was more traditionally Welsh, but one more associated with the comparatively gilded youth of Llandovery, Rydal and Christ College Brecon than with miners' sons who went to Queen Elizabeth Grammar School, Carmarthen – Cambridge. He went for professional rather than rugby reasons, realizing that his opportunities in teaching would be limited without a degree, but inevitably collected three blues and the Cambridge captaincy. He arrived at Cambridge as a full international, first capped in the 1966 Arms Park clash with Australia which also saw the Wales debut of Barry John. There was, however, little hint of a new golden age in the making. Wales went down 14–11 to what was then regarded as its first defeat by Australia (the 1927–8 New South Wales Waratahs, who beat Wales 18–8, have since been upgraded to full status). With neat circularity his Wales career would also finish against the Wallabies, though with no better luck, losing his only match as captain 19–17 at Sydney twelve years later.

Gerald's first ten Welsh caps and his Cambridge blues were won as a centre. He established himself as an automatic choice for Wales – he was never to be left out, except by his own choice – and won a place on the 1968 British Lions tour of South Africa, playing in the Third Test. Reviewing the 1969–70 Cambridge season, Geoffrey Nicholson talked of his 'sudden gliding moves that split the field'. In 1969 he went to New Zealand with Wales as a centre. All too typically of Welsh ventures to the southern hemisphere, the tour of New Zealand was afflicted by an insanely demanding itinerary, a rash of injuries and horrendous results. But it did bring one lasting benefit, Gerald's move to the wing. Wales had only one fit wing for the Second Test at Christchurch and coach Clive Rowlands concluded that Gerald's pace and elusiveness were better suited to the position than either John Dawes or Keith Jarrett, the other two centres. In spite of Rowlands's ingenious selling of the idea, arguing that 'We've got to use your genius on the wing', Gerald was not wholly taken with the idea. Clem Thomas wrote that 'his reluctance could also have been described as extreme annoyance'. Having played outside-half at school, then first inside- and outside-centre, Gerald had no difficulty in discerning a clear trend in his career. 'The next logical step was touch judge, genius or not!' The move though was an inspired one. As Clem Thomas reported, 'His devastating running in the first half of that test . . . had New Zealand at panic stations . . . even though Wales lost badly'. After scoring two tries in his ten internationals as a centre, Gerald was to score eight in his first eight as a winger. His *annus mirabilis* was 1971 – scoring five tries in four Five Nations matches, before adding three in four Test appearances for the victorious British Lions in New Zealand.

It did no harm either that he joined London Welsh after leaving Cambridge, making his debut just after Christmas 1970 away to Swansea. He completed an all-international XV at a club at the zenith of its fortunes, playing a brilliantly open style of rugby calculated to give an outstanding wing as many opportunities as he might desire. He stayed at Old Deer Park until he moved back to Wales in 1974, joining Cardiff and becoming captain in their 1975–6 centenary year. The move to the wing also made sense in terms of the way centre play was changing. As Rowlands had put it, 'You don't want to get involved with the heavy mob in midfield'. Gerald recalls, 'The change had started with MacRae and Davis of New Zealand. They started a style of big men bulldozing down the middle, which other teams imitated'. It is unlikely that Gerald would have been found wanting defensively – he never was on the wing, and was always good at jockeying larger, heavier opponents into positions where his speed rather than their power was decisive. But even his talent might in time have been blunted, as was that of David Richards a decade later, amid the heavy hitters.

Instead it remained undimmed until his retirement in 1978, high-lighted by an extraordinary performance in a cup tie for Cardiff against Pontypool. Pooler, as was their wont, dominated completely up front. Those who were there insist that Cardiff had possession only four times. Gerald scored on each occasion to ensure a remarkable win. A year earlier his side-stepping run out of defence had helped create Phil Bennett's remarkable try at Murrayfield, second only in Edinburgh memories to his own last-minute effort in 1971 when a wide, arcing run took him clear of the Scottish defence and over the line to create the opportunity for John Taylor's immortal touch-line conversion. But his forebodings about the move to the wing were not wholly unjustified. Even a great wing depends on the service he gets from those inside him.

Gerald was never cut off to the extent that Ken Jones, whose international career concluded with thirteen games without scoring after his historic try against New Zealand in 1953, had been in the 1950s. However, it is surely no coincidence that he was never again so consistent a try-scorer once John Dawes, a magnificent passer of the ball, retired from international rugby at the end of the Lions tour and Wales succumbed progressively to crash-ball fixation. Gerald recalls, 'Too many coaches lack confidence in what their players can do, and think that you have to cross the advantage line as close to the scrum as possible. John Robins always took the view that there are any number of points where you can cross the gain line, and the most important thing was that your players should be good enough passers to ensure that it is crossed'. The *Autobiography* chronicles his frustration that wings were not considered to be creative players. Such a sterile approach also conflicted with his own philosophy of the game. As he was to tell John Morgan some years after his retirement, 'Enjoyment was always important because that is the bottom line . . . the wing can be a very isolated position, and if he doesn't feel as if he is contributing then there can't be much enjoyment for him'.

Like any top-class performer, Gerald took his sport seriously, but he always saw it in context and proportion. There was always a wider range of interests and activities to be cultivated. For this reason he took a year out of international rugby in 1969–70, realizing that his hectic rugby schedule was destroying any other benefits from his time in Cambridge. 'I was after all in Cambridge to take advantage of the opportunities that had been given to me, to gain a degree and to get to grips with English literature. I wanted too, since it was unlikely that the opportunity would occur again, to savour fully Cambridge student life and all that it had to offer.'

That sabbatical meant that he was not available to play against the Springboks. He was also not available for the 1974 Lions tour to South Africa, feeling it unacceptable to seek time off from a job, teaching at Christ's Hospital in Sussex, that he was about to leave. He was revolted by apartheid on previous visits, but also says, 'I believe it is up to individuals to make their own minds up on issues of this sort. You also have to respect the desire of sportsmen to play against the best'. Looking back, he is uncertain whether he would have emulated John

Taylor, who refused to play against the 1969–70 team. 'You can't think hypothetically twenty-five years later, it puts everything out of perspective.' But he emphasizes that there was nothing convenient about not having to make the decision. 'I have never been afraid to make decisions, it was just that on both occasions the decision was made for me by other considerations.'

Gerald's broad outlook and sense of proportion have also informed his rugby-writing for *The Times* over the last twenty years. The ex-player is a mixed asset in sports journalism. He brings with him first-hand knowledge of what it is really like out there, but too often also adheres to what might be called the Trueman doctrine – a conviction that nothing is as good as it was when he was playing and an ill-concealed resentment of those who are now young and vigorous as he once was but is no longer. Gerald is well aware of the dangers of nostalgia. 'You can't live in the past. It is natural to remember the good things, but the danger is that you remember things as you would like them to have been, not as they really were. For instance I remember my childhood as extremely happy, but there must have been some difficult times with my father on disability benefit.' Thus when he is critical of aspects of the modern game, readers know, as they did in the cricket analysis of Sir Leonard Hutton, that the opinion is judicious and thought through.

As well as straightforward analytical intelligence, Gerald brings with him the advantage that rugby was always an important part of, rather than the whole of, his life. Rather than resent the men who enjoy the youth he once enjoyed, his experience of top-class rugby informs a humanity in his treatment of players. He knows how tough the game is, and how cruelly public the experience of defeat or failure. 'We are far too prone to concentrate on the negatives, to emphasize what players can't do, rather than what they can. Players know when they haven't done well and there's no need to rub it in. My preference is to emphasize the strengths of players.' In this spirit he has been an enthusiastic champion of players of instinctive class like Robert Jones and Gregor Townsend, and one of the few journalists to have covered the Arwel Thomas–Neil Jenkins battle for the Welsh outside-half shirt in detail without belittling either.

It hasn't all been rugby. His friendship with the journalist John Morgan did not just produce *Side-Steps*. It was also the foundation for his key role in Welsh media and public life as chair of HTV Wales – Morgan was one of the driving forces behind the original franchise bid and was responsible for recruiting Gerald to the board. He says: 'People should take responsibility for their own patches. Wales is my patch and I want the best for it.' That aspiration was also reflected in six years as chair of the Wales Youth Agency, whose staff appreciated both the public profile his appointment brought them and the serious commitment he gave to the post. The HTV role also provided an outlet for a lifelong fascination with politics, implanted by his father, who hero-worshipped Aneurin Bevan. Gerald is discreet about his own allegiances, other than saying that he sees Wales's future within Great Britain. 'We need to have our own level of control in Wales, but each part of Britain is closely dependent on the others and we need to maintain that relationship.'

C. L. R. James is not known to have taken much interest in rugby. But he would have had little difficulty in recognizing and admiring Gerald Davies, not just as one of the most exciting players of what remains Welsh rugby's most exhilarating era, but as someone whose excellence in and enthusiasm for sport fitted into a wider context. It was James who asked 'What do they know of cricket who only cricket know?' He would have understood that one reason why Gerald has brought so much to rugby is that he knows a lot else besides.

*Thanks are due to Gerald Davies for agreeing to be interviewed for this chapter.*

# J. P. R. WILLIAMS

Chris Williams

*I just love playing, I'd much rather play than watch, that's why I still play now. It might seem bizarre, but I just enjoy it. There's still, in my experience, no better buzz than being in the shower after a game, having had a really hard game, and you think, 'I really enjoyed that', feeling absolutely knackered, you've got bumps and bruises everywhere and you think, 'Oh! I'm knackered'!*

    J. P. R. Williams, interviewed by the author, Bridgend, May 1999*

The nine-year-old ginger-haired boy with tortoiseshell-rimmed spectacles summarized the game in a sentence scrawled across the centre pages of the programme: 'Newport scored first but from then on it was London Welsh's match.' It was 3 April 1972 at Rodney Parade, and the visitors had won 11–3. In the *Western Mail* (headline: 'Classical Exiles crack Newport on title march') J. B. G. Thomas put it more eloquently: 'Shrewd, efficient London Welsh took another step towards the *Western Mail* championship when they beat Newport with a splendid display of modern rugby. A large, holiday crowd watched a hard, sporting match in which London Welsh were always too competent and too well together for Newport to achieve control.' Sixteen minutes into the second half, full-back J. P. R. Williams had kicked a penalty to level Newport's earlier score. Then, on a blind-side move, Williams had interchanged passes with Billy Hullin and Jim Shanklin before crashing over for the try that put 'the Welsh' into a lead they were to keep. London Welsh won both the *Western Mail* championship and the Middlesex Sevens in 1972, and the Welsh Rugby Writers Club made Williams their 'Player of the Year'. Earlier in the season he had become the first Welsh full-back to score two international tries when he added to that scored against England in 1970 with another short-range blind-side burst at Twickenham, stepping around Bob Hiller and diving through Peter Dixon's tackle to reach the same corner. When Wales played New Zealand that December the official programme notes

---

*Unless otherwise indicated, all quotations are taken from this interview.

christened him 'the greatest full-back in the history of Welsh rugby'. For that aforementioned small boy the fact that he shared the great man's surname (and would later model his signature on a prized autograph collected in 1975) confirmed the judgement of adults: throughout my sporadic, undistinguished eighteen-year rugby career J. P. R. Williams was my role model, full-back my preferred position.

When the National Eisteddfod visited Bridgend in 1948 the *Glamorgan Gazette* boasted that it was 'commercially and geographically the very heart of the Principality. Equidistant from the two great industrial centres, Cardiff and Swansea, it serves as the headquarters and sorting house of the various industries of Mid-Glamorgan – coal mining, farming, light industries and seaside resorts'. With the conversion of its wartime munitions factory into an industrial estate Bridgend was set to capitalize on Wales's 'second industrial revolution', and by spring 1949 was beginning to enjoy its prosperity. In the first week of March its three cinemas showed *The Birds and the Bees*, the revue ('direct from Salford Hippodrome') *Fanny Get Your Fun*, and Peter Lorre in *The Beast With Five Fingers* ('not suitable for children'). Bridgend Technical Institute staged a demonstration of 'marzipan modelling and cake decoration', with its centrepiece a four-foot marzipan statue of the duke of Windsor in full naval uniform, Cardiff City fans joined a rail excursion to London (departing Bridgend at 6.53 am), to see the Bluebirds away to Tottenham Hotspur, and the town's gamblers contemplated the fact that Manchester United were 7–4 favourites to retain the FA Cup (they did not). Bridgend RFC had recently been displaced from the Brewery Field by Bridgend Rugby League, and were instead playing on Newbridge Fields, with the teams changing at the former Island Farm POW camp. An Egyptian performer named Kitao, billed as 'the man they cannot kill', visited the town. He swallowed fire, washed in broken glass, survived attempts by twelve men to strangle him with a noose, and allowed swords to pass through his body. The highlight of his act was to lie on a bed of nails whilst six men stood on him and broke large rocks on his chest with a sledgehammer. Unsurprisingly, the *Gazette* editorial asked (surely neither for the first nor last time) 'What is Welsh culture?'

Although born in Cardiff on 2 March 1949, Wales's latter-day Kitao, John Peter Rhys Williams (the man they could not quell?) quickly became one of the 13,000 inhabitants of Bridgend. His father had been an army surgeon, his grandfather a miner from the Rhondda valleys who had finished his career as a colliery manager in Gilfach Goch. His mother, also a doctor, was the daughter of an industrial finance manager from Rochdale ('I'm half-English. I don't admit to it very often'). Together they had taken up general practice in Bridgend, living first in Ogmore-by-Sea and then later at the surgery, Ashfield (complete with tennis court), on Merthyr Mawr Road. John, along with his three younger brothers Phil, Chris and Mike, was to grow up in an active, sporting environment (remarkably, all four were to play rugby for Bridgend Under-15s, become Welsh junior tennis champions, and study medicine). When John was just six months' old he was given his first rugby ball by Dr Jack Matthews, alongside whom father Peter had played for Cardiff Medicals. As the brothers grew up they would play the game on nearby Newbridge Fields, and be taken to Porthcawl beach to practise catching in the high winds. Music was another keen interest: John played the piano, was first violin in the Glamorgan Youth Orchestra, and a chorister at Nolton (Anglican) Church, where he made firm friends with the Rhondda-born rugby enthusiast the Revd Canon Haydn Rees. Going to Laleston County Primary School, he encountered teacher Billy Morgan, the current Bridgend full-back. Morgan moved Williams from fly-half to his own position ('I wasn't very pleased with [this] at the time, because full-back was the next move to being out of the team'), and not only watching Bridgend (now back at the Brewery Field) but also playing for the under-11 Bridgend Juniors team became regular pastimes.

For the young Williams, however, rugby had to compete both with tennis and with his parents' ambition that he should follow them into medicine. At ten he joined his father in Bridgend Tennis Club, beginning a climb that ended in him beating David Lloyd to win the British Junior Men's Tennis title at Wimbledon in 1966, and permitted him to contemplate the possibility of a full-time career in the sport. In addition, at ten he was sent to Bryntirion Prep. School, as a preliminary to going to Epsom College (which had a tradition of sending pupils on to medical school). However, Williams, not wanting to go to public school, rebelled and, after a year at Bryntirion, he entered Bridgend Boys' Grammar School. Here he came under the collective influence of

Illtyd Williams (heavily involved in Bridgend rugby), the Olympic gold-medal-winning long-jumper Lynn Davies, and the Neath and Wales full-back Grahame Hodgson. Hard work in the gym began to pay off and, on 11 March 1964, Williams won his Welsh Schools Under-15s cap ('the biggest thrill I've ever had in my life') in a season that saw Wales (with Allan Martin, Phil Bennett, and J. J. Williams) take the Triple Crown.

In these early years, Williams developed his trademark of fierce tackling and courageous defence. At this time he was 'a tiny little boy . . . smaller than Phil Bennett', and relished rugby's physical challenge as a means of proving that he was not as puny as he appeared. Moreover, as a doctor's son who had been driven to and from primary school in his father's Rolls-Royce, 'I think I had to prove to everyone else that I wasn't the privileged lad who was born with a silver spoon in his mouth'. When, in 1966, Williams won a tennis and rugby scholarship to go to Millfield, the public school with a formidable sporting reputation, he encountered a different attitude: 'in Wales at the time the grammar school were the toffs . . . yet when you went to a public school in England you were at the bottom, you were thought of as a Welsh boyo from the valleys'. Williams's reaction, whichever sport he was playing, was to harness his natural aggression and pride to convince himself of his self-worth. He won three caps for Welsh Secondary Schools in 1967 and left school that year to go to St Mary's Hospital Medical School in London.

By the time John Williams began his first-class career in rugby union, with a debut for Bridgend at Bristol on 30 September 1967, he was no longer the insubstantial figure of his early teens. Six feet one inch tall, he weighed thirteen-and-a-half stones (eventually rising, by the end of his career, to over fifteen stones). His early reputation was built on his defensive solidity but, playing nineteen regular games for Bridgend in that first season, as well as others in the try-oriented Floodlight Alliance ('it was made for me, that competition really'), he attracted considerable attention for his willingness to run the ball in attack. Never more than a competent kicker of the ball to touch, and an inconsistent ('reluctant') place-kicker, Williams's career might well have been different had it not been for the Australian Dispensation which outlawed kicking direct to touch outside one's own twenty-five. Now there was the potential for running the ball from what hitherto had been regarded as defensive positions, and the attacking role of the full-back was revolutionized: 'It was quite an opportunity for me because I was never a great kicker . . . so it meant that I had to run with the ball: it suited me down to the ground.' Williams was also fortunate in that there were, as J. B. G. Thomas put it, 'few outstanding full-backs in Wales at the moment'. At the end of the 1967 season Keith Jarrett had emerged as a glorious talent with his record-breaking display against England, but he had been injured for the November game against New Zealand, allowing Aberavon's Paul Wheeler to win his first cap. When Jarrett returned to the Welsh team it was at centre, and Wheeler was dropped after the opening game of the 1968 Five Nations season. His replacement, Swansea's relatively small Doug Rees, was primarily a kicker, and when the Welsh selectors announced their tour party to visit Argentina in September, the *Western Mail* hailed 'the remarkable rise to fame of a young all-round sportsman'. As the only specialist full-back on the tour, John Williams seized this outstanding opportunity to establish himself at the highest level, playing in all six matches and being one of only a few players to return with an enhanced reputation, along with the nickname of 'Canasta' (basket), in recognition of his ability to field the high ball under pressure. Tour captain John Dawes took his chance equally well, persuading the young full-back to join London Welsh, rather than to continue to travel back and fro between London and Bridgend.

By 1968, London Welsh was one of Britain's top club sides, playing running, attacking rugby and winning fulsome tributes from supporters, neutrals and opponents. Williams's game flourished in this liberal atmosphere alongside Dawes, Tony Gray, John Taylor, Mervyn Davies, and (later) Gerald Davies. Displacing the talented Gareth James at full-back, Williams enjoyed an outstanding debut against Richmond before returning to the Brewery Field to kick three penalties, a conversion and score a try in a comprehensive victory over Bridgend. Williams's first full cap came, as anticipated, on 1 February 1969 against Scotland at Murrayfield. It was the beginning of an international career that continued (with one game missed through injury, and one season's temporary retirement) until February 1981, and saw him finally retire as the (then) most-capped Welsh player, with fifty-five full caps (five as captain), and eight Test appearances for the British Lions. It encompassed three Grand Slams (1971, 1976, 1978), six Triple Crowns (1969, 1971, 1976–79) and two Lions Test series victories (1971 in New Zealand, 1974 in South Africa). Significantly, Williams played eleven times against England, being victorious on each occasion (he was injured for the 1974 defeat), yet in six appearances for Wales against New Zealand (including the 1974 unofficial Test) he was never on the winning side. And although his playing style seemed ideally suited to rugby league, the progress he made in the medical world, together with his father's hostility to the professional code ('it was tantamount to being a traitor'), meant that this was never seriously considered.

In retrospect, it is difficult to imagine that, once in the Welsh side, Williams was ever likely to be left out. He made an impressive start against the Scots in a 17–3 victory, with J. B. G. Thomas praising his 'big heart'. Playing in all Five Nations games as well as against New Zealand (twice) and Australia had, by the end of the season, more than compensated for any inexperience. When, in November 1970, as a seven-year-old sitting high up in the South Stand, I saw him for the first time playing for Wales Under-25s against Fiji he had the authority of a veteran. If he was rated as the greatest Welsh full-back ever by 1972 (unrivalled, surely, by any occupant of that position since), by 1974 many observers thought J. P. R. Williams the most spectacular and outstanding full-back in the world.

Such acclamation clearly involved recognition of his attacking flair, but this was always founded on an immense defensive reliability. As a tackler, he was almost faultless. Full-backs rarely have the opportunity to tackle from behind, or even from the side, and so Williams perfected an uncompromising head-on tackle that left the attacker in no doubt as to his commitment to bring them to ground. Wing Maurie Collins was stopped by one such deathly embrace on his way to what otherwise would have been a certain try in Wales's victory over Otago on the 1969 tour. Two years later and Williams made a similar *coûte que coûte* effort to bring down Brian Going as the Lions defeated North Auckland 11–5. Later in his career he developed the 'big hit', a virtual body-check which usually resulted in the attacker going down and Williams staying on his feet. Occasionally tackles were mistimed, or even missed: in the Second Test in New Zealand in 1971 a partly-concussed Williams was unable to prevent Bob Burgess from reaching the try-line, and in the 1972 match against Scotland he suffered a broken jaw when he caught Billy Steele's boot in the face. The intense Triple Crown decider in Dublin in 1978 saw Williams late-tackle Mike Gibson and, in 1976, the Argentinian wing Gauweloose beat him for pace. However, when Williams made an error, he calmly endeavoured never to repeat it. The key example is the 1976 game against France, with both sides still in contention for the Grand Slam. Within minutes of the match beginning, France took the lead when a Welsh mid-field move broke down just outside the twenty-five. Fly-half Romeu moved right, briefly drawing the Welsh full-back before passing to the pacy wing Gourdon, who was able to slip out of Williams's outstretched arms to score in the corner. Wales clawed their way back into the game with penalties and a J. J. Williams try, although left-wing Averous scored another try for France when he was dubiously awarded the touchdown (after a kick ahead by Aguirre) when it looked as if the Welsh full-back had grounded the ball first. None the less, with minutes to go, Wales were leading 19-13, when France were awarded a penalty twenty yards from the try-line on the right. Scrum-half and captain Fouroux, thinking quickly, dummied left before passing right to Skréla, whose pass to Gourdon, steaming down the touch-line, cut out J. J. Williams, and the winger's speed took him past the despairing arms of Trevor Evans. A try seemed certain, when Williams appeared and executed an awesome shoulder-charge which left Gourdon tumbling head-over-heels into touch within inches of the line. Williams's unwavering relish for the battle was never more evident than at that moment.

As a full-back expected to catch the high ball, Williams was frequently on the receiving end of a physical hammering, and never more so than when playing in New Zealand. In the First Test in 1969 Wales were overwhelmed 19–0, but Williams's indomitable resolve earned him the admiration of the All Blacks. The *Western Mail* reported, 'In a remarkable display of fearlessness and courage he stood up to intense pressure without ever flinching. Often he found himself isolated from support and having to deal with high kicks that arrived at the same time as a bunch of charging New Zealand forwards, but every time he emerged with the ball clutched tightly to him.' Understandably his positional sense took some time to adjust to the demands of international rugby: there was the occasional knock-on or dropped catch, and at Stade Colombes in 1969 he allowed the ball to bounce after a kick from Villepreux, resulting in a try for Campaes. Nevertheless, his heroism in withstanding aerial bombardments against the most ferocious of opponents was unsurpassed, his fallible moments a reminder of his mortality.

If there was ever a player who exemplified *courage sans peur*, it was J. P. R. Williams. This message was brutally relayed to a shocked rugby public in December 1978 when he captained Bridgend (to whom he had returned for the 1976–7 season) against the All Blacks. A month earlier he had led Wales to within minutes of victory against New Zealand at Cardiff, only to be cheated by a combination of gamesmanship and inept refereeing, as the opposition forwards tricked Roger Quittenton into awarding them a penalty at a line-out. Bridgend, in the penultimate game of the tour, offered a final opportunity to redress that wrong. Early in the first half at the Brewery Field Williams, after catching a kick ahead, was pinned to the ground at the bottom of a ruck, well away from the ball, when he was viciously and repeatedly raked by prop John Ashworth. The resultant four-inch gash necessitated eight stitches, but Williams, despite losing two pints of blood, returned to play out the rest of the game (won by New Zealand 16–7). Photographs of Williams's dramatically-wounded face caused an outrage which the New Zealand management exacerbated, first by appearing to deny that the incident had happened at all, and then by sending Ashworth on as a replacement, days later, in the tour's final match against the Barbarians at Cardiff. Williams himself was a combative player (excessively so in one notorious incident involving Tommy Bedford with the Lions in South Africa in 1974) but was never accused of cold-blooded foul play.

Intrepid in defence, Williams could be audacious in attack. A most remarkable example of his daring came in the 1971 Grand Slam game in Paris, when Roger Bourgarel carried a frighteningly fluid attack to within ten yards of the Welsh try-line. As the French wing moved diagonally towards the right corner he was half-tackled by Barry John, and twisted inside to pass to scrum-half Max Barrau. With great vision Williams anticipated the move and took the pass himself to race three-quarters of the length of the field before linking with Denzil Williams who put Gareth Edwards in at the corner. Later that year, playing for the Lions against Hawkes Bay, Williams caught an opposition drop-goal attempt that rebounded off his posts before setting out on a foray which involved six passes and ended with Gerald Davies scoring under the posts. If this was, as he put it, 'crazy rugby', he was one of the most crazed. His readiness to set out on belligerent sorties into enemy territory stemmed, in part, from a realization that it was precisely at such moments that the opposition was most disorganized, and from a tigerish determination to get involved in the hurly-burly of the game, rather than remain a detached observer. (It is significant both that the player he most admired was the French back-row dynamo Jean-Claude Skrela and that in Australia, in 1978, in an injury-depleted Wales side, he played as an emergency flank-forward.) In only his third game for Wales, captain Brian Price asked him to try to stay *behind* the three-quarter line if possible! That only rarely did he get stranded may be ascribed to the telepathic understanding he developed with his wings (particularly Gerald Davies who was 'a revelation, he seemed to be able to read what I could do'), his meticulous timing and intelligent reading of the game, and to a dogged ability to stay on his feet and wait for help to arrive when, ultimately, he was caught. Against Scotland in Cardiff in 1978 he collected a kick from Dougie Morgan on the left between the Scottish ten-yard line and the twenty-five. Socks round his ankles, long hair streaming behind him he jinked inside as he charged upfield. It took four Scottish defenders, including Gammell the right wing, first to hold him, and then to bring him to ground, as Bill McLaren gasped 'he really is an abrasive customer for a full-back, isn't he!' When the ball came back, Gareth Edwards and J. J. Williams combined on the blind-side to give Derek Quinnell the space to rumble in from more than twenty-five yards out.

Williams's six international tries (five of which were against England) came from more conventional attacking play, with him being brought into the line as an extra weapon, often at short range. This was the case with his last in a closely-fought game at the Arms Park in 1977, when, with Wales leading by a single point, the ball came back from a line-out on the left. David Burcher made the half-break for Williams to take the ball, dummy to his right, side-step to his left and round Hignell at full-back for the decisive score. The 1976 game at Twickenham saw him at his finest as a finisher. Having received seven stitches in a facial wound early in the game Williams was initially used as a decoy in a first-half attack as the ball was thrown out to J. J. Williams on the left, only for

J.P.R. to take an overhead pass on the inside and crash through a tackle to reach the line. Then, with minutes to go, the ball came out to Bennett from a Welsh scrum inside the English twenty-five. Running in on a scissors with the fly-half, Williams dodged past the tiring English forwards and swerved inside, breaking Hignell's tackle and taking David Duckham over the line on his back. Both the MBE and the Rothmans' Player of the Year Award followed.

Often Williams joined the line not to score tries but to create opportunities for others. In only his second international he took the ball, sold the Irish cover a brilliant dummy and put Stuart Watkins away for a run which ended with John Taylor diving over. Regularly his wings benefited from Williams's incursions and accurate (sometimes fingertip) passing. As defences became alive to his particular threat so he was used as a crash-ball or decoy runner, keeping mid-fields honest in order to make space on the flanks. As a creator, he often did more than just pass the ball on. Against Scotland in 1979 he took the ball from Terry Holmes about thirty-five yards out on the right. Advancing into the Scottish twenty-five he jinked past scrum-half Lawson before chipping the ball perfectly over the heads of the defence for debutant wing Elgan Rees to catch it and go clean over in the corner. And, although kicking was not his forte, he will always be remembered for his magnificent long-range drop goal against the All Blacks in the Fourth Test in 1971, a moment which clinched the series victory for the Lions.

His career ended first in climax, and then in anti-climax. In 1979 he captained Wales to their fourth Triple Crown in a row and, six weeks later, Bridgend to their first Challenge Cup victory, against Pontypridd. That season Bridgend topped both the *Daily Telegraph* Merit Table and the *Daily Mail* Anglo-Welsh Pennant. Controversy over the publication (and profits) of his 1979 autobiography *JPR*, combined with the strain of more than a decade of performing at the top level, persuaded him to follow Gareth Edwards, Gerald Davies and Phil Bennett into international retirement. But the desire to play burned on, and although only a sporadic member of the Bridgend XV the following season, he still played in their 1980 Cup Final success against Swansea. The impending arrival of the All Blacks for the centenary match in November prompted Williams into a number of outstanding club performances and into making himself available again for international selection. There was little doubt that he remained the best full-back in Wales and, although Wales lost heavily (3–23) to New Zealand his customary heroic resistance ensured that he was not blamed. A final win was managed against England the following January, but defeat in Murrayfield led to his being replaced by Maesteg's Gwyn Evans. J. P. R. Williams's last major first-class appearance was for Bridgend in their 1981 Cup Final defeat by Cardiff.

J. P. R. Williams was one of the 'greats'. He was not the fastest player, not the best kicker, not the most dazzling runner, although his abilities in all three areas should not be underestimated. Whatever shortcomings he had, he worked very hard to overcome them, analysing his mistakes, keeping himself extremely fit, and maintaining his mental and competitive edge. As he wrote in *JPR*: 'there's only a certain amount of natural talent available to any one person; the balance of what makes one athlete differ from the rest is mostly hard slog, persistence and an underlying belief that anything is possible'. That he managed to stay at the top of the sport whilst forging a highly successful career for himself as a doctor is testimony to his single-minded industriousness.

It is probably true to say that, as a player in Welsh rugby's modern 'golden era', J. P. R. Williams was admired, respected and revered rather than loved. A private, even shy man, his background, education and work, combined with his living, for nearly a decade, outside Wales, meant that the Welsh rugby public felt they enjoyed less intimacy with their heroic full-back than with some of his comrades. (When, on my way to watch the Varsity Match in 1983, I realized that we were sharing the same railway carriage, I attempted to interest him with the comment that not only did we share the same surname but that my parents also lived on Merthyr Mawr Road: he remained distinctly unimpressed!) Williams himself did not seek adulation and appeared uncomfortable when confronted by it: rather than needing the sustenance of public acclamation his drive and dynamism came from deep within. The fact that he believed that he inherited his 'phenomenal competitive spirit' (which Gerald Davies considered to border on the 'frightening') from his English-born mother emphasizes that his sense of 'Welshness' was a complex rather than a clichéd one, and his lack either of the Welsh language or even a marked accent were early rendered irrelevant by those five tries and eleven victories against the English. For my own part, born in Wales but growing up in England (soccer-mad Swindon, to be precise), I realized my national identity, as have many others, through sport, both as a player and as a spectator. Slow-moving, short-sighted, for many years smaller than most, I was never going to make much of an impact on the field. My career peaks were three (almost wholly unsuccessful) years as captain of my comprehensive school's XV, a few games for the Balliol First XV, and one red-jerseyed appearance (at full-back!) for Cardiff University's Fourth XV. Retirement came at the age of thirty (while J. P. R. Williams continued to play) after I broke my hand attempting to hand off a mechanical engineering student, playing for the History Society on an afternoon when I should have been sitting on the University Senate. Nevertheless, studying J. P. R. Williams (on more than one occasion I went to see him play with the clear intention of monitoring his positioning and tactics) and doing my best to tackle and catch and counterattack as he did, represented a public and private affirmation of my own 'Welshness'. For, as Gareth Williams wrote in *Heart and Soul*, 'in identifying with our sports heroes, we are really spectators of ourselves'.

# PHIL BENNETT

## Colin Baber

If I tell you that I live in a house named 'Y Strade' in Lisvane, Cardiff, and that adorning my office at the Cardiff Business School are a framed photograph of the immortal team that conquered the 1972 All Blacks, an aerial view of Stradey Park and a grog of Phil Bennett (the only one I have ever owned or indeed wanted) then you will know exactly where I'm coming from. So, when my old sparring partner Peter Stead rang me in March, like any good sospanite I quickly fired a broadside before he had half a chance. 'I liked *Heart and Soul*', I said, 'but there was one glaring omission.' Before I could continue, Peter interrupted: 'Yes, I know and that's why I'm phoning, I'd like you to write a chapter on Phil Bennett.' What a labour of love for me and what an admission for such a cycloptic All Whites supporter as Peter to agree that the greatest thorn in his team's side should ever be accorded space and acclaim. This was recognition enough that our subject was someone very special. Our verbal jousting continued as it always does, not just with Peter but with many friends, supporters of the various clubs that constitute the closely knit Welsh rugby scene. I even suggested that my fee should be donated to the Rest Home for Deranged Swansea Forwards which is being built above Limeslade Bay. There I go again, my only excuse is that it is inbred. After all, this is the stuff that Welsh rugby is made of and I make no apologies.

Phil Bennett, or Benny as he is universally known west of Loughor Bridge, symbolizes what I understand as the heart and soul of Welsh rugby. He was the consummate club player, captaining Llanelli for a record six successive seasons from 1973 until 1979, and at the same time was an international performer of the highest repute. Apart from the five games he played for Aberavon as an eighteen year old (he couldn't stay away any longer) when faced with the daunting competition of Barry John, then securely Llanelli's outside-half, Phil played all his senior club rugby for the Scarlets. As a youth player he distinguished himself as captain of an invincible Felinfoel team and with brilliant international performances. Indeed he has lived all his life in Felinfoel, a village at the northern extremity of Llanelli, as has his wife, Pat, and he has always worked in the town, for which he is the sports development officer.

Llanelli is Phil Bennett, and increasingly as he matured as a player he became the very kernel of the Scarlets. Yes, rugby is the ultimate team game and Phil would always be the first to accord to his team-mates his fulsome praise. But, for me, he was always the star attraction. I remember my father talking in the same vein about Albert Jenkins, Llanelli's star centre of the 1920s. Yes, Cardiff would have loved to sign Benny, so would Swansea, as would many Northern league scouts but he modestly reflects that there would have been no point as they all knew there was only one club for him. Those were the days and I am eternally grateful that they were.

The heart and soul of Welsh rugby are those clubs which play with varying degrees of competence, week in, week out, representing communities which are geographically, culturally and spiritually close, yet in rugby terms far removed. Yes, things have changed quite radically since the advent of professionalism and, undoubtedly, there is still more to come. But, in the end, the game can only be as strong as its clubs. Of course, the national team is the pinnacle, the ultimate symbol and outcome of the health, efficiency and success of the game in Wales. But it can only be that, not the converse. To confuse this issue is to tempt self-destruction, something to which Welsh rugby has come perilously close recently. At the time of writing it does seem that the internecine brinkmanship which has plagued the game might at last be ending and that the interests of the national team and the clubs can be reconciled.

The game of rugby is to the Welsh far more than a simple athletic contest, it permeates the very essence of everyday life and the national psyche. Many who have never watched a match will always be greatly concerned as to 'how did the boys do' the previous Saturday, and many who have never played the game will vociferously explain why a seasoned international played badly or well. There is of course nothing wrong with this, and most countries will have their symbolic penance.

The bond between the rugby club and the community which it represents has always been a central feature of the cultural life of south Wales. Phil has never forgotten this and it is a relationship to which he more than most gives full credence. Nowhere is this better illustrated than in Felinfoel. As a boy I saw Felinfoel as the location of the Morris Motors factory and the bus terminus for visits to Swiss Valley, a local beauty spot. But the real heart of Felinfoel is its rugby club of which

Phil is the proud president. Felinfoel also has, of course, its brewery which is especially famous as the producer of Britain's first canned beer in 1935. Thus Llanelli, euphemistically known as Tinopolis because of its many tinplate works, provided both the raw material for the manufacture of the cans and the thirsty drinkers of the village's famous product. But in rugby terms it is the community which has bred Phil and to which he in turn has shown the utmost loyalty. Indeed, Felinfoel Rugby Club which was founded in 1876 played host to my university team in 1963 in an end-of-term tour to south Wales. We were soundly thrashed, but I'd like to think that Phil watched me that day even if he can't remember it! It certainly seemed as if the whole village had turned up to watch, and to ensure that we were properly fed and 'watered' and then entertained. The English boys in our party simply could not believe the occasion. The main talking-point concerned an incident the previous year when we had entertained the Felinfoel party at the Three Tuns Bar in Holborn. We had also been well beaten that day at our ground at New Malden, but during the evening celebrations a Felinfoel worthy, Sam Tripp, in dancing the obligatory 'zulu warrior' had cut his foot on broken glass. Little did Mick Jagger know, a fellow student then, that it was Sam Tripp of Felinfoel who had interrupted one of his regular Friday night 'gigs'! Sam was quickly despatched to St Phillip's Hospital at nearby Lincolns Inn Fields only to be told that it was a specialist VD hospital. Fortunately, Charing Cross Hospital was just down the Strand and quickly administered repairs. But as we found out a year later, all Felinfoel was agog to learn the truth of Sam's visit to a hospital specializing in sexually transmitted diseases, and the students of the London School of Economics saw just how closely knit south Wales village life could be.

It must have been the spring of 1962 when I first saw Phil play. I was home in Llanelli swotting for fast-approaching exams. I was bored reading about the imperfections of the American capital market and so I went to meet my cousin Alan, then a first former at Coleshill School. My interest was quickly drawn to a rugby match between the school's XV and the juniors (Under 15s) of the local grammar school, and in particular by the home team's diminutive outside-half who seemed to be playing a different game from the rest. He was mature beyond belief and with a devastating side-step that invariably followed a convulsive jink and a kick that threatened to explode the heavy ball that schools rugby used in those days. These were talents that surely could not have been learnt. He seemed to beat hapless opponents at will, first in scoring a try and then making another for a tall blond forward. Portents of great things to come surely! He so dominated proceedings that I would not have been surprised to see him waltz across the lily pads over nearby Pontwym. On leaving I met Mervyn Bowen, Coleshill's rugby master who proudly informed me that the little imp's name was Bennett, the blond forward's was Quinnell and that they both had another year in school. They were only just fourteen!

Little did I know it then but I had for the first time witnessed the precocious skills of a boy who was to become my all-time sporting hero. When I was younger my heroes had been either soccer or cricket players. My father, himself a fine amateur wicket-keeper had avidly followed the Scarlets until 'Albert' retired in 1932 but then transferred his allegiances to soccer, I suppose in sympathy, as my parents moved house close to Stebonheath, the home of the town's team. Thus my sporting inclinations were not directed towards Stradey Park, now some distance away, and my heroes were Denis Compton who played soccer for Arsenal and cricket for Middlesex, Stanley Mortensen who scored a hat-trick against Bolton in Blackpool's 4–3 win in the Matthews FA Cup Final of 1953, and 'Big Dunc' – Duncan Edwards, the Busby Babe and Manchester United wing-half, so tragically killed in the 1958 Munich Air Disaster and whom I was convinced could have walked into any rugby team in any position. In 1954, Jock Stein, subsequently the great Celtic manager came to Stebonheath as player-manager and fired unbridled enthusiasms amongst us aspiring teenage superstars with open coaching sessions both meaningful and inspiring. But Stradey in those days did not hold great dreams for me.

In 1964 after abortively sampling the industrial world with BSA, the guns and motorcycle makers in Birmingham, I found myself teaching history and economics back at Llanelli Grammar School which, at the time, was full of academic and of course sporting potential. Terry Price, a sixth former, had already played against Wilson Whineray's All Blacks and had international honours for both athletics and cricket. At one of the teachers' regular Friday evening drinking sessions, I remember asking Hywel Thomas, a former Scarlet and loyal committeeman who had moulded Sevens teams which had conquered all before them in winning the Rosslyn Park Public Schools Sevens a record four consecutive times, which of his charges he tipped for future greatness. After qualifying the potential of a few, he quickly proceeded to extol the virtues of Phillip Bennett who had recently dropped a goal from a prodigious distance when captaining the Welsh Schoolboys against England at Twickenham. 'But surely', I said remembering the little imp I saw performing his magic on People's Park the previous year, 'he's too small'. Never one to suffer fools gladly and with a 'what do you know about it, Baber, you're just a soccer player' tone he simply reflected that if Bennett was any bigger then he would merely need eight forwards on his side, and no one else!

It was then, I think, that the full reality of rugby's significance to us Welsh came home to me as Hywel's eyes filled with tears – the Buckleys perhaps! – and he proceeded to treat us to a diatribe of how 'this boy' had everything, that he would stand up to the closest scrutiny, to how precious is the position of the outside-half, and how so very rarely is a jewel like Benny unearthed. Indeed I have never forgotten this 'lesson', especially in the interminable debates between fans over the comparative virtues of individual players. Focus on the position of outside-half is particularly intense in Wales, as books written by Frank Keating and Alun Richards make evident. In the end, however, this must be a highly subjective exercise which is the result of substantive tangible observation as well as inbred parochialism. But I know my preference now, even if I didn't then.

Benny was then forgotten. I moved to Cardiff to start a new career at the university but always failed to appreciate the seemingly perennial drift of young talented three-quarters, all internationals, who made the journey from Stradey Park to see if Cardiff's Westgate Street was really paved with gold. That is what many in west Wales felt at the time, and I admit to a deep cynicism that has not completely left me. But Barry John and Gerald Davies then came to Stradey in 1964, quickly became the fans' favourites, and calm returned. In those days a regular weekend trip down the A48 to Llanelli with a young family to visit grandparents seemed quite natural, and I quickly became a fervent supporter of the Scarlets. In 1967 I was devastated when Barry John followed the golden trail to the Arms Park. But this was just the occasion for which Benny and it seems Llanelli had waited Since his debut against Swansea in November 1966 Phil had only been a bit player at Stradey but then thank God the golden trail dried up. The shadow of John loomed large for Phil during his early years at Stradey and it says so much for his character and abilities that he was able to emerge from it successfully and that by the end of his career it was felt, at least in Llanelli, that he had completely transcended his predecessor's achievements.

The 1970s saw a decade in which Welsh rugby reached the heights of achievement and endeavour. The best, most entertaining rugby anywhere, ever I believe. If the first decade of the twentieth century was known as the golden age of Welsh rugby then goodness knows what precious metal could describe the 1970s – platinum? Wales was the outstanding team in the northern hemisphere and within Wales Llanelli, in any measurable terms, was the dominant club for which Benny was the outstanding performer. The catalyst for the brave new world must surely have been the successful British Lions tour of 1971 which brought together a group of highly talented young players orchestrated by a deep-thinking charismatic coach who encouraged his players to express their prodigious skills. On their return from the land of the long white cloud the players, especially the Welsh, assumed almost legendary status, particularly Barry John who was duly crowned. Benny would have felt rather peeved not to make the tour as number 2 to John, but I for one, somewhat selfishly perhaps, see his omission rather benevolently as the decade saw Phil accomplish so much for his club, which was not always the case for some of the tourists.

Although Carwyn James was never to coach Wales due to the myopia of members of the WRU he nevertheless cast the die for the unparalleled success of the 1970s. I only had one conversation with Carwyn, in Toronto in the summer of 1973 when I was a visiting professor at the university there. The fact that Llanelli were touring Canada at the same time must have escaped my wife's attention when she agreed to accompany me with our three children and my mother to drive the length of that vast country The ulterior motive should have been obvious, and I was able to watch Llanelli and Benny play four times that summer in places almost 3,000 miles apart in Ottawa and Victoria BC. When we met, Carwyn while extolling Benny's virtues and skills, almost as an aside reflected that his only fault was that he lacked sufficient arrogance both as a player and a person! Incidentally, my only meeting with Phil was also in Canada that summer when we met him, his wife Pat and Delme Thomas and wife on an evening stroll in Winnipeg.

The Canadian tour was the culmination of Llanelli's centenary season, and what a season it was both for the club and for Benny himself. Barry John had just retired the preceding summer, physically and emotionally drained as he found the adulation thrust upon him in the claustrophobic environment of Welsh rugby impossible to shoulder. So the situation was ripe for Benny to give full expression to that amazing range of skills that I had first witnessed in People's Park a decade before. He did not disappoint, and in that centenary season he offered a strong hint of the many magical things to come.

On reflection there are four dates which stand out in my memories of Llanelli. On 7 May 1945, I remember sitting on my father's shoulders in Town Hall Square celebrating VE Day to the strains of Calon Lân; 19 September 1964, was the day I married my wife Pat in St Paul's Church – the short journey to the reception at the Thomas Arms Hotel was interrupted by the traffic heading towards Stradey Park where West Wales were to play the touring Fijians; 29 July 1965, when our first child was born in Glasfryn Maternity Home. We were then living in Cardiff, but as I was convinced that Alison would have been a boy there was no choice over the birthplace! Finally, 30 October 1972, the day that I and all Llanelli remember in crystal clear terms, when the Scarlets defeated the All Blacks. No day, no sporting occasion could surely ever assume greater significance in the communal psyche as does that grey autumn Tuesday.

After lecturing I rushed off down the A48 with a Newport supporter, a rabid Cardiff fan from west Wales (I've never been able to understand such sentiments!), and a Cockney colleague who was to see his first rugby match. We got down to the Apple Tree in time to catch a couple of pints of draught Bass, and some pre-match atmosphere. After persuading Stan the postman, the pub's resident (and illegal) bookie, to lay me generous odds against a Scarlets win and a spread bet which included 9–3 (Stan was no mug) we hurried off down to Stradey which was already jam-packed with 24,000 or so others and managed to dig our way on to the Tanner Bank as far as the 25-yard-line at the town end. I have been at many sporting occasions in different parts of the world but nothing has ever come close to the experience of Stradey that day. To describe it as spiritual does exaggerate I suppose, but it cannot have been far short. Those of us privileged to have been there witnessed a momentous occasion.

The game itself needs little mention. The world of rugby knows the scoreline better than any other game ever played – Llanelli 9 Seland Newydd 3 – thanks to Max Boyce who also reflected that the beer was piped down from Felinfoel. But thank God, Phil Bennett also made that journey and this must have been his greatest triumph. Few, however, not even the Glynneath minstrel, could have appreciated that Phil had deliberately aimed his penalty attempt at the upright so the ball would deflect into the welcoming arms of Roy Bergiers to score the vital try. Yet another of Carwyn's fiendish ploys! My lasting memory came right towards the end of the game when the All Blacks were menacingly threatening the Llanelli try-line. They threw into a line-out, Delme Thomas outjumped Andy Haden and 'Chico' Hopkins passed out to Benny who skipped outside the fast approaching Alistair Scown and kicked the sweetest touch-finder there has ever been. It must have been forty, no sixty yards, who cares! I can remember the dejected faces of the New Zealand forwards to this day. Within seconds the final whistle went, we had beaten the unbeatable and pandemonium broke out. Our little town and our little man had triumphed over one of the world's great rugby nations. It was far more than just a game. Carwyn James had once again out-thought the mighty All-Blacks and Benny and the fourteen other Scarlet Warriors gave practical reality to his orchestration. I just could not return to Cardiff with my companions as there was further celebrating to enjoy. And, yes, I did hear a few of the old boys who frequented the Apple Tree admit that they could at last die happily and I did enter a few of Llanelli's pubs that night and the following day to find that the beer had run out.

What a start to a centenary season. The rest of Benny's career might well have been an anti-climax, but his character and ability would dictate otherwise. If beating the All Blacks in Stradey was not enough then Phil was also to play in the Barbarians team which served up the equivalent of rugby caviare in beating the All Blacks at Cardiff Arms Park. Indeed, Phil, one of only three of the Baa-baas (along with Tommy David, another Scarlet, and Bob Wilkinson) who had not toured New Zealand with the 1971 Lions, had cast the die for that fabulous feast of rugby football. After twelve minutes he danced mesmerically out of defence leaving four of the helpless All Blacks stranded and thus set up that never-to-be-forgotten try which was so dynamically completed by Gareth Edwards. Unfortunately, Phil was not successful in his third game against the All Blacks, when Wales lost 19–16 in December 1972. Indeed, he had the chance to level the scores in the closing minutes but failed with a relatively straightforward but long-distance kick. On that tour the All Blacks defeated all four of the Home Countries.

Also in that centenary season Llanelli defeated Cardiff in the WRU Challenge Cup by 30–7 in what I still say was the most comprehensive defeat of Wales's self-styled leading club and Benny was brilliant. Llanelli completely dominated the early days of the Cup. They appeared in the first five finals and, after losing to Neath in the first in 1972, they won the next four, a record unlikely to be equalled. The Cup presented Benny with yet another arena in which to exploit his talents and again he did not disappoint, winning the first two presentations of the Lloyd Lewis Trophy as the best player in the 1975 and 1976 finals, first against Aberavon and then against Swansea. During that magical season of 1972–3 with Benny starring, Llanelli also won the Floodlight Alliance Final (in which only tries counted) for a sixth successive year and the Welsh Snelling Sevens by defeating Newbridge in the final with a record 52–6 victory. Benny then captained Llanelli for six successive seasons after succeeding Delme Thomas in 1973. No Welsh club has ever experienced such success or played such attractive rugby and no player has been so effective or dominant on the club scene in modern times as Phil Bennett.

But although Phil maintained a high level of commitment to his club rugby and only rarely disappointed his adoring Scarlets fans either by not turning out or by not contributing more than his fair share of endeavour and skill, I feel that his international career was never quite accorded the heights of praise that it really deserved. I have already alluded to the reason for this: Benny was never one of the 1971 Lions. He was never accorded the status of king; even though, for some of us, his achievements transcend those of Barry John, he is seen in a rather lesser light. There is no doubt that Barry was a hard act to follow when he retired prematurely in 1972 at the age of twenty-seven. The king was dead but the new king was to find his accession rather more difficult than one might suppose. Despite his tremendous contribution to club, country and the Barbarians in that 1972–3 season Phil was not able to make what should have been a smooth transition into international rugby. The unreasonable expectation Welsh rugby has of its outside-halves, coupled with the great national disappointment expressed on John's retirement, especially in causing the break-up of the classic half-back partnership with Gareth Edwards, ensured this. Thus in 1975 the 'Big Five' reverted to type and for Wales's first game against France Benny was dropped without any explanation and only six months after he had competed so superbly for the British Lions in South Africa. The tragic loss of his and Pat's first baby soon after his return combined with Phil's low physical state after that demanding tour must have undermined his emotional preparedness for the international arena. A month later he regained his place as a substitute for the injured John Bevan, only to be left out of the Welsh squad at the start of the 1976 international campaign. Yet again the Big Five were to confuse the issue completely, choosing John Bevan to play in the first international against England with David Richards as understudy. Typically, Phil did not receive the news direct from the WRU but from a journalist's phone call. But then the hand of God intervened, and if Maradona's claim to divine intervention in putting England out of soccer's world cup in 1986 attracted notoriety then the injuries to Bevan and Richards could only have been seen in a benevolent light. That season Benny went on to score a record thirty-eight points out of 102 thus becoming the first Welsh player to score 100 points in his career and helping Wales to a Grand Slam under Mervyn Davies's captaincy.

Phil Bennett played twenty-nine times for Wales, the first two out of position; the first as a wing substitute (Wales's first) for Gerald Davies against France in 1969, and the second as centre against Scotland in 1970 and then as a substitute for J. P. R. Williams against Scotland in 1972; and the last eight as captain. In his last three seasons of international rugby, Wales won two Grand Slams and one Triple Crown only to lose to France at the Parc des Princes in 1977 by 16–9. In his last match for his country, against France in Cardiff, he scored two tries and converted one in a 16–7 victory. He scored 166 points for Wales, and in that last game passed Tom Kiernan's European scoring record. If the forty-five points he scored for the British Lions are added then that last match saw him pass Don Clarke's long-held world record of 207 points. All this from a player who had not always been the main kicker for Wales in an era when average international scores were much lower than they would become over the following two decades. But what a finale – Phil retired from international rugby the same time as Gareth Edwards whom he had partnered on twenty-six of his twenty-nine appearances.

Although Phil failed to make the Lions tour to New Zealand in 1971 he did tour twice with the Lions; to South Africa in 1974 with the most successful Lions team ever and as captain of the Lions in New Zealand in 1977. Willie John McBride's Lions took South Africa by storm in the early days of the anti-apartheid movement. Apart from the last Test which ended in a 13–13 draw, the Lions won the other three Tests and ten provincial games with gas to spare. Willie John and his forwards tamed the giant Springbok packs allowing his backs to cut the South Africans to ribbons. Phil, along with J.P.R., Gerald, J.J., Gareth, Andy Irvine, Mike Gibson and others scorched over the High Veld and showed what British rugby was about. Phil's finest game was undoubtedly the Second Test, which the Lions won 28–9. Phil had exorcized the shadow of King John in no uncertain terms and Wales would have a stable presence at number 10 again. Or would we?

The Lions tour to New Zealand in 1977 was an unhappy one failing to live up to the high standards set by Doug Smith and Carwyn James six years earlier or by the unbeaten Lions in 1974. Phil was appointed captain, largely on the basis of his success in leading Llanelli and Wales. But from the start the tour was blighted. At least five key members of the prospective Test side had made themselves unavailable – Gareth, Gerald, J.P.R., Fergus Slattery and Peter Dixon – and both Geoff Wheel and Roger Uttley were forced to withdraw through illness. Neither did the tour party's relationship with the travelling press group make for a happy time. Add to all this the almost weekly addition to the injury list, and the tour's reputation as an unhappy one is understandable. Phil by his own admission did not play well and it is little wonder. It was indeed a minor miracle that the Lions almost drew the Test series, winning the Second Test, 13–9, and losing the Fourth Test and last by a mere point.

Thankfully, Phil was soon able to erase the unhappy memories of the New Zealand tour the following season, which ended with Wales winning another Grand Slam and Benny retiring from international rugby with those two tries against France and the scoring records. He went on to play for his club for a further three years with his last game against Northampton in April 1981. Unfortunately, I did not witness his swansong. It was typical of him that he made no grand announcement that he was finishing, no fuss, just like the way he played. He had played 412 games for the Scarlets, scoring 2,532 points including 132 tries.

In conclusion, I suppose I should admit to two disappointments. The one is that my political leanings (not to mention a lack of finance) made a visit to South Africa in 1974 a non-starter for me. But I would have loved to have gone. The other is that I would love to have seen Gareth my son who plays scrum-half for Bristol play with Phil. What a partnership!

# TERRY HOLMES

Trevor Herbert

In 1976 I moved to Cardiff from London, where I had spent the previous decade. I had gone to London as a student and ended up working there. Those years were the best to be in London if you were Welsh and a rugby fan. The great London Welsh side of the early 1970s drew the London Welsh community together, and the twice annual visits to Cardiff for the Five Nations home internationals were rituals of unparalleled pleasure. The stream of emphatic victories and the style that typified their achievement promoted a self-confidence that our English friends and colleagues must have found unbearable.

When I went to live in Cardiff, I was struck by how little I knew it. As a boy in the Rhondda I had been taken there no more than four or five times. I could remember almost nothing about those trips, because so frenzied was my excitement at the prospect of visiting the great city that I was mesmerized to the point of amnesia by the end of such days out. How could I not have been? The castle, the arcades, the market, the trolley buses: it was all too much for my youthful innocence to digest. I do recall though that I understood hardly anything of what the local people said. My mother told me this was because they had a 'Cardiff accent'. I asked whether it was Welsh, and my father, with what I came to regard as undue decisiveness, said 'No'.

I was to learn how wrong my father had been, when, after a year or so of indifference towards Welsh club rugby, I started to watch Cardiff play. I had been attracted by the prospect of seeing Gareth Edwards, but soon found that his appearances in routine games were infrequent. The more regular inside-half was Brynmor Williams – a player who would have gained considerably greater celebrity if he had played at another time. On Saturdays and some Wednesdays I would go, with an increasing enthusiasm, to the Arms Park terraces, and I soon became fascinated by the distinctiveness of the place. It had not especially occurred to me that Cardiff Rugby Club was more than a stage for the stellar talents of Gareth Edwards, Cliff Morgan, Barry John and their like, whose roots lay elsewhere. I had regarded it in terms similar to those London clubs like Harlequins and Wasps whose names carried no hint of their locality because they did not relate to a community in the way that – say – Neath, Bedford, Leicester or Llanelli did: they merely provided a focus for rugby-playing city slickers. I had not realized that the core culture, the heartbeat, of Cardiff Rugby Club, was the city, its suburbs, its people and their flavours. The players who came from without had to prove their skills and character not just in the club but to the gatherings on the terraces.

At this time the young Terence David Holmes was about to emerge from the shadows of Gareth Edwards and Brynmor Williams to become one of Cardiff's greatest stars. In the years of transition that followed the 'golden era', he ignited much that was to be kindled in the national team. But at the Arms Park he was a yet greater hero: the urban Welshman, the archetypal if not typical Cardiff player. No player could have been more a product of the city. Holmes was born on 10 March 1957, at 74 Churchill Way, Cardiff, a spot now occupied by one of the most central of the shoppers' car parks. His parents were Irish Catholics; he never called them 'mam' and 'dad', but Phyllis and Dai. He was brought up a Catholic, was an altar-boy at the Catholic cathedral, and following the family's eviction to the Fairwater district of the city, he went to Bishop Hannon School, where he was introduced to rugby by the PE master, Roger Goode. His ties to an extended family – both parental and married – have always been strong. In childhood, his mother seems to have been the greatest anchor. She worked on a fruit-and-veg barrow in a lane off Queen Street. His father had been a sailor who later drifted between a variety of other jobs. He was a kindly, carefree man, well-known in the bars of the city. He appears to have taken only a passing interest in his son's sporting career, and was famously spotted by Terry Holmes riding a bike through Cardiff wearing his son's Welsh rugby team blazer, replying to Holmes's mild protestations by shouting, 'Don't go on boy, it's only a bloody jacket'.

The Catholic community in Cardiff has been strong since the main period of immigration towards the turn of the century. On fine days in the parks of the city, you can still spot the Catholics by the sports they are playing. Among the recreational practices typical of, if not unique to them, is baseball or 'rounders'. Such recreations functioned critically to initiate both the socializing and the athleticism of working-class boys like Holmes. Those who gravitated to rugby played for one of the plethora of school teams or boys and youth clubs, and hoped to progress through representative teams to Cardiff Rugby Club. It was this predictable path along which Terry Holmes passed rapidly. He went to the Cardiff club from his school team. By 1976 he had played for the Welsh Youth team for three seasons and broken the record for the greatest number of caps. The brightness of his talent was already apparent in the senior game. On 21 March 1975 he captained the Cardiff and District Youth team to a victory over Bridgend Youth, to win the coveted D. G. Griffiths Trophy. Less than twenty-four hours later, the seventeen-year-old made his debut for Cardiff against their most vehement rivals, Newport. In the next decade he would play in 193 games, score 123 tries for the club, and be captain for the 1984–5 season. Apart from a single game for Glamorgan Wanderers, and leaving aside representative matches, he never wore senior rugby union colours other than the blue and black of Cardiff.

The emphasis that many have put on Holmes's strength and physical bulk, and his capacity to act as an extra back-row forward, does little justice to the breadth and subtlety of his game. Undoubtedly Holmes – 6′1″ and always over 13 stones – was big for an inside-half. His lethal capacity to strike from the base of a five-yard scrum was one of the hallmarks of his play: one felt that he would charge optimistically at a brick wall if he suspected that the try-line lurked behind it. But his game was intelligent and it had stealth. He was seldom predictable, and he seemed to sense spaces and movements and how to exploit weaknesses in his opponents' lines of defence. The attention that his opponents devoted to him allowed him to absorb defences, opening up a yawning space into which the ball could be lobbed for another blue-and-black clad figure to run liberated. Holmes did not merely play well – he controlled games. He was an instinctive player, and possessed the single ingredient that all great backs and half-backs share: the ability to change the tempo and tone of a game in a single instant by an apparently ordinary but incisive piece of play.

Even when Gareth Edwards retired, Terry Holmes was not an automatic choice at inside-half for Cardiff. Indeed, his selection for the Welsh tour of Australia in 1978 was as a second string to Brynmor Williams. It was on that tour that he won his first cap and asserted his presence in the side. By the 1980 season, no one seriously doubted that he was the best scrum-half in Wales, and that his strength and intelligence were to be the basis of the Welsh game plan. Following the 1979 victory over Scotland, the *Western Mail's* J. B. G. Thomas singled him out as 'the outstanding player on the field. A man of strength, determination, skill and constant endeavour and every bit as impressive and effective as was Gareth Edwards at his age'.

In 1975 the celebrated partnership with Gareth Davies had begun, when the two were picked to play for Cardiff against Pontypool. It was Holmes's second game for the club and Davies's first. The two players were often characterized as being quite different: Davies was smooth, light-footed, Oxford-educated and Welsh-speaking; Holmes was the burly, street-wise Cardiff urbanite, by that time working in a scrap business. In fact, the success of their partnership came from their similarities: both were from unambiguously working-class origins, both (despite the different expression of it) possessed a depth of pride in their Welshness, and both played instinctively and with a sense of celebration. The understanding between the two men was often clichéd as 'telepathic', but they played together so many times – more than 200 times, according to Davies's estimate – that it would have been surprising if they had not reached a fairly clear understanding of each other's game. What was not always fully acknowledged was the extent to which a third man, Cardiff's English number 8, John Scott, shared and influenced the Cardiff half-backs' attacking edge. It is a pity that the Scott-Holmes-Davies combination was never unleashed in a Lions team.

Holmes's period as the Welsh inside-half spanned an important period of transition. When he first played for Wales in Cardiff against the All Blacks in November 1978, J. P. R. Williams, Steve Fenwick and J. J. Williams were still in the side, as was the Pontypool front row. This was the game remembered for the notorious Andy Haden line-out incident which led to the New Zealanders winning by the smallest margin. Wales deserved to win that day, and had they done so, no one would have been especially surprised, for the momentum and self-confidence built by the sides of the mid-1970s was still the common currency. Even at the end of the 1979 season, the 27–3 win against England was greeted with the headline 'Wales Look Ready for Another Great Era'. The pattern continued; the 1980 win against France saw Holmes ('the Cardiff human hurricane') score in the twenty-third consecutive home nations victory at Cardiff. But England's 17–7 defeat of Wales at Cardiff in 1982, their biggest win since 1921, signalled the unnerving beginning of the time when Welsh victories had to be hoped for, rather than confidently anticipated, even though Wales lost only one of the next six games in which Holmes played.

In his final full season, 1984–5, a new cohort was emerging: Jonathan Davies and Paul Thorburn won their first caps. In the eight years he played for Wales, he had won twenty-five caps and captained the side. His caps were not continuous because he sustained injuries that kept him from international duty, but his place was never really insecure. Injuries were to blight his career and prevent him from making a mark as a British Lion. He was selected for the tours to South Africa in 1980 and New Zealand in 1983 but sustained serious injuries that abbreviated them. On a couple of occasions he broke an ankle, the ligaments in his knee were often damaged, and he had a tendency for dislocations to his shoulders. There was nothing especially frail or vulnerable about his physique, but his reckless disregard for personal safety on the rugby field, and his tendency to play simultaneously both a forward's and a back's game, placed him in danger on most occasions that he played.

Holmes had always seemed like a good prospect for rugby league, and as early as 1979 Salford had made a move for him. But his ambitions in the union game were always paramount, and his attachment to Cardiff powerful. In the autumn of 1985, however, circumstances coincided to prompt the move north. He was twenty-nine years of age, and a career as a celebrated but unpaid union player had fulfilled most of his ambitions, but provided no direct financial security. In the days of amateurism, Cardiff were famously and truly amateur: there were no hidden benefits which surrogated for direct payment. Gareth Davies, who had already resigned from the Welsh team, had intimated his intention to leave the game within a year. The key partnership of this era was about to be fractured. Holmes was to captain Wales against Fiji in November 1985, but he was already entertaining the view that Welsh interests would be served if a new half-back pair were to mature in time for the 1987 World Cup. The young Jonathan Davies was obviously brilliant. Holmes liked playing with him, but he sensed that the baton was being passed to a new generation. Wales beat Fiji 40–3 and Holmes scored a try, but following a minor knee injury, 'the lionhearted Terry Holmes' (as J. B. G. Thomas described him) left the field early to 'thunderous applause'. Only he knew that it was his last game for Wales.

There is a folklore about the tone and manner in which union players have been seduced by league clubs. This folklore has been given extra relish by the absurdly protectionist, prejudicial and rarely rational behaviour of sectors of the union game. The story of Holmes's transfer reveals nothing salacious, disreputable or even particularly clandestine, but in the period when negotiations were taking place, the confidentiality and discretion that befits such matters were properly observed. Predictably, this discretion stimulated rumours and anticipation in both Wales and Yorkshire, leading to especially intense expectation of his first game for the great rugby league club Bradford Northern. A few days before the Fiji game he had been contacted by the northern club and was told there was interest in signing him. He took part in no negotiations but agreed to think about it. His game against Llanelli at Stradey Park on 23 November was to be his last for Cardiff. The following Tuesday he travelled to Bradford with only his brother-in-law Tommy Foley as a companion. He negotiated the provisional terms of his contract in the boardroom of the club, and this was followed by a medical test. He was to sign on 3 December.

The move received contrasting coverage in the newspapers of Bradford and south Wales. In Wales his impending departure caused Mrs Pamela Naysmith, a 40-year-old Cardiff housewife, to organize a fund to raise the £80,000 that was being paid for him, so that he could be kept in Wales. 'It is time' she said, 'that Welsh rugby supporters stopped crying into their beer and dug deep into their pockets.' In Bradford the prospect of his arrival reopened well-worn debates about the merits of union players in the league game, and raised questions about Holmes's age and apparent vulnerability to injury. There was palpable suspense in the few days before the deal was struck, as newspaper headline writers spun lines like, 'Speculation growing about Northern move for Holmes' and 'Holmes keeps Northern waiting'. One paper referred optimistically to the re-establishment of Wales as the 'nursery of rugby league'. Ray French, the doyen of league journalists, thought that a player with Holmes's profile would stir the 'sleeping giant' that Bradford Northern had become, and proffered the thought that he could be in the Great Britain side within a year.

Most in Wales felt that Holmes deserved every reward that he could get from the league game. He had been a good servant to club and country, and even his detractors acknowledged the burden he had carried at the base of the Welsh scrum. It was his reputation for strength and courage that made the prospect of his arrival so attractive to Bradford. The club was on a downward spiral and had recently sold the great Ellery Hanley to Wigan for £150,000. Much was made about the 'mouth-watering prospect' of Holmes teaming up with John Woods at half-back. Less than a year before, Woods had moved from Leigh to Odsal Stadium, the Bradford Northern ground, for £65,000. Bradford needed Holmes's charisma as well as his physical presence. His was the first major transfer from Wales since Clive Griffiths went to St Helens from Llanelli for £27,000. But the comparisons that were being drawn most conspicuously were with two yet earlier transfers: David Watkins and Terry Price. Bradford needed to get the turnstiles clicking by capturing the popular imagination with the prospect of a new hero. One commentator, writing in the week that Holmes was to sign, and lamenting the dwindling number of spectators at Odsal, observed that when Terry Price joined the club in the late 1960s, 'more people turned up to watch his first training session than were at the club match last Sunday and 13,000 turned up for his first game'.

The first match that Holmes played for Bradford was away against Swinton. The anticipation could hardly have been higher. There was the expected media attention, a flotilla of cars carrying friends, family and supporters from Wales, and a gate three times the Swinton average. The pressure on him must have been immense. He had been on the pitch for barely thirteen minutes when, in a hard but fair tackle, his shoulder was decisively dislocated. Amazingly, out of stupidity, embarrassment, ill-placed bravery or whatever, he continued to play – even continued to tackle – until the pain overcame him. I remember watching the television pictures of him leaving the field. He looked a pathetic sight, carrying a devastating injury and the weight of £80,000 worth of expectations. Seven weeks later he was back, in the Bradford 'A' team against Batley 'A'. Two minutes into the second half, the same shoulder slipped out of its socket. The criticism of him and of the wisdom of Bradford's strategy in buying him was as vociferous as it was predictable. For Holmes and those close to him it was a catastrophe. He had shown himself to be as vulnerable as his worst critics had predicted he would be. Privately he entertained the idea of retirement, having spent a total of less than an hour on the rugby league field; but his sole utterance to the waiting press was, 'I will be back'.

In the spring of 1986 he underwent yet more surgery. By late August the headlines in *The Rugby Leaguer* read 'Welsh Wizard Raring to Go'. The first two games of the new season saw Holmes playing a decisive role in victories against Widnes and Hull Kingston Rovers. He started scoring tries, the type that had been typical of his union career. Suddenly the press was proclaiming the need for Bradford to revive their 'pathetic' pack of forwards to balance with their brilliant running backs, Holmes, John Woods, Phil Ford, Steve Donlan and Terry Simpson. On 7 October 1987 Bradford played Castleford in the final of the Yorkshire Cup. It was in this match that he tore ligaments: it was his final injury. He had been enormously popular in Yorkshire. People admired his self-effacing bravery and his refusal to whine, and they always waited expectantly to see the brilliance that they had admired in his union game. In fact, they saw only glimpses of it for, despite his stoic efforts, Holmes never controlled games as he had done in rugby union, which is what Bradford and the rugby league public so desperately wanted of him. The injuries which made his league career so tragically short were obviously the prime reason for Holmes's comparative failure in league. But if he possessed any defect, it was not in his underlying skills and certainly not in his appetite for the game and passion for his club. There was perhaps a deeper schism between the two codes than he had realized. He had played the union game on the basis of sophisticated instincts that he often shared with other key players, and these instincts did not transpose to the league code as automatically and effortlessly as he needed them to. He was a natural player outside his native environment. His sense of space and timing were firmly entrenched in the union game. 'The only similarity between league and union', he was quoted as saying, 'is the shape of the ball and the goal posts.'

He had been happy in Yorkshire, but had not disguised the strength of his roots in Cardiff, from where his wife Susan also came. When he had left, the Cardiff secretary had sent him a commendable but unpublicized letter in which he thanked him, wished him well and emphasized his freedom to return to the club which he had served so selflessly. In 1991 he started his coaching career at the club, a protégé of the Australian coach Alec Evans, to whom he was assistant between 1991 and 1998 (except for a year as head coach in 1996–7). His old partner Gareth Davies was also to return to the club as its chief executive.

He took over as head coach again in 1998, and there followed a period that was almost surreal in its absurdity. Tensions between the WRU and the Swansea and Cardiff clubs were fuelled by entrenched conservatism, petty politics, blind ambition, envy, indifferent management and a near total collapse of common sense. A dispute, from which only lawyers drew profit, resulted in the two great clubs becoming all but disenfranchised from the Welsh Rugby Union that they had helped galvanize for more than a century. They settled for a series of Anglo-Welsh 'friendly' fixtures which started well enough, but became increasingly meaningless as the teams' opponents realized that, in a game played for prizes, they were playing for nothing other than fairly meaningless statistics. The Cardiff club, privatized and professionalized, did not do badly. It lost just eight away games and retained a home record that had endured since 1997, but on the terraces there was an eerie sense that all was not well and that the club's true soul was ebbing away.

A single association with Cardiff's traditional competitors remained in the shape of their eligibility for the SWALEC Cup. After playing lesser sides in the earlier rounds, Cardiff were drawn against Llanelli in the 1999 semi-finals. The game was seen as important and by some even as symbolic. Not only did it represent the traditional rivalry between two of Wales's élite clubs, but it was also a test on the field of play of matters that had been squabbled over the previous year in committee rooms. Llanelli won 39–10, but the game was as notable for the extent to which it exposed the ineptitude of the Cardiff team as it displayed the Scarlets' skills. Before the game the Llanelli coach Gareth Jenkins was asked to predict the outcome. He extolled the importance of 'the emotion and spirit of a club' and said that the side with the biggest spirit would win the game. Sadly for Cardiff, he was right. The club possessed one of the most expensive groups of players ever to have been assembled in Welsh rugby, but their performance lacked almost every element that Holmes stood for.

In the aftermath, Terry Holmes announced his intention to resign from the club that had been part of his being for almost a quarter of a century. He was not a bad coach – indeed to my mind he had the talent to be a great one – but if he had a weakness, it was his innocence. He failed to appreciate, maybe he was incapable of appreciating, that the players in his charge did not, as a matter of native instinct, become fired with the will to win in the way that he did whenever he stepped onto a rugby field. He resolutely and consistently refused to criticize his players, and though the club promptly announced the appointment of Lynn Howells as his successor, Holmes, with scrupulous attention to duty, did not go away and sulk. He was there with his team for each of the four remaining games.

There is a certain dignity and enigma about Holmes which is rare in rugby. He is the classic urban working-class hero. He has drawn sustenance from the streets of Cardiff just as others have from the valleys and hills of the Welsh hinterlands. He wrote that the Cardiff club had turned a directionless working-class boy, who might have ended up as 'a mindless yob or a no-gooder' into a man with a purpose, and that Cardiff RFC taught him that the most important things in life were 'firstly people and then ideas'. Many institutions would proudly embody such words in a 'mission statement', but in Holmes's career we see their realization.

There is a moment that I recall with clarity, which seems in several different ways to typify the flavour of Holmes's presence in rugby. I was interested to discover that he too remembers it in his autobiography, even if in somewhat different terms. It was a mid-week game in Bath in 1984. I had been persuaded to go by a friend, who insisted that our trip include a visit to 'The Brain Surgery', the only pub run by the Cardiff brewers S. A. Brain outside Wales. When we got there, we found the place awash with Cardiff supporters – not gangs, but individuals or middle-aged couples, betrayed by their ties and scarves, showing little regard for each other, but all paying tacit acknowledgement to the temporary status of the place as a cultural oasis. It was there that I first heard talk that Holmesy might go North, even though there was no substance to those rumours. A man whom I had not previously met asked me if I had heard the rumours. I told him I had not, and he said that he 'could not bear the thought' of Holmesy not playing for Cardiff again. We spoke about the game and the merits of the home side. His wife said, 'Holmsey's playing tonight. I never feel we are going to lose when Holmsey is playing'.

By the time we got to the game, there were 16,000 before us, and we managed to squeeze in near the goal-line which the Bath team was to defend in the second half. Bath had played well, and with minutes to go led by less than one score. Cardiff was awarded a scrum five yards from the Bath line, and I felt relaxed: the outcome seemed inevitable. Holmes would pick up the ball after the Cardiff pack had given him a yard, and roll irresistibly over for a try – we had all seen it a hundred times before. Then the most singular of things happened. Holmes put in, and the referee Laurie Prideaux immediately penalized him for feeding the ball crooked to the scrum. It was ridiculous; Cardiff had one of the best packs in the business, with a front row of internationals. In any case, I saw that ball go in – it was the one detail of that match which I was able to observe clearly – and I will swear until my dying day that it went in as straight as an arrow. There was a millisecond of blunt and confused silence. Holmes and *both* teams looked at Prideaux with incredulity. Mr Prideaux, who had made his decision with considerable confidence, suddenly averted his gaze, and from all corners of the stands and enclosures the word 'NEVER' was shouted, murmured and chanted as if it were a rehearsal for a choral speech contest. This was not mere disappointment at a game lost: a more important matter was finding expression. The word was being used *literally*, for the Cardiff fans felt affronted: Holmes never fed a crooked ball or committed a cynical act.

In the programme for his final game as Cardiff coach on 8 May 1999, Holmes appealed for the club to nurture more local children in rugby, and for it to rediscover its roots, and he stressed the need for its players to be proud to wear the blue-and-black jersey. None of the many great players who have worn those colours could have invested such words with more weight. He stands as an example for his game, and above the tribal vicissitudes that have sometimes afflicted and tarnished it.

*I am grateful to Dr Eric Bowers who kindly loaned me material from his private archive when I was preparing this article.*

# GARETH DAVIES

Siân Nicholas

In 1974 my father interviewed Gareth Davies for a place to read chemistry at King's College, London. He remembers a self-contained young man who talked happily about his interest in rugby and mentioned in the course of the conversation that he was a Wales schoolboy international outside-half. As the interview ended, my father suggested, 'Well, if you come to us you can play for London Welsh' – they needed a new number 10 – 'or, I suppose, you could go to UWIST and play for Cardiff.' Gareth declined the attractions of London Welsh and went to the University of Wales Institute for Science and Technology, where he played briefly for Llanelli before playing for Cardiff, Oxford University, Wales, the Barbarians and the British Lions. But it is not just his twenty-one caps for Wales, his celebrated half-back partnership with Terry Holmes, or his retirement from the international game in protest at his treatment by the WRU selectors, that mark his particular contribution to Welsh rugby. Unusually, it is the career he carved out *after* his playing days, as BBC Wales head of sport, and especially as chief executive of Cardiff RFC, that singles Gareth Davies out as one of the most influential men in Welsh rugby.

Like so many Welsh outside-halves, Gareth Davies's early life seems to have fated him to play for Wales though, as with so many, the reality strayed from the stereotype. He was born and brought up in the west Wales mining village of Tumble, seven miles from Llanelli. He followed Carwyn James and Barry John to Gwendraeth Grammar School (where he was followed, in turn, by Jonathan Davies), and was encouraged to develop his natural game by the school rugby coach, former Wales wing Ray Williams. Yet although his mother encouraged his love for the game, his father, a miner in the Blaenurwen and Cynheidre pits, discouraged such frivolities, would not watch him play, and insisted that Gareth concentrate on academic success. He managed a happy compromise, doing well enough at his schoolwork to gain a place at university, and at the same time gaining not just school honours but Welsh Secondary Schools caps at both rugby and cricket. Not many Welsh internationals confess in their autobiography that their greatest disappointment on leaving school was not to have become head boy.

While gaining schoolboy rugby honours, it was his village side, Tumble RFC, that gave him the most encouragement and opportunity to play rugby. Traditionally, the next step was Llanelli, and while settling in at university he was pleased to be offered a few games when Phil Bennett was unavailable. More unexpected (though a welcome solution to the burden of travelling westward several times a week) was a telephone call from Barry John himself, inviting him to play for Cardiff in a team of rugby legends. Davies's first game for Cardiff was in November 1974 against Penarth. A week later, after being picked against Llanelli, he was sidelined when, in his first experience of Welsh club bureaucracy, his former club refused to grant him clearance to play. His first 'official' game for Cardiff was the traditional Boxing Day match against Pontypool at Pontypool Park, the 19-year-old outside-half playing for the first time with the 18-year-old Terry Holmes, Cardiff's untried third-choice scrum-half. It was a daunting occasion on which to begin such a remarkable rugby partnership, but both acquitted themselves well though it was Davies, with a flawless kicking perform-ance and two dropped goals, who seemed most obviously the player to watch.

Cardiff RFC was a very different proposition to Llanelli. Llanelli, Welsh-speaking, insular, jealous of its local connections and traditions, looked askance at the city slickers in the east, the 'Cardiff Athletic Club', whose rugby operation had long been almost synonymous with the Welsh rugby establishment. One member of the Llanelli committee told Davies that he would learn more about rugby sitting in the stand at Stradey Park than playing for Cardiff. But the Welsh-speaking west Walian soon found his feet at Cardiff under Gerald Davies's captaincy. He successfully combined his studies with playing for Cardiff and UWIST (with whom he won the UAU title with a dropped goal in the last minute), toured Canada with the Barbarians, and made the Welsh squad, understudying Phil Bennett, in 1976. At the suggestion of former Wales scrum-half and Oxford Blue Onllwyn Brace, he took time out from Welsh club rugby to take a diploma in education at Oxford Uni-versity. On a wet day at Twickenham in December 1977, Oxford University, with Davies controlling proceedings at outside-half, executed a ruthless ten-man game to beat Cambridge for the first time in six years. He returned to Cardiff tipped to make the full Wales team.

The first cap soon came, on Wales's bruising 1978 tour of Australia. Davies was in the happy position of being partnered in the First Test, not, unfortunately, by his Cardiff team-mate Gareth Edwards (who, like Phil Bennett, had declined to tour), but by his other Cardiff team-mate Brynmor Williams, and then in the Second Test by his *other* Cardiff team-mate Terry Holmes. He made his Five Nations debut in the 1979 quadruple Triple Crown winning team, and by the 1980 season he and Holmes were acknowledged as the outstanding half-back partnership in the international game. They were the undisputed first choice half-back pairing for the 1980 British Lions tour of South Africa, but both were injured early on and played together only once, in the opening game.

As a player, Gareth Davies's poise, elusive running, ability to take a pass, good or bad, and capacity to soak up pressure or even turn the tide of a game with soaring touch kicks over the heads of the opposition, marked him out as the natural successor to the great number 10s of the past. For Cardiff he proved both a great tactical player and a consummate matchwinner. In a Wales team still dominated by the great figures of the 1970s, he fitted in seamlessly. The resemblance to Barry John, not only in style of play, but in stance and physique, was impossible to miss. At his best, his play seemed effortless. His 'telepathic' partnership with Terry Holmes, one of the longest standing in the game, was decisive, both for club and country and, despite their very different backgrounds, they and their families became close friends. They came as a pair: when in 1982 they were approached to go to South Africa to play for Natal, they discussed it together and turned it down together.

As a non-goal-kicking outside-half, Davies scored forty points for Wales, including nine dropped goals. He always regretted never having scored a try for his country, although he secured victory for a combined England–Wales XV against a Scotland–Ireland XV with a spectacular last-minute touchdown. Possibly his greatest game for Wales was the bitter confrontation against England at Twickenham in 1980. After Paul Ringer's controversial dismissal in the opening quarter, Davies's relentless tactical kicking kept Wales's fourteen men in contention until almost to the final whistle – only to be cruelly thwarted by a late penalty.

However, Wales was an ageing team, losing the habit of winning against a new generation of opponents. Holmes and Davies were criticized for insufficiently expansive play. Davies himself was a self-confessed reluctant tackler ('I just don't *like* tackling'). While Barry John's fragile grace and Phil Bennett's sparkiness had inspired both admiration and affection, Davies seemed just too casual, too aloof, to attract similar depths of loyalty. In 1981, after Wales lost heavily to Scotland in Murrayfield, Davies was dropped along with almost the entire back line. Reinstated in 1982, he found himself squarely in the firing line, as newly appointed Wales captain, as outside-half, and as a player out of form. Wales were convincingly beaten by Ireland at Lansdowne Road, Davies missing a possibly try-saving tackle. The Welsh forwards orchestrated a victory over France at Cardiff, but against England at Twickenham the loss of Holmes with a shoulder injury early in the second half was a decisive blow. Davies was again heavily criticized for both his play and tactics: for opting to face a swirling wind in the first half, for failing too often with his touch-kicking (the first English try started from a missed touch-kick), and for missing a reasonably easy drop-goal attempt. In the last game of the season, against Scotland at Cardiff, the Welsh backs set out to run the ball – with disastrous results. Scotland shattered Wales's fourteen-year undefeated home record in the championship, 18–34, the highest score (then) registered by a visiting international team at Cardiff. Three of Scotland's five tries came from Welsh handling errors – the first by Davies himself when, on the attack and with two men (and the whole of the National Stadium) calling for the ball outside him, he chose to chip ahead into the Scottish 22 straight into the arms of Scotland wing Roger Baird. One error of judgement but, to many watching, this disastrous move marked the moment Welsh rugby's glory days finally came to an end. Seven players were dropped after this game, but it was Gareth Davies who bore the brunt of the blame.

At one point in the next two years Davies was apparently fifth choice for the national team, behind Malcolm Dacey, Bleddyn Bowen, Geraint John and Paul Turner. He responded by playing the best rugby of his career for Cardiff. Partnered week in week out by Terry Holmes, supported by John Scott, Cardiff's formidable English number 8, and surrounded by the best players Cardiff could attract, he scored a club record 383 points in the 1983–4 season, and only narrowly missed breaking his own record with 365 points in 1984–5. He twice equalled

Barry John's feat of four dropped goals in a match. After his performance for Cardiff against the touring Australians in 1984, Australian coach Alan Jones commented, 'Wales must be a red hot side if they can afford to leave him out'. In the Five Nations Championship in 1985, with Dacey injured, Davies found himself once more beside Holmes in the Welsh team. But it was an unhappy comeback. He clearly did not enjoy his return to a team that was demoralized by poor results, resentful of John Bevan's prescriptive coaching techniques and reeling from the retirements of captains Eddie Butler and Mike Watkins. After marking his return in emphatic style with a dropped goal in the forty-seventh second in Wales's unexpected victory over Scotland at Murray-field, Davies's form collapsed as Wales were outplayed by Ireland at Cardiff and outlasted by France in Paris. Against Ireland, even his tactical confidence seemed to desert him as he stuck too rigidly to Bevan's running game plan. In Paris, he missed several touch-kicks as well as a reasonable dropped-goal chance at a crucial moment of play. With Dacey now fit, and the young tyro Jonathan Davies in eye-catching form at Neath, Davies's place in the postponed England game seemed under threat. What no one expected was the selectors' decision to announce the team nine days before the match – and two days before Dacey and Gareth Davies faced each other in a club fixture – with A. N. Other written in at number 10. No one had bothered to tell Davies he had not been picked: he heard the news from a Cardiff committee member the night before the team was announced.

Davies's response, his dignified announcement of his retirement from international rugby and his decisive outplaying of Dacey the following Saturday, brought him more sympathy from the Welsh public than he had received throughout his international career. Jonathan Davies's sparkling debut in Wales's unexpected victory over England turned spectators' attentions to the future rather than the past. But the manner of his departure seemed to exemplify the problems at the heart of Welsh rugby, notably the managerial incompetence ('the selectors wouldn't last very long in business'), and the thankless status of its most loyal players. Although as Wales captain Terry Holmes advised him to stay, as his friend he confessed he would have done the same thing. Gareth Davies retired from club rugby at the end of that season, with a still undefeated club record of 2,753 points in 326 games.

In his autobiography, Gareth Davies outlined a future beyond rugby that centred around family, golf, and his job at the National and Provincial Building Society. In fact, he quickly moved on to a successful stint as assistant director for Wales at the CBI, and in 1989 was appointed BBC Wales head of sport. The appointment of a former rugby player was hardly a precedent (he succeeded Cliff Morgan and Onllwyn Brace in the post), but eyebrows were raised at the appointment of someone whose experience of broadcasting extended little further than pre- and post-match analyses and appearances on *A Question of Sport*.

In fact, Gareth Davies's skills were well matched to the times and the challenges facing the BBC in the early 1990s: the introduction of management and business disciplines under the new director-general John Birt, and the increasing competition among television companies for the rights to sports coverage. His managerial background, business skills and strategic sense stood him in good stead. During his tenure, the BBC Wales sports department (long pilloried among other sports bodies as the BBC Wales rugby department) expanded its coverage both in broadcast hours and sports covered. Moreover, he was instrumental in signing exclusive television contracts with the Football Association of Wales (FAW), Glamorgan County Cricket Club, and the Cardiff Devils ice hockey team, ensuring that television sports coverage in Wales – as well as radio coverage in two languages – was among the most diverse in the country. Most significantly, Davies negotiated a £1.3 million contract with the WRU to broadcast live club matches for the first time. Extraordinary as it may now seem, this was against stiff opposition from the leading Welsh clubs themselves, who feared the 'overexposure' that live television coverage might bring. Davies was clearly held in high regard by the BBC management (newspaper reports tipped him for 'higher things' in Cardiff or London), and his job could have been a sinecure. Instead, after five years in the post, and just after successfully orchestrating – against a concerted challenge from BSkyB – a three-year contract to secure the Five Nations coverage for the BBC, he suddenly announced his move to another institution struggling with change, Cardiff RFC.

In the early 1990s, English clubs, sponsored by millionaires with deep pockets and an eye to the opportunities that the expected deregulation of rugby would bring, began a scramble to purchase all-star teams, with the promise of trust funds in anticipation of the move to full professionalism. Cardiff was one of the first Welsh clubs to retaliate in kind. In early 1994 Cardiff's own millionaire backer, Peter Thomas, a longstanding enthusiast and former player at the club, led a search for a chief executive of Cardiff Athletic Club, Cardiff RFC's parent body. Although candidates such as Gerald Davies, Gareth Edwards and Welsh coach Alan Davies were mentioned, Gareth Davies was from the earliest stage Thomas's choice. It was a job unprecedented in Welsh rugby, with a salary to match: advertised at £50,000, it was £5,000 more than the secretary of the WRU himself earned. Davies, like everyone else, knew that rugby union was changing and looked forward to helping steer that change. No one anticipated it would change quite so fast.

During his first two years in the post, Davies was chiefly engaged in turning round the affairs of the biggest and administratively the most complex rugby club in Wales in the new era of spiralling financial commitments. His first public pronouncements sought to bring some discipline and sanity to proceedings, as he lambasted players who, he claimed, were 'holding Welsh clubs to ransom' with their demands for 'cars, cash and jobs'. He deplored the IRB's reluctance to police the anarchy into which semi-professionalism was descending, and the WRU's reluctance to plan for the long-term future of the Welsh game. In October 1994, marked out as a 'progressive' element in the Welsh game, he predicted a 'painful revolution', and warned that there was not enough money in the game to ensure the survival of all of Wales's clubs.

During the 1994–5 season, unscrupulous recruiting, disaffection with the points-at-all-costs mentality engendered by the Heineken League, and higher gate prices to cover unprecedented player expenses, saw Welsh top class rugby in chaos and fans abandon the grounds. The IRB's abandonment of the principle of amateurism in August 1995 opened the floodgates. In September Davies prophetically announced: 'What we have to realize in Wales is that we are in a different world now. We cannot survive on past attitudes and past traditions.' He moved quickly to secure Cardiff's position as the most powerful professional force in Welsh rugby by brokering the purchase of Jonathan Davies from Warrington, a coup that made front-page headlines across the rugby-playing world. He was also instrumental in the formation of First

Division Rugby Limited, a negotiating body for the leading Welsh clubs. In December, Terry Holmes returned to his old club as coaching director, and Cardiff became the first Welsh club to put its entire squad under contract and demand transfer fees from English raiders. Recognizing that the new game respected no frontiers, by January 1996 he and his counterpart at Leicester RFC, Peter Wheeler, were leading discussions with the Scottish clubs about the future of the club game in the British Isles. On 1 February 1996, in a move supported by 80 per cent of Cardiff members, the Cardiff rugby club separated itself from the athletic club as a private limited company; by May, Cardiff Rugby Football Club Limited had raised £3 million in a share issue to members. 'The days of leading clubs being run by amateur committees have gone', Davies announced. The progressive had become the revolutionary.

Of the succession of disputes between Cardiff and the WRU from 1996 that culminated in the withdrawal of Cardiff and Swansea for the entire 1998–9 season, one day someone may have the time and patience to write a full account. The search for a formula that might protect the international game as the prime focus of rugby union, while allowing individual clubs to pursue their own interests, proved all but insurmountable, as clubs demanded full autonomy in order to finance their spiralling wage bills, and the English and Welsh unions demanded loyalty contracts from both clubs and players. The clubs wanted to be Manchester United or Real Madrid, carving fame, fortune and dividends out of the European game; the WRU feared becoming a new FAW, relying on the goodwill of English clubs to release players for begrudged international duty. Most outsiders simply looked on aghast as the tightest-knit union of clubs in the rugby game went about tearing itself to pieces. Gareth Davies, Cardiff's strategist and public face, was at the forefront of it all.

The stumbling block was, of course, control and the financial rewards that would come with it. Cardiff's impressive run in the first European Cup in 1995–6 was predicted to net the club up to £250,000: in fact, crowds were far below expectations and the WRU proved reluctant to release television and sponsorship money. The revenue from televising club competitions became the chief focus of contention between the clubs – led by Cardiff/Davies – and the WRU, and led to

Davies backing BSkyB's bid for television rights for club rugby at the same time that the WRU was fighting a rearguard action to defeat Sky's bid for the Five Nations. By summer 1996, less than a year after the game went professional, the Cardiff wage bill was an estimated £750,000 for the following season and rugby union itself appeared threatened by bankruptcy. A transfer frenzy over the summer saw almost eighty players sign for Wales's twelve leading clubs, including four current Wales internationals to Cardiff. As the first year of full professionalism drew to a close, the *Western Mail* described rugby as 'weaker, more confused and more divided than at any time since the dispute over expenses spawned rugby league 103 years ago'. The 'undignified scramble' for money had 'set club against club, club against country and country against country'.

The 1996–7 season began with the fixture list in confusion, club finances in chaos, and the WRU threatening to expel the twelve leading clubs for pursuing independent negotiations for an Anglo-Welsh league. As ITV withdrew a £15 million coverage deal from the Heineken European Cup, Cardiff contemplated a season deficit of £500,000. With clubs unable to budget for the following season, Davies predicted that the Welsh game could realistically support no more than four fully professional clubs. Cardiff led the way in rejecting WRU moves to secure administrative control of the game, notably the demands, first, that clubs sign ten-year loyalty agreements in return for places in the European competition the following season and, second, that the WRU control all television and sponsorship negotiations during this time. Cardiff refused to sign more than a four-year agreement that would take them to the end of the existing television contract and leave them free agents thereafter, and went to the High Court for adjudication. Meanwhile, other, less single-minded, Welsh clubs were in financial meltdown. In 1997 Llanelli was forced to sell Stradey Park to the WRU to cover its debts. In July 1998 Neath, who had pipped Cardiff to the Championship just two years previously, went bankrupt with debts of over £600,000. Cardiff itself, now with twenty-four internationals on the playing staff, contemplated losses of over £1 million for the 1997–8 season. Courting the hostility of the other Premiership clubs, Davies for the first time publicly broached (in the match programme for the Cardiff–Llanelli fixture) the idea that Cardiff might look outside Wales and join the English league.

In the 1998–9 season Cardiff, joined by Swansea, carried out their threat to withdraw from the WRU, and instead ran a fixture list of 'friendlies' against English opponents. The first matches attracted the highest crowds for club rugby matches in the whole of Wales, and both Cardiff and Swansea won convincingly against the leading English clubs. However, as the season progressed and the official commitments of the England clubs took their toll, the quality of the opposition teams fell and crowd attendances declined (though neither as much as some commentators maintained). In November 1998 Davies's pivotal role in the new rugby order was confirmed by his election to the five-man management board of English First Division Rugby. The WRU's attempts to punish the rebels backfired: both Cardiff and Swansea refused to pay £150,000 fines. Further developments took on an Alice in Wonderland quality. The IRB considered fining the WRU for 'allowing' Cardiff and Swansea to defy them, but instead fined the RFU for 'failing to stop' English clubs playing the Welsh rebels. Rumours that Cardiff might buy up Bedford RFC to gain entry to the Allied Dunbar League were denied by Davies in February 1999. The turning-point may have been the appointment of Graham Henry as Wales coach, and his palpable annoyance at the shambles into which Welsh club rugby had descended. Over the spring and early summer of 1999 an agreement was finally made by which Cardiff and Swansea would be reinstated (to the dismay of some loyalist clubs who saw their hard-won places in Europe disappear). The WRU would finally hand over Cardiff's missing television revenues, and drop their legal action against Swansea to recoup money lent to them (to finance, among other things, the purchase of Scott Gibbs).

It was a victory of sorts for Davies. But traditionalists took some comfort when Cardiff were comprehensively defeated by Llanelli in the semi-final of the 1999 SWALEC Cup. However cash-strapped and demoralized as a club, Llanelli still had the resources, perhaps simply the pride, to beat the expensive rebels. The saddest part of the defeat was the resignation of coach Terry Holmes, the last Cardiff British Lion born and bred in Cardiff, and throughout the season a loyal opponent of his former half-back partner's strategy against the WRU.

Having got some, at least, of what he had held out for, Gareth Davies left Cardiff in June 1999 for the chairmanship of the Sports Council for

Wales. At the time of writing, Cardiff RFC Ltd has readvertised his post as 'operational director', with particular emphasis on business administration; the club has just announced its summer signings, including that of Neil Jenkins. Welsh rugby looks forward to the 1999–2000 season with Cardiff and Swansea back on side. But the long-term future of the European Cup, the British League, even the long-term future of many of the greatest clubs in Wales (though *not* Cardiff) still hangs in the balance.

Gareth Davies was not one of the very greatest Welsh number 10s, but on his day his play rivalled that of any of his predecessors. For Cardiff he showed what an outside-half of natural grace and ability could achieve when supported by an outstanding scrum-half, a rock-like number 8, and a great team around them. For Wales, his talent – even when combined with that of the phenomenal Terry Holmes – was insufficient to vitalize a squad relearning how to lose after the glory days, or to accommodate new training regimes that stifled his ability to dictate play and finally destroyed his confidence as an international player. His natural flair and style were underpinned by tactical and strategic skills which, when applied in the business environment, saw him directing change in some of the most complex organizations in Wales. Eschewing a life of punditry and the after-dinner circuit, as the head of BBC Wales sport he led the way in marketing Welsh rugby as a live television sport for the new media age. As Cardiff chief executive he attempted to take Welsh rugby kicking and screaming out of the amateur era, and ruthlessly demonstrated both the enormous opportunities and the brutal realities of the professional game. What he did at Cardiff may not have cast the game in a pleasant light or made him popular in the Welsh rugby heartlands. But in 1999 only the most innocent or hopeful observer would deny that Gareth Davies's competitive, unsentimental and above all commercial vision of the new Welsh rugby order may yet prove the way of the future.

# ARWEL THOMAS

Huw Richards

'When Arwel Thomas has the ball, a try is always likely. The trouble is you can't be sure at which end.' Perhaps it takes one outside-half to provide the definitive summation of another. Thus Barry John crystallized the mix of exhilaration, apprehension and occasional downright infuriation inspired by Arwel Thomas in his attempts to establish himself definitively in John's former shirt in the national team in the second half of the 1990s.

The mythology of the Welsh number 10 is well established. Max Boyce provided its theme tune, but the product retailed by his fictional factory was there long before – the logical consequence of a style of play to which creativity, the unexpected and an element of deception were essential. This approach, as Gareth Williams has pointed out, responded both to cold logic and to Welsh preferences – dealing practically with problems set by the larger, stronger players fielded by England and Scotland at the same time as appealing to a Welsh sense of the theatrical. The consequence has been one of the cultural paradoxes in which rugby abounds. New Zealand, whose self-image is that of an individualist, frontier society traditionally plays rugby whose collectivism might have been condemned as excessive by Stalin. The England team of the everyman-for-himself-and-sod-the-hindmost Thatcher years practised Stanley Baldwin's creed of 'Safety First'. Collectivist Wales has always prized individual genius, and above all the improvisational mid-field playmaker. It is not absolutely necessary that this genius should be an outside-half. Gwyn Nicholls and Bleddyn Williams did the job formidably well from centre, as might Albert Jenkins if the selectors of the 1920s had not been afflicted with terminal confusion. But since the 1950s and the era of Cliff Morgan, the focus has been on the outside-half. He is not necessarily the best player. The scrum-half succession represented by Gareth Edwards, Terry Holmes, Robert Jones and Robert Howley is unmatched for consistent quality by any position in any national team in the world, save perhaps New Zealand open-side flankers. But mythical status has passed by the number-9 shirt, although not all of its individual wearers. Glamour and charisma are the designated lot of the other half.

James Thurber once wrote that most middle-aged Americans fell asleep to images of themselves striking out the New York Yankees. Many of their Welsh counterparts spend their dreaming hours side-stepping the last All Black tackler – the New Zealanders are still the opposition of legend, whatever the momentary pleasures of beating England – in a red number-10 shirt to win the World Cup. To be the embodiment of national myth and childhood dreams imposes an immense weight on mere flesh and blood. Theodore White, in one of the most vivid passages of *The Making of the President: 1960*, talks of the transformation accomplished at the moment when a president is elected – when he ceases to be a mere politician and becomes half-man, half-embodiment of the constitution. While there is no guaranteed four-year term of office, a Wales outside-half undergoes something of the same change.

As Arwel Thomas himself has acknowledged, it means that both the rewards of success and the penalties of failure are disproportionate: 'When I do have a bad game, everything is my fault. When I have a good game it's all down to me. Of course, rugby is not like that but that's just part and parcel of the position I play and the way people view the No 10 jersey in Wales', he told *Rugby World* in 1998. Those pressures were redoubled by the national team's struggles in the 1980s and 1990s, particularly after Jonathan Davies had tired of the short-sightedness and backbiting of the Welsh scene and moved to rugby league. Jonathan was undoubtedly the greatest of the players who went to league in this period and his loss a devastating symbolic blow, although whether it was actually more damaging in playing terms than the departure of props Stuart Evans and David Young is questionable. But what it un-doubtedly did was to fuel the desire in Wales for a prolongation of the outside-half tradition, an Arthurian figure who could lead us back to greatness. The misfortune of the men who actually had to fill the position was that they were measured against the Arthurian ideal, and the greatest feats of Messrs Morgan, Watkins, John, Bennett and Davies, in their years of maturity, behind half-decent packs. For a nation with a rich history, we have a poor collective memory. All of the acknowledged greats had their contemporary critics, and most shared the experience of being rejected by the selectors – Bennett on one extraordinary occasion, also immortalized by Max Boyce, relegated to third place in the national pecking order.

We are also prone, particularly in the bad times, to what Americans term the quarter-back controversy, where the battle for the key position in the team takes on wholly disproportionate importance. Such debate is often essentially philosophical, a matter of how one wants to play the game, with the claims of control and reliability pitched against those of imagination and flair. Hence the debate between proponents of Glyn Davies and Billy Cleaver in the post-war years, or those of John Bevan and Phil Bennett during Bennett's brief exile from the team. It has parallels elsewhere – many New Zealanders would rather have seen Frano Botica than Grant Fox at number 10 for the All Blacks in the late 1980s, a sizeable English minority was not reconciled to the consistent preference for Rob Andrew over Stuart Barnes, while Scotland has never quite seemed sure whether the exotic talents of Gregor Townsend belong at outside-half or centre.

To write about Arwel Thomas is also to write, by implication at least, about Neil Jenkins. While Byron Hayward briefly threatened to complicate the issue (it must be admitted that as an ex-boxer he would probably have landed a better punch on the persistently irritating Philippe Carbonneau than Arwel accomplished in one of the more comic moments of his career at Parc des Princes in 1997), and Jonathan Davies provided a brief coda to his magnificent career when Arwel was injured before the 1997 England match, the battle for the number-10 shirt has been a straight fight between Jenkins and Thomas since Arwel emerged as a serious contender in the mid-1990s. Jenkins exudes physical solidity. He is robust, deliberate and methodical in movement, a formidable barrier in defence but has on occasions looked slow in attack. Thomas epitomizes mercuriality – tiny, darting and instinctive, with a sense of the dangerous and unstable. Each stands for certain of the essential values of top-class sport. Jenkins is thoughtfully pragmatic and committed above all to winning. Thomas is no less determined to come out on top, but he is much more self-consciously an entertainer who aims to please both himself and the spectator with his repertoire of tricks and deceptions.

Proponents of the one have been far too ready to slag off the other. As Gerald Davies, who has treated both sympathetically, points out elsewhere in this book: 'We are far too prone to concentrate on the negatives, to emphasize what players can't do, rather than what they can.' The east–west dimension has added an edge. To miss touch or failing to ignite your three-quarter line may be regrettable, but they do not make you deficient as a human being. Neither has deserved the vituperation that has come his way and both have handled the rivalry with greater dignity and sense of proportion than some of their self-appointed champions. While they are very different, they are hardly polar opposites. Both are exceptional goalkickers – the day before Jenkins kicked England to defeat at Wembley with a display of metronomic accuracy, Thomas helped Wales 'A' complete the second-string Grand Slam by taking his total for four games to seventy-seven points. If Thomas is the more exciting attacker, Jenkins left nothing to be desired in this direction with a striking display against France. And if Jenkins is the more convincing defender, Thomas is significantly better than his appearance would suggest, as Will Carling, considerably larger and heavier, found when he was unceremoniously dumped on his backside at Twickenham in 1996. Moreover, they have had the happy habit of inverting personal stereotypes when they meet at club level. A typical example was the draw between Swansea and Pontypridd at St Helens just before the end of 1997. Thomas kicked goals from every-where, while Jenkins launched his rather less starry back division with greater conviction and imagination.

The choice between them has reflected the emphasis and philosophy of the coach concerned. Graham Henry's preference for Neil Jenkins has been rewarded with by far the most accomplished and confident performances of his Wales career, a happy culmination of possibly the longest apprenticeship in international rugby history. The versatility of full-back Shane Howarth, who before he signed for Newport RFC in the summer of 1999 played outside-half for Sale, and of Llanelli's Steve Jones – big enough to play effectively at centre – made Arwel surplus to requirements first for the Five Nations and now for the World Cup. To question Henry's judgement after his achievements over the last year would be quixotic. But the World Cup will be a poorer spectacle for Arwel's absence.

Being in the right place at the right time is an essential element in sporting success, and Arwel Thomas could hardly have done better in his early years. He was born and brought up in Trebanos, the Swansea Valley village whose population of under 2,000 has produced four international sportsmen in the last fifteen years, with possibly a fifth on the point of joining them. Bleddyn Bowen and Robert Jones were complemented in the mid-1980s by Glamorgan fast bowler Greg Thomas, while Rhodri Jones – Robert's younger brother and Arwel's half-back partner – forced his way into the Wales squad for the trip to Argentina.

If Trebanos is an extraordinary 'hot spot' for talent, then so is the club he joined after winning his Wales Youth caps, Neath. While the Welsh All Blacks have not been capable of regaining their dominance of the early 1990s, their achievements since the arrival of open professionalism demolished what stability there was on the Welsh club scene are arguably still more remarkable. Twice they have seen talented squads decimated by the depredations of richer clubs, their future as a force at top level apparently jeopardized. They even went into receivership in 1998. On both occasions they displayed an extraordinary ability to reform and regenerate, locating fresh talent and rapidly regaining their place among Wales's top three or four clubs. Their ability to locate talent is unmatched. As with Bridgend, who lose players to Cardiff as fast as the M4 can transport them, the problem is hanging on to them. While their historic strength has been in the pack, the late 1980s and early 1990s found them producing an impressive succession of gifted attacking half-backs. Jonathan Davies, first and best of the line, argued in 1996 that this was entirely uncoincidental: 'Without fast rucking you don't allow an outside-half enough time to be properly creative. One of the few teams who have rucked fast and efficiently over the years has been Neath. It is no accident that I came through with Neath. They were and are still an outside-half's dream team. Every creative stand-off in recent times in Wales has been produced by Neath. Arwel Thomas, Adrian Davies, Matthew McCarthy . . . no other team has produced halves of that quality.' It was perhaps less helpful that Arwel was rapidly hailed as 'the next Jonathan Davies'. While his size, gamin cockiness, eye for a half-opening and ability to throw the pass which is angled so as to straighten the line and all but compel the man outside to make a break were unquestionably reminiscent of Jonathan – not to mention a century of diminutive deceivers dating back to the James brothers and Swansea's 'Dancing Dicks' of the first golden age – the player of substance is never a mere retread.

There were calls for his inclusion in the Wales team within months of his becoming a Neath regular in 1994. Those advocates included J. J. Williams, never the most enthusiastic supporter of incumbent Neil Jenkins, who said 'Arwel is one of those typical Welsh Valley boys who were born with no 10 on his back. They are cocky and confident in their own natural Welsh flair. Nothing worries them'. It is probably as well that Alan Davies chose not to heed him. 'Cocky and confident' he might be, but Arwel himself told the *Daily Mirror* he did not feel ready for the challenge. And the demoralizing Welsh failure at the 1995 World Cup was certainly one to miss.

Arwel did travel that summer, but not to South Africa. His journey was the rather more modest one across the Severn Bridge to Bristol, anticipating the exodus to England seen a year later when full professionalism set in and the top English clubs started brandishing chequebooks. By the time that happened Arwel was on the way back, this time beating the trend that became clear in 1998–9 as the English clubs' money started to run out by a good couple of seasons. He always was ahead of the game. It was a traumatic year. Bristol, a great club in decline, recruited a 20-year-old with limited senior experience to change a forward-dominated pattern of play – the previous season their leading scorer had been flanker Derek Eves. Living away from home for the first time he had to cope with the consequences of sudden fame when he won his first Welsh caps. He subsequently told Chris Hewett of *The Independent*, his most consistent admirer in the English press: 'I realize I wasn't as prepared as I thought I was, either on or off the pitch. Suddenly there were a million interviews to do. Suddenly, I had television cameras following me to college. When you're not used to that level of exposure, it hits you hard. You end up not knowing which way to turn.' Unsurprisingly, his reported statements that year show that the adjective 'mercurial' applies just as well off the pitch. In January he explained: 'I left Wales partly to get out of the public eye and I think playing rugby in England has given me a lot more confidence', while a couple of months later clubs hoping to take him back to Wales were told: 'The English game is a higher standard because you are playing top-class rugby.' Two months later he signed for Swansea, and by early 1997 he was telling Terry Godwin of *The People* of the importance of exposure in the Welsh media to his chances of playing for Wales. Bristol, understandably, were disappointed. So were fans who would like to have seen Arwel paired with Robert Jones, who made the opposite journey during the same close season. Not only for the curiosity of an all-Trebanos half-back pairing, but for the effect Jones's supreme service, tactical judgment and overall guidance might have had on his game at a crucial period in his development.

While his first cap, and sixteen points, came in a 31–26 victory over Italy, the moment which has fixed itself in the folk-memory as marking his international arrival came eight minutes into the England match at Twickenham. Wales were awarded a penalty twenty-five yards out. Picking himself up after the late tackle which had led to the penalty Arwel realized that England, firmly pre-programmed to expect the obvious – in this case taking an easy three points – were retreating behind their line without paying much attention to what he was doing. Taking a quick tap penalty he launched an attack, and Hemi Taylor forced his way over on the left. In truth the tap penalty was not well executed. He came close to knocking on, and the quick hands of Gwyn Jones and Leigh Davies were needed to give Taylor his chance. But it took imagination and audacity to forgo three certain points and gamble on a possible seven only a few minutes into your Five Nations debut away to the tournament's toughest team. It established a style, a mental outlook and a persona.

Its appeal to a national coach like Kevin Bowring, who had set himself to reassert 'an innate style, something based on intuition and imagination', was obvious. Bowring's term as coach ended unhappily in 1998, just as that of Alan Davies had fallen just short of the World Cup three years earlier. But both served Wales well. Where Davies restored some basic coherence to the Welsh game after the shambles of the 1991 Australia tour, albeit at the price of playing rather uninspired rugby, Bowring gave it back its sense of itself. It doubtless helped Arwel, who would look slight in most company, never mind that of international rugby players, that Bowring's own personal experience predisposed him against the proposition that size is all. A highly accomplished number-8 forward for London Welsh, the commonest explanation for his missing the representative honours that his all-round skills merited was that he was not big enough. Arwel remained the first-choice outside-half for most of Bowring's remaining two years in office. It is hard to resist the conclusion that his exclusion after the Twickenham disaster of 1998 also marked the point at which Bowring, who resigned three games later, also began to lose confidence in himself and his philosophy of the game. Ironically, he was back on the field only a few minutes into the following match against Scotland when Jenkins was injured, and contributed to a somewhat shaky 19–13 victory. But Jenkins was back, and Arwel out of the squad, for the following match against Ireland.

Arwel's spell as Bowring's first choice incorporated a spectacular high point as he first contributed to a three-try burst against Scotland, breaking in mid-field, handing off Gary Armstrong and outpacing Scott Hastings on an exuberant high-stepping run to the line that momentarily looked as though it would carry him into dead-ball territory. It was followed by a dazzling, though losing, Welsh display in Paris in which Thomas impressed both Serge Blanco, who wrote: 'He has a superb vision of the game, and with his obvious talent he is certain to become a major trump card for Wales in the years to come. He is a very, very fine player', and Pierre Villepreux.

There were also desperate lows, notably a miserable afternoon at Lansdowne Road in his first season where he was flattened and seriously shaken in the first five minutes. He should probably have come off, but stayed on to miss touch four times, presenting Ireland with two tries. Two years later he was submerged in the massacre at Twickenham. He had been in doubt with a knee injury and even during Wales's fluent first twenty minutes he looked out of sorts, tentatively flicking passes out and showing little sign of his habitual ability to straighten and ignite the three-quarter line. There were times when he certainly was just not good enough. As he admitted to *Rugby World* in August 1998: 'When I make mistakes, it's no good me simply saying "well that's just because I'm unpredictable". That's just an excuse really . . . If I knew the answer to becoming consistent, then I would do it. But I don't.'

So will he ever get back? He is after all still only twenty-four (he was born in November 1974). Yet Glyn Davies played his last international at twenty-three, Terry Price at twenty-one. There are, however, more reasons than the proliferation of internationals, offering far more chances of a recall than were ever offered to Davies in the 1950s or would have been available to Price had he not gone North, for believing that he might. At Swansea his creativity has been an essential component in the outstanding Welsh club side of the last couple of seasons. In a team long on quality and personality, playing alongside both club stalwarts like Simon Davies and Paul Arnold and world-class performers like Scott Gibbs and Colin Charvis, he is the outstanding popular hero – the name which induces either cheers or groans of disappointment according to whether or not it is announced at number 10 in the All Whites line up. After a tricky start – he was reported as complaining that he was being 'treated like just another player' after he was taken off in a match against Llanelli – he has clearly earned the confidence of coach John Plumtree. As New Zealand birth and South African playing experience imply, Plumtree is hardly a heedless romantic about ways of playing rugby. Arwel's appointment as club captain during Scott Gibbs's absence in the first few weeks of the 1999–2000 season is a considerable vote of confidence, entrusting him with leadership during a crucial period when the All Whites return to a strengthened Welsh League competition, and must do well to ensure inclusion in any British league. It brings with it the hope that responsibility will bring fresh maturity to his game, although without dimming that innate sense of adventure. Robert Jones's return to Swansea can only help. And as well as playing brilliantly at club level, Arwel has also been willing to knuckle down and perform for the A team.

Youthful brilliance has a nasty habit of burning itself out. The trick for any shooting star is learning from occasionally bitter experience without losing the risk-taking exuberance of the early days. Maturity will be of immense benefit if it eliminates the lapses in concentration which have disfigured some international performances, but will be little help if it merely brings predictability. He will not be short of advisers. No Welsh outside-half ever is. One piece of advice he will certainly receive is to get into the weights room and bulk up as did Jonathan Davies and Scott Gibbs to cope with the rigours of professional rugby league or Neil Back – the Leicester flanker whose appearance has been transformed from boy-band member to night-club bouncer – in order to convince the England selectors that he was not too lightweight for the international game. But as Phil Bennett has pointed out: 'If Arwel tried to bulk up like Scott, he could well lose some of his speed, his elusiveness and his nimble footwork – the very skills that make him so special.' Yet, a player whose physical stature is such that one press box observer was heard to joke 'I didn't know Arwel was back in the squad' as Robert Howley led a 6-year old mascot on to the pitch at Wembley, only to receive the reply 'Arwel's grown a bit then has he?', is inevitably at some disadvantage. Graham Henry pointed to the need to tackle seventeen-stone Springbok flankers and suggested 'he might try talking them down'. Japan's struggles at international level, in spite of the technical brilliance and ingenuity of their rugby, are a reminder that brawn is an indispensable element.

But Arwel is also a reminder of the possibilities of rugby. This is not just a matter of appealing to some mythic tradition. He shows that rugby is not just a game for the large and musclebound. He is also a standing reproach to the all-too-prevalent assumption that the safest option is always the percentage one – a lesson that England failed to learn during a period when they had the most gifted squad in their history, with fatal consequences for their chances of winning the World Cup. The argument not infrequently heard is that 'he'd be OK if we had an All Black pack. Without it he's just too much of a risk'. Aside from the obvious point that if Wales had an All Black pack it would not matter too much who played outside-half, this is to ignore the counter-argument that a team which has potentially brilliant backs and fragile forwards should pick the outside-half likeliest to create try-scoring opportunities from limited ball. Under these circumstances the safe option becomes mere damage limitation.

Those who enjoy their sport concussive, pre-planned and athletic are very welcome to American Football, rugby's mutant younger brother. Arwel appeals to those who enjoy the intuitive, the instinctive and the unexpected, given a further Chaplinesque appeal by the sight of a small man getting the better of large ones. As Gerald Davies has written: 'For a Welshman, the game is only real if tinged with elements of dazzling fantasy.' The continuing truth of this was shown by the enormously warm reception given to Arwel by the Millennium crowd when he appeared as a replacement close to the end of the pre World Cup match between a Wales XV and the USA. Arwel the dazzling fantasist was on show in Swansea's SWALEC Cup semi-final against Cross Keys in 1999. Cross Keys may only have been Second Division opposition, but there are few players who, against any opponent, could have matched the moment when Arwel broke, twitched his hips and resumed his run on the same line – his intending tackler having meanwhile disappeared, fooled by that minimal feint. Turning in the press box to locate the origin of the appreciative chuckle behind me, I discovered Gerald Davies, enjoying a fellow-spirit and a moment he might have contrived himself twenty odd years ago.

Arwel will probably never be as reliable as safer players – as Somerset Maugham noted, only mediocrity is always at its best. On his bad days he is uncomfortably reminiscent of Rossini's wonderful summation of Wagner: 'Glorious moments, and dreadful half-hours.' But on the good days he reaches heights – and, more pertinently, angles – undreamt of by most performers and reminds us of why we bother to watch the game at all. Many writers have compared him to Dickens's Artful Dodger. A still more valid literary comparison might be with Arnold Bennett's Denry Machin: 'With what great cause has he been associated? Why, with the great cause of cheering us all up!'

*Thanks are due to Neil Levis (*Times Education Supplement *and* Woodford RFC) *for his assistance with the research for this article.*

# COLIN CHARVIS

Peter Stead

'Charvis to miss final', 'Charvis definitely out' were the typical headlines which both discouraged Swansea supporters and made it difficult for commentators and pundits to predict the outcome of the 1999 SWALEC Cup Final between Swansea and Llanelli. These two old clubs had been playing each other regularly since 1876 but almost everything about this 1999 final was unusual, and it was little wonder that neither expert nor supporter knew quite what to expect. Not only was the game to be played at Cardiff's Ninian Park, a venue new to both clubs and most of their supporters, but it would also be the first competitive game between the clubs for fourteen months. At the close of the 1997–8 season Swansea had 'rebelled' and opted for a season of friendlies against Cardiff and leading English clubs; Llanelli meanwhile was left with feelings of anger and betrayal and with a domestic agenda that looked distinctly unappetizing without fixtures against the two biggest Welsh clubs. The Scarlets had responded positively by winning both domestic competitions and they were going to Ninian Park in search of a treble. They were on a roll and, of course, they had come to think of the cup as their own for they had already won it ten times. Swansea supporters were certainly quite prepared to accept underdog status. Not for a moment did they doubt the quality of their team, but things were not looking good for Ninian Park. Scott Gibbs was doubtful, Colin was 'definitely out', of late the All Whites had not been playing truly competitive games and above all they feared the passion of the Scarlets. Until the start of the 1990s honours had been almost exactly even, but in the last decade Llanelli had usually had the edge in these fixtures, not least in cup games. It was in every respect an intriguing prospect, but one for which the All Whites were already lining up their excuses.

It was a magnificent day at Ninian Park. The old stadium which could, at one time, hold 60,000 was now packed to capacity with a mere 14,500, but at least dressed in shorts and T-shirts they could bask in warm sunshine. The match-day programme confirmed what had become apparent in the last few days: Gibbs would be playing and captaining Swansea and their open-side flanker would be Dean

Thomas. Of Colin Charvis there was no mention: he was not even listed among the replacements. It was time to reflect on his cheek-bone injury, incurred when Tim Rodber had crashed into him at Wembley five weeks earlier, an incident, of course, that had made possible the dramatic last-gasp Welsh victory. Today it would be up to 'Deano', a great favourite of the St Helens faithful: he would let nobody down but the lack of a specialist flanker on the bench was a matter of concern. Suddenly it was time for the team changes. There was only one: 'at number 7 for Swansea, Colin Charvis'. Dean Thomas became a replacement. A buzz commenced that did not subside until half-time. What on earth had happened? Was it a miracle cure or had Swansea, in the later words of Robert Lloyd, 'pulled a flanker'? The Scarlets were clearly unsettled, not least their makeshift full-back Byron Hayward. After early skirmishes it was clear that the Swansea pack had come to do the business, and their brief was to get the ball as soon as possible to a mid-field that would punch holes in Llanelli's defence. Every team dreams of a big match in which the game plan operates like clockwork, in which the drawing-board plans are acted out to perfection. The scrum was solid, Andy Moore was supreme in the line-out, possession assured. Mark Taylor and Arwel Thomas went through gaps and Colin Charvis was there to score two tries and Tyrone Maulin a third. In this devastating first-half burst the game was won and one sensed that there could be no recovery. It was a cramped, restricted Ninian Park pitch with little room on the flanks: what was needed was tight control and sudden injection of pace in the middle and that is what the Whites had provided. The sheer pace of things had done for Llanelli and, in that respect, the Charvis ruse did seem very much part of the plan. Swansea appeared to be a yard faster, not least because the white boots of Colin Charvis were having roughly the same effect on the Swansea team as that of the rabbit at a greyhound race. It was a poor second half, but when Deano came on as a replacement and scored an injury-time try it rounded off a perfect day for Swansea fans. 'The Turks', the traditional enemy, the infidels from the west, had been decisively beaten 37 10. Of course, it had all started with that Charvis ploy.

Ninian Park was of immense significance for the All Whites. It was a justification of their rebellion and a demonstration of the excellence that had throughout been their sole ambition. It was a reminder too of their huge significance in Welsh rugby as a whole, for five members of the team that won the SWALEC Cup had also played at Wembley in the victory against England. Indeed, after that game those five players had been invited to the Guildhall to be personally congratulated by the lord mayor of Swansea, an unprecedented occasion which fully indicated the city's sudden awareness that there were top-class sportsmen living and playing locally. It was in many ways a good end to the season for Colin Charvis who, as he set off for Argentina, could take pride in the increasingly favourable press notices that his appearances had been prompting. Undoubtedly, it was his two tries against Argentina at Llanelli in November 1998 which represented a turning-point in the general perception of him as an international player. Confirmation had come in Paris in March when he had twisted and dived to score the first Welsh try and generally starred in the great Welsh victory. For the *Evening Post*'s Mark Orders he had been 'outstanding' in that game: he had 'combined speed with industry, superb handling skills with impressive power' and turned in 'a barnstorming all-round perform-ance'. In the England game Neil Jenkins, Chris Wyatt, Scott Gibbs and Shane Howarth were clearly the heroes but Charvis came more and more into the game and had a very good final quarter. It was not at all inappropriate that it was his late desperate charge that led to the game's denouement. By the time of his unexpected but superb Ninian Park performance he was being described as 'a world-class player'. It was the time of year for picking imaginary Lions sides, and the general feeling was that if he did not make the Test side he would certainly be in the squad.

Meanwhile he was definitely in one team, for *Wales on Sunday* journalist Suzie Brewer had selected him for her 'Dream Team'. These things are not unimportant; whilst the priority for any Welsh team is to win matches it also helps considerably if they can capture the imagina-tion of a Welsh public crying out for sporting heroes and cultural icons. Chris Wyatt was generally adjudged to be the Welsh player of the Championship in 1999 and he was also identified as 'the number one heart-throb', but Colin Charvis was not far behind. For Brewer he was 'poetry in motion'. This judgement was a reflection of the extent to which Welsh television now promotes rugby as family entertainment, and it is also proof of the power of the visual image generally. There is little doubt that Colin Charvis is photogenic. Look at any illustrated match report of recent Wales and Swansea games and there is sure to be a dramatic shot of Charvis on the burst or diving for the line. Perhaps it is his colour that attracts the camera but more likely it is the look of intensity on the round face, something highlighted by the smallness of the head, the shortness of the neck and the steep slope of the shoulders. We are always shown a player determinedly going about his business. The most memorable shot is that of his try in Paris: as he twists through the tackles of two Frenchmen, one of whom is in the process of ripping off his shirt, it is surely a bionic arm that stretches out to ground the Gilbert ball. Inevitably, he is frowning. The camera has not captured many smiles, but there is one charming shot of Ben Evans kissing him at the end of the French game and Colin with eyes wide shut just about looks as if he is enjoying it.

The media coverage of the game in Wales inevitably leads to over-hyping and to an exaggerated emphasis on personalities, yet Colin Charvis remains utterly realistic about the state of rugby in Wales and his own place in it. The great Wembley win over England gave him his twentieth cap (including three as a replacement), but the statistic that pleased him most was that this was his tenth victory: just a couple of months earlier ten losses had been offset by only seven victories. He had hated that, just as he had been greatly embarrassed by the scale of some of the defeats. The experience of conceding fifty-one points to France and ninety-six to South Africa invited a degree of modesty and encouraged a realistic perspective. He was embarrassed not only on his own behalf but for his country too. 'How could the WRU put out such teams?' he asked as he noted how many of his colleagues failed to respond to the demands made by the coaching staff and consequently fell by the wayside. Above all he appreciates the extent to which things have improved under the new coaching regime. There has been a targeting and subsequent recruitment of key players in order to eliminate the glaring areas of weakness. From Steve Black comes the motivation, and from Graham Henry a clinical analysis of how the opposition can be beaten and a specific detailing of precisely what has to be done in every game. Of course confidence is increasing, but there is a great awareness of how much further there is still to go. Naturally Charvis is conscious of how this applies in particular to back-row play.

For years this had been one of the great strengths of Welsh rugby, but perhaps in no area of the game had the decline in quality compared to other nations been so apparent. In 1999 Welsh fans were greatly encouraged by the contributions of Brett Sinkinson and Colin Charvis, but says Colin 'we are still way behind'. For him, the lessons to be learnt are those taught by the back rows of England and France. There is a degree of arrogance in the English pack but they have a collective policy. They work hard and they achieve vital turnarounds. These turnovers are the key and it is the abrasive French who are the masters of catching the opposition unawares and then going on to score themselves.

Colin Charvis loves to analyse back-row play, all the while struck by the singularity of the position. Indeed, he would be a very effective shop-steward for the back-row union. It is, of course, a somewhat undefined position. Every other player is under pressure to be good and effective at a particular skill: they have to pass, throw, shove or jump, but for the back-row forward the skills required are less specific. It is also very much an 'in-between' position. They are men in the middle, 'neither here nor there', aware of the backs being coached on the one side and the power-house forwards on the other. It is also a job in which natural instincts have to be curtailed as priorities are worked out rationally. Initially, Charvis as one of nature's number 7s judged everything in terms of the number of tackles he made in any particular game. He used to boast about his eighteen tackles: now he is happy with only twelve if he is allowed to fulfil obligations in other respects. Obviously the better the front five are playing, the fewer tackles he will have to make and the more opportunity he will have to get to breakdowns and to link up with his backs. If they are doing badly then the back row is sucked in to help out and their creative attacking game-winning potential is lost. Here in one sentence we have an insight into why it is in recent seasons that Wales has either played only adequately or very badly.

He makes no secret of having always wanted to play at number 7, although he has played at number 8 for Wales and is now usually handed the number-6 shirt. When he first came to prominence in the mid-1990s he was immediately identified as a great sevens player and the success he enjoyed at Dubai, Hong Kong and Tokyo and other tournaments suggests that this is his natural milieu. He is always at his most devastating in open expansive games, but the extent to which he has worked at being an all-round back-row player is very apparent. In the *Planet Rugby* figures for the 1999 Five Nations Championship he was second only to Neil Back as a successful tackler, having made thirty-two and missed four. Increasingly obvious is his determination to get to the breakdown and to win the ball. One's initial image of a player running with ball in hand has given way to one of him bending over to forage. And this perhaps leads on to another aspect of back-row play, for there is always the need for controlled and targeted aggression. Quite consciously and deliberately the need for aggression has to be assessed. The fact is that throughout matches back-row forwards are never able to forget their responsibilities. As the game swirls around them they have to ask whether they are 'earning their keep'. There is a constant need 'to prove themselves', for they are only as good as that last tackle or turn-over. It is a position in which those seeking anonymity can easily find it. Alternatively glory beckons. Charvis talks about his game very much like the professional entertainer he has become. 'For an hour and a half I have to be an extrovert' and so it becomes a matter of 'switching on and then switching off'. Scott Gibbs has referred to him as being 'enigmatic' and that is probably because of his need to switch off occasionally. Players have sometimes looked and seen that their number 6 is asleep in the corner of the dressing-room.

It is a pleasure to listen to Colin Charvis talking about rugby and the lifestyle that it has given him. He talks clearly, intelligently, frankly and patiently with only a hint of an English Midlands accent. All the while he stresses the obligation he feels to fulfil responsibilities towards the supporters of Swansea and Wales. Nevertheless, he is angered by the bandwagon of criticism that follows spectacular defeats. 'We don't choose to lose.' He very much appreciates BBC Wales's coverage of games and particularly enjoyed their 'we are rebels as well' attitude to Swansea's successful cup campaign in 1999. He greatly values Eddie Butler's independence and wonders whether his tendency to say exactly what he feels is related to his 'essentially English background'. In his view, Butler was spot-on in immediately claiming that there was nothing wrong with Rodber's Wembley tackle. What does annoy him, however, is the tendency of the press and programme-writers to create stereotypes. Writers and profilers like to fit players into categories, and at one point Charvis felt it necessary to register a heartfelt protest via the internet: never again did he want to see a player profile that spoke in terms of 'favourite food – pizza, favourite film-star – Demi Moore, last holiday – Tenerife'! Meanwhile nobody shows such interest in his degree in civil engineering or in the fact that when in the OTC he passed his Regular Commission Board and went to university as a Royal Engineer cadet.

As a rugby player Charvis is classically a product of Queen Mary Grammar School, Walsall, where he was a school prefect, captain of the firsts and passed A-level with amongst other things a B in mathematics and an A in general studies. He was born in Sutton Coldfield in 1972, the son of a father who had left Jamaica when he was fourteen and who had gone on to become a technician in the RAF and then an electrician. His mother, who was white and who died when Colin was fifteen, was the daughter of a Cardiff man who had gone to the Midlands to work for Rolls Royce. His mother's early death meant that he was almost solely in touch with his father's side of the family, many of whom had been in the Forces and from whom he picked up both his interest in a military career and the sense of dignity and self-discipline which made him proud of his school uniform, his briefcase and his way of talking properly without needing to swear. Naturally enough, they wanted him to be a cricketer, but soccer was a bigger attraction and his ambition was to play for Aston Villa at Villa Park and Old Trafford. No wonder he was later proud to play at Wembley: that was an ambition fulfilled, although like some other Welsh players he actually hated the place. But he was too big for soccer and, in any case, he had become a grammar school boy and therefore a rugby player.

From school he had gone to Central London Poly to study engineering. At first he had decided 'to be cool' about his rugby background and to understate his claims. In fact, he turned up late with his boots in a bag having missed the early trials as he had been with the army in Germany. 'You lied, didn't you?' said coach Glanmor Richards who quickly saw that he had a real player on his hands. Very soon, 'Have you got any Welsh in you?' was the question directed at the 18-year-old Colin Lloyd Charvis. The positive response led to his playing for London Welsh and later for the Wales Under-21 side against France at Cardiff. Five years after going to London he was playing for Wales. 'It was a Cinderella story', says Charvis, and indeed it was all a little fortuitous. What was crucial was that he loved London Welsh and that clinched the question of his rugby identity. He loved the atmosphere and the superb location with all the surrounding bars and restaurants. He still feels a strong loyalty to the club and would not mind ending his playing days there in the distant future. What is vital is that the London Welsh recovery continues, and he heartily endorses Graham Henry's policy of wanting to make it a leading British club so that any Welsh exiles wanting to play in the London area would naturally gravitate there. While playing for London Welsh he became a regular viewer of *Rugby Special* and, increasingly, he noted that Swansea were the stars of the short Welsh snippets that were shown. He noted how well they played at home, especially when Aled Williams was on song at outside-half. This was his kind of rugby. But meanwhile there were degree exams to be taken, to be followed quite probably by a career in the Royal Engineers.

The Swansea team of the mid-1990s was one capable of achieving a degree of success but very much wanting to do better. Constantly, the All Whites were being reminded of the difference between good players and great players and between what could pass for successful rugby at the local as compared to the international level. Throughout the decade the club was being forced to come to terms with the qualities and standards required at the highest level of club rugby. Under coach Mike Ruddock the All Whites had won the Welsh championship in 1992 and again in 1994. The club obviously liked the idea that it was the best in Wales. However, in October 1994 the All Whites entertained South Africa and having taken a seven-point lead went on to lose 78–7. On that day the South Africans, responding to perfect playing conditions, slipped into the form that would earn virtually the same players the World Cup just eight months later. It took the All Whites a long time to recover from that disaster, as was indicated by their unexpected failure that season to finish in the top four of the Welsh championship. The only consolation was victory over arch-rivals Pontypridd in the WRU Cup Final. Lessons were learnt that season; the squad needed strengthening and above all league games had to be won both home and away. The failure to finish in the top four had cost the club a lucrative fixture against Fiji and might well have resulted in exclusion from the new Heineken European Cup had they not won the Welsh Cup. It had been a very close thing and, in retrospect, we can see that it was in the summer of 1995 that Swansea realized that detailed and ambitious long-term planning was needed in respect of tactics, personnel and finance if the club was to survive at the top. This was the summer that saw centre Mark Taylor and flanker Colin Charvis arrive at St Helens.

Charvis was needed as a back-up player for Swansea's existing talented and beloved back row. The All Whites had always been proud of their open rugby and in particular of the way that dynamic back-row forwards linked up with each other and with the backs. The tradition of Clem Thomas, Mervyn Davies, Trevor Evans, Gareth Roberts and Richard Webster lived on, and it was one which Geoff Atherton and Baden Evans, two former back-row men now prominent in the affairs of the club, were eager to sustain. The men in possession were not only good but they were all in their separate ways great favourites of the St Helens crowd, very much club heroes. This was particularly true of number 8 Stuart Davies whose presence in the side was always taken as a guarantee of total effort and probable victory, and number 6 Alan 'Santa' Reynolds whose tremendous bursts and crunching tackles were precisely what many All Whites fans paid their money to see. At number 7 was the fearless crash-tackling Rob Appleyard, who like Stuart Davies had scored in the Cup Final and was obviously destined to emulate his colleagues by playing for Wales. Could Charvis survive in this company? Was he capable of replacing any of these talismanic figures? There were many who thought not, including the scout who went on the club's behalf to Old Deer Park to make the initial reports on the London Welsh flanker. Mike Ruddock and Baden Evans were forced to check for themselves. Doubts were resolved; clearly here was promise. On arrival at St Helens the newcomer was for some weeks listed under the try-scorers as Chervis, which did not bode well. His arrival proper came in the game against Newport on 14 October 1995. What All Whites supporters remember most vividly from that day was Gareth Rees's unfortunate tackle on Swansea's captain, Tony Clement, a tackle which put him out for the rest of the season. But it was a game that the All Whites went on to win 78–6 and of their eleven tries four were scored by Colin Charvis. By December he was on the front page of the programme, a magnificent action shot by John Harris of Colin in full stride, one hand clutching the ball to his chest, tongue out in concentration, inevitably scowling. He went on that season to score a total of eight league and seven non-league tries to end up third in the club's point-scoring table. Here was a player very much in the Swansea mould, the number-7 shirt was rightly his.

Once again though, it had been a disappointing season for Swansea. There was no silverwear to show and defeats by Munster and Toulouse had indicated the demanding level of European competition. In the summer of 1996 the club had to face the challenge of professionalism, and a much tougher fixture list would bring games against leading British and European clubs. The Whites had responded by signing ten new players including Scott Gibbs and Arwel Thomas. Clearly a new era had opened for the supporters and the players. In his first amateur years Colin Charvis had worked at St Helens as a marketing executive and schools-liaison officer. Now he became a fully fledged professional negotiating his position at the club with manager Baden Evans and with a London agent to secure wider commercial and media deals. He was acutely aware of his status as a prominent sportsman in his own right, but he was also very much a member of a group of players in Swansea whose priority it was to secure the international status of the club. The players were now driven together as never before. They travelled together, the single men often lived together and they all went out together although there were a number of different cliques. There was plenty of time to tease each other about who had the best car, the best-decorated flat, the best girl-friend, the best collection of CDs and the most fearsome dog (Colin's was a German shepherd). They were all experts too on each other's injuries and at times the club seemed cursed to suffer in that respect. It was suggested at one stage that the All Whites could offer their whole squad to a television company as the cast of a long-term *Casualty*-style soap opera. For ten months Colin was plagued with groin and knee injuries: he missed the 1997 Cup Final and had to sit out four internationals before making his way back via the replacement bench. Above all at Swansea there were great friendships, with Andy Moore, with Deano Thomas and others. A commitment to the All Whites meant far more than just playing on match days. For they were now, undoubtedly, a band of brothers.

The coming of professional rugby to Swansea involved a squad of talented players fulfilling fixture requirements of a bewildering variety; the quality of the opposition varied enormously and so did the size of the crowd. The leading Welsh clubs were striving to achieve higher standards and yet supporters were being alienated by one-sided games, ridiculously inflated score lines, unusual kick-off times and excessive coverage of live games on television. At St Helens the fans were never quite sure what to make of victories of 82–18 over Newport, 63–18 over London Irish, 62–16 over Gloucester and 71–10 over Dunvant, especially when later in that 1996–7 season they were to lose 12–42 to Llanelli at St Helens and 26–32 to Cardiff in the Cup Final. One thing that was as true as ever was that the All Whites were usually at their best playing at St Helens. The unique quality of the playing surface certainly suits the Swansea style, and this considerable asset is something often commented on enviously by visiting players. Charvis makes the point that this is one reason why the All Whites have no reason ever to fear a British league, for the high-scoring, one-sided victories that the team would record at home would ensure that they would never be relegated. This was the kind of confidence that carried Swansea through John Plumtree's first season as coach in 1997–8. That season the club won its third Championship title in seven years, winning all its home games and indeed only losing one away game at Llanelli. The All Whites only won two of the six Heineken Cup games, but paradoxically it was the two excellent games against the Wasps both narrowly lost which proved that the players and the supporters needed to have regular access to rugby of a higher quality. The seeds of the rebellion that was to come in the summer of 1998 were planted in those two games. In September 1997 the Wasps had won 31–25 at St Helens after having been behind 18–10 at half-time, largely through a brilliant second-half display inspired by a back row which included Lawrence Dallaglio and Chris Sheasby. This was undoubtedly world-class back-row play and it was an object lesson that was taken to heart by Swansea's back row of the day (Appleyard, Moriarty and Dean Thomas) and by everybody else at the club. This was the level at which the All Whites needed to compete all the time.

In 1999 Colin Charvis found himself playing for two New Zealand coaches, both of whom were faced with the task of proving match by match that their respective teams, Wales and Swansea, could operate at the top level. The players were now under the control of arch-motivators and of experts capable of pinpointing every weakness in the opposing teams. At Swansea there was the additional advantage of having Kevin Hopkins as a brilliant organizer of the backs. With all this support and guidance available the players are all too aware that ultimately it is they who have to deliver. But inevitably things sometimes go wrong and the team underperforms. After all, even the very best players are unable to do it every match and once the troops sense that 'the stars are not up for it' things quickly begin to unravel. With striking frankness Colin Charvis talks about the effect on the rest of the team if the front five are being outplayed, if Scott Gibbs is having a quiet day, or if the outside-half or full-back are kicking badly. At club and international level all these things can happen, the danger is always there. At the national level there is a big reliance on Neil Jenkins, an extraordinary kicker, a great all-round tactician and according to Colin 'an awesome thinker about the game', a back who is unusually interested in such details as where the prop should place his feet. The All Whites meanwhile remain essentially a mood team, exuberant and extravagant when playing champagne rugby at home, but sometimes looking as if they were meeting each other for the first time when playing on alien territory. They admit that they were not really at their best when winning the cup at Ninian Park: it was perhaps a 70 per cent performance.

Yet again the squad needs strengthening, at least at full-back and possibly on the wings as well. Quite naturally it is Colin Charvis's ambition to retain his place in successful national and club sides. He is proud of what he has achieved and grateful to rugby both for its material rewards and for allowing fulfilment in a variety of ways. The ambitious St Mary's pupil is still very much in evidence. A driving ban encouraged him to look for an indoor hobby, and the outcome was a passion for computers and the internet. He feels very strongly that too many Welsh players have responded to professionalism by just content-ing themselves with jobs at the clubhouse rather than developing themselves outside the game as do English players. Certainly, he resents the way in which Welsh rugby does not expect its players to be intellect-uals or indeed to show any degree of emotional or psychological complexity. Some colleagues have coined the name 'Montserrat' for him, presumably because of his unpredictability. The truth is that there are times when he wants to be his own man and not just another Welsh forward existing merely to be a Grog model. The St Mary's boy chose to fulfil himself as a professional rugby player rather than as an army officer. He still reflects on that decision. At school and in the Royal Engineers they readily identified him as a leader. He was always told that he would be a leader. Perhaps we should think of him as being in service behind enemy lines. That is certainly how they will remember him in Llanelli. Unexpectedly and very coolly he had turned up late at Ninian Park, his boots in a bag, and not for the first time he went on to steal the show. Thank goodness for that Welsh grandfather.

# CHRIS WYATT

Alan Evans

Christopher Philip Wyatt did not make the most auspicious of starts to his career in international rugby. In a decade when caps were given out in a cavalier fashion that would have had men such as Roy Thomas, Colin Bosley, Elwyn Williams and others, who played in so many trial matches but never got the call to wear the three feathers on their chest, shaking their heads in despair and frustration, the arrival of yet another utility forward in, of all places, the Sports Stadium in Harare for a few minutes' play as a replacement lock against Zimbabwe seemed to be nothing more significant than the further confirmation of the devaluation of the Welsh cap.

That Wales should score eight tries and forty-nine points against Zimbabwe in June 1998 was soon consigned to the irrelevance it always threatened to be as three weeks later the same Wales tourists suffered the indignity of fifteen Springbok tries against them and only avoided the unwanted distinction of the dreaded century of points conceded when a final opposition attack broke down. Chris Wyatt won his second cap that day, this time for forty-minutes' play as a replacement flanker, and when the Springbok machine next faced Wales at Wembley five months later and Wyatt, now a first-choice selection as a lock, failed to secure Henry Honiball's kick-off and then fumbled the ball thrown to him at the first Welsh line-out there seemed little reason to revise initial impressions that here was yet another so-called modern forward destined for rapid obscurity.

Little did we realize that long before that same 1998–9 season would run its full course Chris Wyatt would be regarded as one of the key players in the revival of Welsh international rugby on the field and one of its blossoming personalities off it. Even when we found ourselves fourteen points up after half an hour against the Springboks at Wembley, the attention-grabbers were the familiar boot of Jenkins, the driving legs of Charvis and the two Quinnells, and the agreeable try-scoring habit of Gareth Thomas. After all, Wyatt may have been 6'5" tall, and he may have been 17 stones plus of all-action natural athlete as Graham Henry had assured us, but it was twenty-five minutes before he won his first line-out and he did seem to be slow in getting to grips with the pace of the game around the field. But something had caught our eye at that first line-out. Instead of standing and waiting for the ball, the Welsh forwards had arrived only as Jonathan Humphreys was about to throw it in – and in Chris Wyatt's case he was the last man of all and, unless our eyes were deceiving us, the ball had actually left the hooker's hands as in one movement the rangy lock got to the line, went up and fed the ball back quickly to Robert Howley.

This was precision timing with a vengeance. Henry had indicated in the days leading up to the match that the line-out, like the scrum, merely served as a means of restarting a game from set play. There was nothing unusual in this; Carwyn James had said much the same thing twenty-five years earlier. It was deep into first-half injury time before the next Welsh line-out ball came against the Springboks and, sure enough, Humphreys and Wyatt went through the same drill and again the ball was in Howley's hands before the opposition had moved. Now we saw the true benefits of this slickest of restarts as the blind-side wing Dafydd James burst through the mid-field and Gareth Thomas was sent hurtling along the right touch-line, testing the Springbok defence to the limit. Moments later the whistle for half-time went, but all present realized that a far more important signal had been made: that the Wales team under its new coach had reassessed its line-out tactics and that Chris Wyatt was a key man in the whole operation.

As the international season unfolded, everyone realized, too, that there was more to Chris Wyatt than mere line-outs and fancy drills. His background in the game was hardly conventional. Born in the Malpas area of Newport but educated up to the age of twelve in the Isle of Wight and then Suffolk before returning to the Queen's Comprehensive School in the centre of his home town, he showed no great aptitude or affinity for rugby until he went to Pontypool College for his post-16 qualifications. It was his PE lecturer there, Phil Jones, together with the WRU referee Paul Adams who pointed him in the direction of the oval rather than the round ball. Within no time he was selected for Wales Youth against England as a lock-forward, though one with an appetite for loose play, all arms and legs and a bit of running around but without the hard graft and body-on-the-line commitment to succeed in the top flight. As a keen fisherman, he still appreciates the exaggerated note in current match programmes that he won three youth caps; the game against England when he was in the same pack as Andrew Lewis and Barry Williams was, in fact, his only appearance at that level.

Over the years, the lock forwards who have won the hearts and minds of the Welsh public have either been the spectacular leapers into the sky like Roy John, Delme Thomas and Bob Norster, or the no-nonsense maulers and masters of clandestine skullduggery such as Brian Thomas, John Perkins and Geoff Wheel. Very few have been expected to combine their particular quality with a general mobility and ball-handling contribution around the pitch, though to be fair to Norster there were many occasions when he came closer than most to fulfilling the criteria of an all-round forward. Perhaps the most gifted of all in recent times was Dick Moriarty, capable of rotating between flank, number 8 and lock as easily as Derek Quinnell had done a decade before but less successful in controlling his volatility and maximizing his potential.

Expectations of Welsh lock-forwards, as indeed of the props who scrummaged in front of them, were based on the mantra established over generations that to win rugby matches the backs required just 40 per cent of ball possession and their native wit and cunning would do the rest. That, after all, was how both Cardiff and Wales had beaten the All Blacks in 1953, how the Welsh backs had spearheaded the 1971 Lions' historic series win in New Zealand, and how even way back in 1933 Watcyn Thomas had led Wales to the first-ever win at Twickenham because, as J. B. G. Thomas later concluded, 'The pack was doing well and heeling smartly and it was up to the backs to win the match.'

So team selection over the years was based on the principle that the pack had to be ball-winners and, when they did the job they were there for, those spring-heeled lock forwards would be heroes in their own right – but when the supply of line-out ball dried up, or worse still their methods of getting it in the first place failed to find favour with the referee, they quickly became the villains of the piece. Thus the embarrassment of a World Cup match against Australia when only four line-outs were won in eighty minutes, or the sheer agony of that final line-out in 1978 when the All Blacks Oliver and Haden fell to the ground and all Wales watched helplessly as McKechnie's last-gasp penalty robbed them of glory. Or the ecstasy of that earlier spring afternoon at the Arms Park as Delme Thomas, with a little help from his friends, won five line-outs on the south touch-line against a wooden

English pack followed in quick succession by four second-half tries in the north-east corner, including a hat-trick for Maurice Richards, and a left-footed dropped goal by Barry John.

As the strategies and resulting ebb and flow of the game changed in the mid-1990s, nowhere was the shifting requirements of what made an effective player more evident than in the lock-forward position in general and in the line-out techniques in particular. The successful lifting of the Delme and Denzil duo in the early 1970s had necessitated, or so it seemed at the time, changes for the better in the laws that would see the emergence of giant practitioners such as Bayfield in England, Norm Hadley in an emerging Canada, and Derwyn Jones in Wales. All were very much ball-winners rather than ball-carriers. The laws changed again as along came John Eales and Ian Jones and, suddenly, where there had been bulk and power, there was suppleness and pace. Instead of catchers who could run, the search was on for runners who could catch; in other words, be relied on to restart the game at the line-out and then be just as effective and influential as the game unfolded in other parts of the pitch.

For a forward like Chris Wyatt the question would be whether he could harness his own mobility and ball skills into a wider game that would require, at most, thirty or so line-outs, half of which would be 'own balls' with an expectation of 100 per cent success. By the start of the 1998–9 season, his progress had been typically erratic, reminiscent of the Moriartys and the younger Quinnells before him. A couple of seasons of senior rugby at Newport, then another at Neath saw him alternate between lock and number 8, and the attention he drew from the national selectors seemed to be based on little more than the fact that his speed and size and general usefulness as a utility player marked him out as being a bit different from the run-of-the-mill Welsh forwards of his generation. The minor selections duly arrived. A season as lock-forward for the Wales Under-21 team and then packing down alongside Gareth Llewellyn in a wretched match for Neath against the 1994 Springboks followed by a game at blind side flanker for Wales A and then half a match for Wales against South East Transvaal on tour in Witbank suggested that no one quite knew where Wyatt's true position lay. In the summer of 1997 he went with the Wales squad to North America and played four times in the back row without ever threatening to break into the Test team. It was on his next tour to Southern Africa that his first caps came as a replacement against Zimbabwe and South Africa, but caught in the debris of near humiliation in the Springboks' fifteen-try massacre at Pretoria the notion of a 'breakthrough' to the big time was not one that readily sprung to mind.

The arrival of Graham Henry as national team coach in the autumn of 1998 was to herald many changes in Welsh rugby in general and the fortunes of several individuals in particular. The playing styles of established stars were reassessed and in some cases, such as Neil Jenkins, overhauled. Some were discarded altogether and new faces with new qualities brought in. Typical of Henry's new approach was in the second row of the pack with the press announcement for the team selected to play South Africa in the return fixture at Wembley citing, 'The lock pairing of Craig Quinnell and Chris Wyatt brings together Wales's most mobile and athletic middle row combination ever.' Quinnell was the 20-stones-plus powerhouse with handling and running skills that tempted him, or so his detractors said, to develop an appetite for the fancy stuff around the field which, together with his apparently explosive temperament, left little time for the hard graft of traditional lock-forward play. And, at first, Wyatt was tarred with the same brush, with the added problem that he was regarded as merely a lighter version of the wayward Quinnell. As the long international season ran its course and Wales moved on from the Springboks at Wembley and Argentina at Stradey Park to the unique demands of the Five Nations Championship and then a summer tour to Argentina, both Craig Quinnell and Chris Wyatt were to prove their critics spectacularly wrong. Not only were they athletic and mobile. They were supremely fit, hard-working and influential in the new Wales of Graham Henry.

Under other coaches, Chris Wyatt may have remained little more than a journeyman utility forward, useful on tours both on and off the field and good fun to have around. Henry, though, was suspicious that here was a real if untapped talent that needed to be developed, set challenges and put to the test. From that first hesitant line-out at Wembley when the wandering Wyatt arrived late and left empty-handed to the glorious afternoon against the English six months later when at a conservative estimate he bagged a dozen clean catches of his own, culminating in that acrobatic leap that allowed a juggling Scott Quinnell to send Scott

Gibbs on his path to glory, he was to repay fully the new coach's faith in him. Out of uncertainty and scepticism there grew an expectation and acceptance by the increasingly up-beat Welsh supporters that whatever plans the backs had to conjure their patterns in mid-field and beyond, Chris Wyatt would provide them with the ball. And it soon became evident, too, that he had the speed and skill of his own to join them in the mazy running that went hand in hand with the multi-phase rugby that quickly became the team's trademark.

Against Argentina at Stradey Park, line-outs were won with remarkable skills including, or so it seemed, an ability to adjust one-handed takes at the top of the leap before delivering the ball to Howley on the proverbial plate. As early as the eleventh minute the extra dimension that Chris Wyatt brought to the team was very evident. Having caught an opposition kick-off with a competence that had eluded his predecessors in the red jersey for more years than most of us cared to remember, he reappeared in the same sweeping move eighty metres up-field, an attack of thrilling ambition and speed of execution featuring Neil Jenkins, Dafydd James and Gareth Thomas and several switches, to take centre Mark Taylor's pass and with a swivel and one-handed pass of his own Wyatt sent Colin Charvis on the final surge to a breathtaking try. Next came Scotland at Murrayfield and, amidst the deflation and disappointment of an unexpected and unnecessary defeat, an even more spectacular team try of the highest quality featuring seven phases of play after another Wyatt catch at the back of a line-out. Somehow, he was to appear four times in a build-up that was to end with him again being the final link, this time between Jenkins and Gibbs, and again displaying a one-handed pass not found in the coaching manuals but born of inspiration and genius.

The merits of that Murrayfield try paled into insignificance alongside the final result. Observers who had shaken their heads in disapproval and doubt about the line-out ploys since they were first unveiled at Wembley now had their say: only one man jumping and no variations; and probably illegal for good measure; not good enough in Scotland up against a pack coached by Jim Telfer. Yet Wyatt and Wales had already won three line-outs before, twenty minutes into the game, Ed Morrison, a referee for whom Wales had the highest regard, suddenly ruled the late arrivals at the throw-in out of order. For the rest of the game the Welsh forwards, including Wyatt, had to be standing and waiting before the ball came in. The doubters' worse fears had materialized – and Graham Henry was not amused. The inevitable comments about fussy northern hemisphere referees were given an airing but would there be a change of thinking by the coach and, if so, would Chris Wyatt survive? The Australian Scott Young took charge of the next game against Ireland and then the Scottish referee Jim Fleming awaited them in Paris – there was a feeling that if the French hit-men did not blow Wyatt aside, then the letter-of-the-law Fleming surely would. But Henry stuck by his guns. He publicly disapproved of refereeing interpretations that 'slowed the game down' and assumed that Wales would be allowed to proceed with their fluid rugby. No official complaint about Morrison's refereeing was made and no further clarification was sought. Wales moved on to their next games with the same line-out techniques, though with the occasional use of Craig and Scott Quinnell as front jumpers, and for Chris Wyatt it was a case of onwards and upwards.

Against Ireland and Italy, Wyatt's take and feed set up tries for Craig Quinnell without fuss, bother or much opposition, and later still in Buenos Aires the combination took one step further as the Pumas, now expecting the full force of the Quinnell charge from Wyatt's catch, were left watching helplessly as he simply offloaded the ball to Brett Sinkinson whose turn it was to dive over unchallenged. At last we had a pack of forwards who were thinking on their feet. To assistant coach Lynn Howells it came as no surprise. He had worked with Chris Wyatt as he came through the ranks of Wales Under-21 and Wales A, and Howells will happily admit that the lock is a willing learner, keen to do well, and whose success at the highest international level is the source of particular satisfaction amongst the team management.

As the national squad prepared to go to Argentina in May 1999, another feature in Chris Wyatt's character became apparent. Consistent success and a customer-friendly style on the field was attracting increasing media coverage and public relations work for the team and its individual players off it, and Chris the 'natural' as a rugby player proved to be something of a performer in front of the cameras as well. These days there is no shortage of ideas for ways to promote live television rugby in Wales with the trailer being used as a device to attract audiences. Even so, Chris Wyatt's cameo performance as an archetypal

Argentinian barman left S4C viewers pondering his likeness to Antonio Banderas rather more than rugby fans had considered him a born-again Geoff Wheel or Brian Thomas. The television producers, apparently, were more than a little impressed and as Welsh rugby became a marketable product again there seemed little reason to doubt that Chris would become a key player in more ways than one.

Once in Argentina, the smell of the greasepaint swiftly became a thing of the past as Wyatt the player again took centre stage and the Welsh team resumed its run of success. It could all have been so very different with a 23–0 deficit after thirty minutes of the First Test in Buenos Aires. Wales clawed their way back into the game with three line-outs won by Wyatt on the left touch-line, leading to tries by Dafydd James, Sinkinson and finally Wyatt himself. This was a try that represented all that was good about Chris Wyatt. He won the ball with yet another huge leap and then reappeared moments later at Mark Taylor's side to take his pass and with a triumphant lunge of his long arm, the ball again grasped securely in one giant hand, he claimed his first international try. Wales had taken the lead for the first time and his season, too, was complete. It goes without saying that when Wales won the Second Test and the series a week later, the team's only try and a Neil Jenkins drop goal had their origins in set-piece possession won by him.

The team returned from Argentina as heroes. For the first time ever a northern hemisphere nation had won a Test series there and not without displaying great strength of character. Earlier impressions that here was a squad winning over a previously disillusioned public were confirmed. Not for twenty years had the men in red reached out to an audience of admirers beyond the rugby diehards. Now their profiles and activities were filling the front and middle pages of the newspapers almost as regularly as the sports sections. Where there was once J.P.R. and Gareth, Benny and Barry, or Gerald and Basil Brush, there was now Jenks and Shane, Garin and Gibbsy, Alfie (Gareth Thomas) and the Mighty Quinn (or Quinns). Oddly, amidst the growing familiarity of the nicknames and first names, Chris Wyatt seemed to be still just 'Wyatt'. It need not have concerned him. For whereas the team as a whole were undoubtedly winning the hearts and minds of the public, he was touching their soul – a man of indomitable spirit and buccaneering profile who satisfied their sense of adventure.

In the summer of 1999, Chris Wyatt stood on the threshold of even greater achievements. Chosen as player of the year by the rugby writers of Wales; highly respected by the Scarlets of Llanelli as an utterly dependable clubman who had already clocked up over a hundred games for them in less than four full seasons; courted by the media as a charismatic figure to parade in the shop window of the game; and, most of all, a Test player of stature who was expected to cover every acre of the new Millennium Stadium as no lock-forward before him had ever roamed over the old Arms Park. The demands on him would be high, but his exceptional improvement during the previous twelve months when line-outs were won as never before, cover-tackles materialized from nowhere and daring runs and swivel passes became commonplace, left everyone with the feeling that such demands on Chris Wyatt were entirely realistic.

Nothing, of course, was certain. What could not be taken away, though, were those indelible images of the winter of 1999 and a resurgent Wales when the numbers 1 to 15 on the jerseys became almost meaningless, when everyone was simply a player who was expected to contribute ball-winning and ball-carrying, tackling and running, when no match was won or lost until the final whistle, and when, in Graham Henry's world, losing teams held meetings and winning teams had parties. Chris Wyatt had good reason to anticipate many parties.

# BEYOND THE FIELDS OF PRAISE: WELSH RUGBY 1980–1999

Dai Smith and Gareth Williams

The Dutch of the seventeenth century were great innovators and their pre-eminence was recognized across Europe in manufactures, agriculture, trade and shipping. Yet by the end of the next century they seemed incapable of keeping up with the progress outside their boundaries, and the former undisputed leaders were overtaken and displaced (by the English). They lost their lead in devising the carto-graphical aids and navigational techniques that would have enabled them to sustain their supremacy and they were equally slow to adopt new and improved methods in what they had been good at, ship-building. In 1775 a Dutchman wrote: 'We are no longer innate in-novators and originality is becoming increasingly rare with us here. Nowadays we make only copies whereas formerly we made only originals.'

In 1980–1 Welsh rugby, walking tall, crossed the threshold of its second century. On the way in, it managed simultaneously to graze its head and stub its toe. The next twenty years would see it flailing to stay upright, when it was not flat on its face. Success breeds complacency, and complacency and readiness to change are mutually exclusive attitudes. Change implies imaginative effort and hurts vested interests whose unshakeable conviction it is that if something has worked well in the past, it will continue to do so in the future. Welsh rugby was in for a rude awakening. In fulfilment of one of its centenary aims of making 'a significant contribution to rugby knowledge and thinking', in September 1980 the WRU hosted a world conference for coaches and referees, attended by 150 delegates from forty-seven countries. Given Wales's results over the previous ten years, based on playing and coaching innovations that had been widely exported and which had achieved for Wales status as one of the game's leaders, this was not an entirely illusory perception of its world-wide position. However, this conference was the last time Wales would play any decisive role on the world stage until in August 1995 the International Rugby Board, for the previous hundred years rugby union's bow and arrow in the age of the stealth bomber, overnight reversed a century of history and under the Welsh chairmanship of Vernon Pugh announced that the game was going professional – although just a month earlier, the WRU had issued a 23-point document warning of the consequences if the game abandoned amateurism. Four years later the Rugby World Cup, another innovation unheard of in 1980, would focus even more attention on Wales, who by then, buoyed up by a sequence of extraordinary, and more to the point out of the ordinary, victories over France, England, Italy, Argentina and South Africa, was beginning to recover international self-respect and internal stability after the most painful twenty-year period in its history.

## Decline and Fall

The warning signals announcing the descent of the Dragon into two decades of doubt, desperation and near disintegration had come early and fast. Graham Mourie's All Blacks repaid their invitation to the centenary celebrations with conclusive victories, within fifteen days, over the four foremost Welsh clubs, before completing the whitewash by inflicting on Wales, in a game fittingly sponsored by Crown Paints, their heaviest home defeat (23–3) for ninety-eight years. Countries nearer home also began exposing Welsh shortcomings. There were fortuitous victories in 1981 over England (21–19) and Ireland (9–8), with Tony Ward in ebullient mood, cheekily showing the ball to the opposition, darting and sniping to inspire two tries against three kicks from a Welsh XV content to push the opposing pack around the park all afternoon but with little else to offer. Two narrow home wins, and two away losses, were sharp reminders after the similar record of the previous season that the 'golden era' was history. There were clearly limited returns from forward domination alone, but Welsh rugby was reluctant to learn it: later in 1981 an unexceptional Wallabies side inflicted a 37–6 thrashing on a Pontypool pack which included seven internationals. The following year Scotland dismembered Wales 34–18, their biggest total against Wales since 1924, and so ending Wales's run of twenty-seven Championship home games without defeat.

By the end of that year Wales had recorded only five wins out of thirteen, and were propping up the championship they had dominated throughout the 1970s. The next year, 1983, they suffered their heaviest away defeat in fourteen years, 24–6 to Romania in Bucharest. The victory over Ireland in Cardiff that season would have been savoured more had anyone anticipated it would be the last home win over the Irish for the rest of the century; more faltering performances mocked the 'third in the world' tag Wales had adopted after a one-point victory against fourteen Australians in the defeated semi-finalists' play-off in the inaugural World Cup of 1987 (having already been drubbed 49–6 by New Zealand), and after managing only one win in the Five Nations that year. The Triple Crown in 1988, the last of the century, brought some relief, but instead of consolidating it with a tour to Canada or Japan, a demoralizing visit to New Zealand saw Welsh decline accelerate with terminal velocity.

In 1990 and 1991 Wales went through two successive Five Nations campaigns without a win, and for the first time ever conceded more than a hundred points in the Championship. In 1991 England won at Cardiff for the first time since 1963 (not everyone agreed this was a record to be well rid of) and later that year a calamitous tour of Australia saw the Wallabies become the first side ever to score six tries against Wales in an official international (no caps had been awarded against Fiji in 1964). In the early 1990s both England and Scotland beat Wales three times in a row for the first time since the 1920s, from 1988 to 1994 Wales never managed two consecutive Championship wins, and between 1995 and 1997 Ireland beat Wales on four successive occasions for the first time ever (the 24–23 defeat in the 1995 World Cup being perhaps the most numbingly depressing in Welsh history). While on-field ineptitude plumbed depths beyond the imaginings of even *Titanic*-sleuth Robert Ballard, off-the-field hype soared into the realms of fantasy: 'We will be a very difficult team to beat . . . this side is as skilful as the sides of the sixties and seventies', declared caretaker coach Alex Evans.

The claim was as unreal as the coach's sudden appointment was mystifying, for by this time the administration of the Welsh game was in constant turmoil. Investigative committees had been set up, reports commissioned and their belated proposals (seventy-eight of them in the 1990 'Quest for Excellence') partially accepted, partially financed. In June 1985 one such committee of reform reported, in terms that would haunt the stadium millennialists in the winter of 1998–9: 'Soon we shall have one of the most modern rugby grounds in the world. It will indeed be woeful if we do not have a team to match its magnificence.' John Dawes, coaching organizer throughout the 1980s and a member of that committee, harboured concerns that the greater financial investment in the future of the game it proposed was being diverted into yet further ground development. He warned in 1987 that 'we are light years behind in fitness, strength and determination', and pointed to a reluctance to accept that 'we have been overtaken'. Welsh rugby was paying the price of a complacency engendered by and, to the percipient, already discernible in the 1970s: what if Ray Williams's 1975 proposals for a league structure, originally mooted in 1908, had been adopted at the time or pushed more successfully in the 1980s?

Ray Williams, as sage as he was visionary, had been the catalyst who brought about the coaching revolution, and arguably laid the foundations for the playing success, of the 1970s. Appointed coaching organizer for Wales in 1967, he broke down barriers of suspicion and conservatism by charm and drive. His failure, as he moved up and through the Union hierarchy, to effect wider structural changes earlier, or indeed at all, was galling to him but not entirely unexpected. One of his last acts as secretary of the WRU was an impassioned appeal to the clubs – 'however illustrious some may be' – not to imagine, in 1988, that the 'destiny of the game in Wales' was really in their hands any longer.

> The structure that we have at the moment must be changed. It is largely an accident of history and is certainly not durable enough to sustain the game in Wales in the years to come. Success goes to those who plan properly. We cannot have a small group of clubs putting up the barriers and saying that things must always stay the same. I don't believe they are thinking about Welsh rugby. They are thinking about themselves. I appeal to them for the sake of Wales, to think again. I appeal to them to cast off the old ideas, to join us in trying to create a better structure and a better game for all the players and all the clubs. What England, with their leagues are doing now, we were talking about in 1975 – and could have had established by 1981. Today there are real signs that we're losing ground in terms of quality and excellence. Yet still some people are turning a blind eye and pretending it's not really happening. Unless we grasp this nettle, and get planned development approved and organised, the game in Wales faces grave problems.

In 1990, two years after he left office as, effectively, the last of the WRU secretaries to wield real influence, Williams saw a national league structure at last introduced. But the attendant reorganization of the Welsh game had not followed. The key proposals of the 1990 report, urging a major overhaul of the game's administration to include a board of management with a chief executive, regional directors instead of district representatives, and provincial-style unions to replace the then-current counties and districts, became casualties of the acrimony which engulfed the WRU over Welsh involvement in South Africa's rugby centenary celebrations. The Union's own commissioned report detailed a saga of frustration laced with farce. Relating to events in 1989 it was not presented to the Union until 1991 and not released to the clubs for another two years, another example of the WRU burying its head in the sand only to expose its thinking parts. Although the vacuous slogan 'keep politics out of sport' was shown to be particularly meaningless in the 1970s, Welsh rugby continued to maintain links with apartheid South Africa, confirmed by a 306 to 62 mandate by the clubs in 1984, though there was no expectation of any immediate fixture by which they could actually implement the decision. The following year the WRU sanctioned a tour by Crawshay's XV even after the South African government had declared a state of emergency in the black townships.

The fatal attraction of the Republic to rugby players' basic instinct that the game alone, and their own enjoyment, was paramount was an unfailingly disruptive force in world rugby. The 1986 New Zealand 'Cavaliers' tour, sponsored appropriately enough by Yellow Pages and organized by the fertilizer mogul Louis Luyt, was condemned even by the NZRU who retaliated by punishing the renegades, though they could not have been too disappointed to see new talents emerge in their place like Wayne Shelford, John Kirwan, Grant Fox, Alan Whetton, Sean Fitzpatrick and Michael Jones who won the first World Cup the following year. When the top Welsh players were themselves similarly courted in 1989, the WRU chose to leave it to the individual, and paid dearly for its ambivalence. There was farce in the clandestine airlifting of players from a squad session at Aberystwyth, and fall-out when the shenanigans led to the morally principled resignation of the incorruptible David East only eight months after succeeding Ray Williams as secretary in November 1988. The subsequent inquiry conducted by Vernon Pugh QC unearthed bizarre evidence of accounts transferred from Luxembourg to the UK but ran up against a wall of rehearsed answers and uncooperative witnesses. When the Union eventually yielded to demands from the clubs for the release of the report in 1993, with Wales again at the bottom of the Championship table, a motion was passed of no confidence in the entire general committee who immediately walked out to be replaced in April 1993 by new blood headed by Vernon Pugh, whose legal expertise and sound rugby credentials rooted in the Aman Valley saw him immediately elected to the chairmanship of the WRU (1993–7) and soon the International Rugby Board as well, successive powerful tenancies which made him the most influential voice in the administration of Welsh and world rugby. With Glanmor Griffiths confirmed as honorary treasurer, injunctions and writs became more newsworthy than any activities on the field, and interpersonal friction saw the rumbustious Denis Evans, appointed secretary in January 1990 as David East's successor, sacked in October 1993, so that assistant secretary Edward Jones became the WRU's fourth secretary in five years. When Ray Williams succeeded Bill Clement in 1981 he had been only the sixth secretary in a hundred years; when Denis Gethin became the eleventh secretary in 1998 he was the sixth in eleven years. Ray Williams himself, who on relinquishing the post of WRU secretary had become the tournament director of the 1991 Rugby World Cup, was in 1993 the first former secretary ever to stand for election to the WRU Committee. In 1997 he stood down from that body, thus ending thirty years' involvement with the Union. Personnel was changing fast on the field, too. Between 1988 and 1992 Wales capped seventy-five players, hired and fired four national coaches (Tony Gray, John Ryan, Ron Waldron and Alan Davies) and, in the locust years after Jonathan Davies's departure early in 1989, chose seven outside-halves in the one position where continuity had historically been a talisman of Welsh international success.

The morale-sapping continuing defeats, the constant revision of the record books as one humiliation followed another, and the apparent inability to find any solution were grisly reminders of an earlier period of depression and disarray. In 1929 Rowe Harding had lambasted the administrators of his own day as 'representatives of an outworn but not discarded tradition', essentially pre-war men in a post-war era, responding to a crisis they barely understood always tardily and often irrationally, losing their way at selectorial level, maladroit in public relations, increasingly unconfident in all their dealings. The similarities with the 1920s do not end there: economic depression, large-scale unemployment and industrial conflict combined to create a climate of administrative myopia, selectorial confusion, critical defections to the rugby league, thinning crowds and clubs reduced to pleading with the Union for financial assistance.

The wider similarity with the 1980s, when industrial Wales experienced its greatest trauma since the 1930s, is striking, the facts starker. In 1981 there were still in south Wales 27,000 men at work in thirty-six pits. By the end of the decade the Welsh coal industry was dead and buried, with only its spirit walking the earth at Tower Colliery, set to become Wales's last deep coal-mine as a workers'-run co-operative in 1995. The steel industry which had expanded in the 1960s and 1970s to take up the job losses experienced in mining haemorrhaged even more dramatically than coal. The work-force in steel and tinplate in 1991 was a third that of 1979. A decline in all manufacturing industry in the UK meant that Wales, a branch plant economy, was knocked even harder. In effect the broader industrial base built up since 1945 proved as vulnerable as the old mono-culture of heavy industry before it. Low wages, poor skills and overdependence on benevolent state direction were no help in the face of state withdrawal and being on the margin of all market-led development. In the 1980s when you left the train at Paddington you almost tasted the indifference of prosperity to deprivation. When Phil Bennett urged his 1978 team on against England with 57 remembered varieties of colonial and capitalist oppression of the Welsh, the rhetoric was as tribal as it was tongue-in-cheek, a ritual before expected victories. The bitterness of the rugby dregs drained down to the next Triple Crown of 1988 did not just lie in the sporting arena: the very essence of the industrial and urban society which had spawned and nurtured Welsh rugby was being systematically dismantled.

The year-long miners' strike of 1984–5 can be debated endlessly for its origins, its tactics and its ending. What is not in dispute is the trauma it inflicted on the hearts and souls of Welsh rugby's most faithful and most innocent supporters: the bobble-hatted fans whose identification with this sport had taken the game to the centre of Wales's popular culture. Yet that centre was definitely not holding. The Rhondda, where over 50,000 colliers had once worked, had no mines left when 1985 ended and a population scarcely many more in total than its mining work-force had once been. The struggle in Wales had been as much social and cultural as industrial and political; the NUM in South Wales adopted the slogan of Cymdeithas yr Iaith Gymraeg (the Welsh Language Society): 'Cau pwll, lladd cymuned' (Close a pit, kill a community). And, in the sense that the major social touchstones of identity as they had impacted upon Welsh rugby were being hastened to their grave, so the kind of community that had fashioned sporting culture out of their material being was, indeed, being killed. In the 1920s and 1930s the way of life continued irrespective of the economic misery suffered; in the 1980s that particular modern way of life lived by most of the Welsh this century abruptly ended. In the central valleys well over 90 per cent of the people were native born in a country which, overall, had a smaller indigenous population than any other of the UK's nations. From here they migrated to the coastal towns, to the new settlements at the mouths of valleys or further afield: for those left behind unemployment, social deprivation and basic poverty were mixed and matched with cultural dislocation.

For all the self-serving claims of government propaganda, the empty rhetoric of a 'valleys' initiative' and a 'sunrise economy', by the early 1990s Wales still lagged behind the other regions of Britain in the key indicators of household income (Mid Glamorgan was the poorest county in the UK in this respect), average gross weekly earnings and annual average employment rates (nearly 30 per cent among the 18 to 20 category in 1994, the worst in the UK after the north-west of England). Outmigration became once again the resort of those of working age who had the means and inclination to move. For rugby players the pull of the magnetic north became once more irresistible; not only, between 1980 and 1991, to eighteen already capped international players but to those on the fringe of selection, like Mike Carrington transferred from Neath to St Helens for £61,000 in 1988, Gerald Cordle from Cardiff to Bradford Northern for £80,000 in 1989, and Kevin Ellis from Bridgend to Warrington for £100,000 in 1991. If the Welsh economy was a more diversified one – by 1990 less than 3 per cent of the Welsh work-force was in coal, iron and steel, more than a quarter in electronics, engineering, business and financial services – it was also a less secure one, a screwdriver economy where some thought Dai was now an abbreviation for Daihatsu. The traditional stereotypes of a heavy industrial past were receding to be replaced by new images of Japanese electronics firms, marinas and theme parks. The biggest indigenous enterprise looked like being the heritage industry.

In sum, an increasing dependence on market forces and commercial calculations made well outside its borders threatened to leave Wales and its rugby very exposed, a danger which became brutally clear when the announcement of the amateur game's embrace of professionalism in 1995 saw the M4 suddenly congested by cheque-book waving agents from English rugby union clubs bankrolled by entrepreneurs whose interest in the game was often little, their hunger for profit unreasonably great. As it entered the 1990s, therefore, Wales was a very different place from what it had been in the 1960s and 1970s, let alone an earlier period. The last two decades of the twentieth century saw Wales undergo a dramatic transformation, and no part of society – politics, culture, education or sport – was unaffected by it.

Yet in strict rugby terms, wherever we look in the 1980s we have a distinct sense of having been here before. There is, for instance, the high profile of the South Wales Police, historic beneficiaries of economic depression, who rose from the bottom (nineteenth) of the unofficial club championship in 1980–1 to fifth position for two seasons in succession just three years later, producing influential administrators in Rod Morgan, a selector until his untimely death in 1989, former chief constable David East who became WRU secretary that year, and a division of international players like Martyn Morris, Bleddyn Bowen, Steve Sutton, Ritchie Donovan, Richie Collins and John Wakeford. A fondness for selecting players out of position had reached the mystifying level of the inter-war period as the selectors cast around for someone who could win some – any – ball at the back of the line-out to compensate for the sweaters, rather than jumpers, further forward. More controversial still was the furious debate over fly-half, which again had resonant historic overtones. Indecision manifested itself here when the selectors got themselves into a hopeless muddle over the respective merits of the astute Gareth Davies and the beautifully balanced runner, fluent distributor and, as he twice demonstrated at Twickenham in 1984, drop-goal expert Malcolm Dacey. By April 1985 the selectors seemed not to have seen enough of either to convince themselves and nominated A. N. Other as fly-half against England. Into the breach raced Jonathan Davies, brash, cocky, oozing self-confidence and with plenty to be confident about. Davies was undoubtedly the most gifted player of his generation, a talent waiting to be fulfilled, only to fall foul of Welsh forward inadequacies, inept management, and an increasingly hostile press. The catalyst of the Triple Crown triumph in 1988 and one of the few to emerge with any credit from that summer's suicidal tour of New Zealand, he left a gaping hole by signing for Widnes in 1989 which meant that within three years Llanelli's Colin Stephens would be the fourth fly-half to be capped in seven games.

As in the 1920s, too, it was thought that might and muscle at forward, endless (often aimless) kicking and the crash-ball behind, would bring their own rewards. What they brought were predictability, lack of imagination and an erosion of confidence behind forwards who relished scrummaging for the sake of it, releasing the ball only when all other options up front had been exhausted. The line-out, meanwhile, was left to its own devices, to become in the absence of Robert Norster through suspension in 1986 and injury in South Africa in 1989, by the early 1990s a disaster area. By then, too, it was apparent that Welsh forwards had completely lost the art of rucking: clearly basic techniques were being either not learned, or not taught. Thud and blunder at forward was complemented by a complete absence of penetration in the mid-field. There was a nice irony in the fact that the Big Five selection panel, called into being in 1924 to arrest crisis, was abolished in 1991 for the same reason; but for all the changes of selectors, coach and players, there seemed no answer to tactical impoverishment, a pervasive technical deficiency, and an overall lack of accuracy, control and discipline.

The heavy defeats that began accumulating after the 52–3 and 54–9 maulings in New Zealand in 1988 showed we had forgotten how to tackle too. Big hits went in, but not necessarily on players with the ball, a totally misguided response to another misconception: that Wales had 'become soft' after the infamous Ringer incident at Twickenham in 1980. While it ill-behoved the FFR's Albert Ferrasse to protest that 'our boys played in fear' against Wales that year, when 'our boys' comprised such submissive citizens as Mm. Paparemborde, Joinel, Paco and Rives, violence that sometimes lurched into criminality became an ugly feature of the Welsh game: thirty-one players from senior Welsh clubs were sent off in 1983–4, three clubs were under suspension at the start of 1986–7 because of poor discipline, the referee walked off in an early season clash between Bristol and Newport and a touch judge was sent off at Pontypool; in 1987 the first player to be sent off in the World Cup was a Welshman. The Union took action to stamp out thuggery at club level while promoting some notoriously abrasive characters to senior positions. Too many clubs prided themselves on their hard men, while envy laced with social prejudice singled out the valley clubs for especial opprobrium: Pontypool was the dominant club in the 1980s, losing friends and fixtures on its way to four championship titles between 1985 and 1988, while Treorchy's promotion to the First Division in 1994 was an intriguing reprise of the 'Rhondda forward' syndrome of a hundred years before.

The coastal clubs were hardly lambs either, but none could manage the particular vibrancy that emanated from the Gnoll where Jonathan Davies's virtuoso performances attracted the biggest crowds in British rugby. Managed by the 'ayatollah' Brian Thomas, coached by Ron Waldron, and supplying nine internationals in 1989–90, the Neath approach relied on constant movement, stamina, a minimalist hair style and frightening the opposition, which worked well enough at club level – apart from some unsavoury encounters with touring sides – to persuade the Union to capitulate to demands to nationalize the Gnoll style with Waldron as coach of Wales.

But international sides were bigger, stronger and less easily intimidated. Neath's undoubted high-scoring club success was no guarantee of a reversal of Wales's national fortunes, and the 1991 Welsh tour to Australia was fatally undermined by internal divisions over the style to be adopted. Dispute over a training regime which emphasized running at the expense of all else led to further hideous defeats and a disgraceful brawl at the final post-match dinner. This marked the nadir of 'the national game'. Once again it revealed that Welsh rugby, Bourbon-like, had learned nothing and forgotten nothing; no single club, whether the Neath nine, the Llanelli seven of 1928 (eclipsed by the

Scarlet eight in Paris in 1993), or the Cardiff ten of 1948, held the key to international success. This delusion became a *reductio ad absurdum* when it was believed eleven Cardiff players might arrest imminent disaster during the World Cup Finals in 1995. It was not even that Cardiff was the best club side that season, Swansea was, and they were sensationally demolished 78–7, including twelve tries, by a South African XV that made elegant full-back André Joubert, who scored thirty-eight points, the talk of Wales in the mid-1990s as his predecessors Marsberg and Morkel had been in the early years of the century.

The 'Whites', as it happened, had not suffered unduly from the depredations of northern scouts, but these were a still further reminder of an earlier period, the inter-war years, when sixty-nine capped Welsh players had joined the rugby league. A new wave of defections now broke over a Welsh game already shipping too much water to stay afloat much longer. Once again it was the damaging 1988 tour, followed by the over-hasty sacking of team manager Derek Quinnell and coach Tony Gray, that precipitated a new exodus of refugees along the road to Wigan Pier. What had been a trickle represented by the occasional high-profile signing like those of Stuart Evans and Gary Pearce in 1987 became a cataract in 1988–9 as Adrian Hadley, David Bishop, Paul Moriarty, John Devereux, Jonathan Griffiths, David Young, Allan Bateman and Jonathan Davies took the money and ran, soon to be followed by Rowland Phillips and Scott Gibbs, until Scott Quinnell became the 164th and last Welsh international to 'go North' in 1994. The following year, what had for a hundred years been a gangplank became overnight an open gangway and the return traffic on it was brisk. The skills and fitness levels that some of the exiles brought back with them led to regrets that more had not followed them north in the first place; but there is no denying the dislocation caused by the loss of a third of the Triple Crown side of 1988.

Everything about that year flattered to deceive: not least the hope for a lasting foundation of success which it had seemed to presage. In retrospect, three exceptional players stand out more sharply than three somewhat unlikely victories and certainly Robert Jones, Jonathan Davies and Ieuan Evans would all have sparkled as individuals in any of Welsh rugby's kaleidoscopic eras. The eyebrow which the scrum-half invariably cocked before firing the ball out to his partner – such as the grateful Rob Andrew whose career Jones ignited on the 1989 Lions tour – was probably a permanent psychological tic brought on by a footling selectorial policy which saw him yo-yo in and out of the Welsh teams he graced by his sheer class. It was his pass, uncharacteristically scrambled, and with his back to his partner – Jonathan Davies – in the Scottish game of 1988 at Cardiff, the ball looping high, out of the clutches of his opposite number, Roy Laidlaw, that gave the Llanelli jester one of his finest moments, Jonathan's try the admixture of instinct and preservation that saw him shoot back with the ball from where the ball had come and away from the calvinistic clutches of Finlay Calder, then kicking bravely and skilfully through the only channel possible, to outsprint the flailing Derek White for the touch-down. It was almost as remarkable, in that 25–20 Welsh triumph, as Ieuan Evans's greatest international try: an improbably multiple side-stepping prance down the touch-line before veering infield to score near the posts. But the truth was that it would be Scotland, this very team in essence, who would take the Grand Slam against England within two seasons, while Wales drove Jonathan Davies to despair and Widnes, Robert Jones to disbelief and Bristol, and Ieuan Evans out of the captaincy which, in the early 1990s, he alone fully deserved. Somehow the elegance and excellence of these exceptionally talented players was not enough. It may be that in a Wales made scruffier and hang-dog in its general life their individual sporting superiority was, sadly, neither here nor there. Even Ieuan Evans was reduced to the pitter-patter of purse-snatcher to save Wales, as he did on a cold tense February day in 1993, by stealing up on a casual Rory Underwood before going hell-for-leather after the ball his toe had purloined. Like the players, these were singular moments but merely moments all the same. Neither on the field nor off it did the Welsh seem to possess anything but a fleeting control of their destiny. All was in flux.

Certainly the Wales to which Jonathan Davies returned in late 1995 was different again from the one he left in January 1989. The centrality and historically privileged position rugby had enjoyed in schools like his own Gwendraeth Grammar were now increasingly challenged by developments implicit in the expansion of comprehensive education (bigger schools but fewer teams) and the changing nature of physical education (now examinable) within a national curriculum which encouraged a wider provision embracing basketball and dance, and which downplayed extra-curricular and team sports generally. These developments were only giving statutory recognition to social changes already underway, and the industrial action taken by teachers in 1985–6 played a relatively insignificant role. Irrespective of any individual action by teachers, satellite dishes and the intrusion of the global mass-media were setting the cultural tone of a deindustrialized south Wales, bringing a new awareness of a cultural pluralism and of alternative forms of recreation and entertainment.

In any case 'old schools' had no difficulty in reasserting their long-rooted rugby tradition after the year-long dispute; newer foundations, all glass and concrete, found it neither necessary or even desirable to invoke, or reinvent, a non-existent past. In these circumstances an increasing role was taken by local rugby clubs, not always to the advantage of those between mini-rugby and senior school age-groups since club houses were not of course educational providers of a graduated and rounded physical education but centres of sociability dedicated to winning games and maximizing bar takings. In the schools themselves, the demands of the national curriculum allied to the popularity of Saturday-morning jobs confined rugby games to mid-week late-afternoon, effectively ruling out most activities in the dark evenings of winter. By the early 1990s fewer than thirty state schools in the whole of south Wales were playing any meaningful rugby on Saturday mornings. Paradoxically, but typical of these unsettled times, Welsh school rugby registered some heartening victories, even defeating the All Blacks: in 1991, the year their seniors suffered their heaviest defeat since 1881 (63–6 in Brisbane, conceding, as in 1881, twelve tries, exceeded by the thirteen yielded to New South Wales, 71–8), the Under-18 side became the first ever Welsh national team to win in New Zealand (17–11 in Christchurch); that year (1991) the Youth XV won the Grand Slam while the Under-21 side went unbeaten for four years. Such successes were spasmodic until buttressed by a cluster of Triple Crown and Grand Slam wins at 'A', universities, Under-21 and Under-18 levels in 1999: whether the structures are in place to ensure these players will feed through to senior level remains to be seen.

For Wales, like eighteenth-century Holland, a country with too narrow a demographic base for it to remain naturally competitive in rugby terms, a disproportionate number of its young men will have to play the game and opt for it as their preferred sporting outlet; and maybe the corrosive acid of constant defeat in the context of wider and more enabling social change has contracted that base beyond even the ability of the sensational victories of 1999 to reverse a longer-term trend of gradual disengagement. These developments have in turn been intensified by the onset of professionalism which has the capacity to bring the game in Wales to the brink of extinction. Within six months of the game going professional in 1995 Llanelli sustained losses of £900,000 and sold Stradey Park to the WRU for £1.5 million; in 1997 they were massacred 81–3 by the All Blacks. Most Welsh clubs are working at a serious loss and unless financial realism or a fairy godmother manifests itself some will soon go bankrupt. The messianic arrival of Graham Henry from Auckland temporarily at least averted what looked like a more profound bankruptcy of technique, method, morale and selection. Alan Davies, (Welsh coach 1992–5), lamenting the absence of a structure to support players, confessed that he had 'neither the ability nor the strength of character to bear the whole burden of the Welsh nation'. His immediate successor, Kevin Bowring, had the furrowed brow for the task but could, in the end, lift neither his own brow nor the nation's burden. It was a task the estimable Henry was brought in specifically to address: the previous year Wales conceded a record 145 points in the Five Nations and 224 in a humiliating five-match tour of South Africa, including a shocking 96–13 defeat in the Test. At the domestic level Welsh rugby in 1999 is still a war zone of unexploded mines, mud-filled craters, empty shells and the terminally wounded fighting for life while the general staff close ranks and look to salvation from the retro-roofed phoenix rising from the debris alongside the Taff. And perhaps, against all the odds, it will rise there in the next century. If it does it will owe much to the life blown back into the Welsh game in the dying embers of a late afternoon in Wembley in the last Five Nations game of this rugby century.

## The Song of Songs

Before it began it was more retro-chic than retro-roofed. Max Boyce, *sans* bobble hat and leek this time but still the rugby troubadour of less troublesome times, had walked onto the Wembley pitch around 3.30 to sing 'Hymns and Arias' (Old and New) to a crowd expecting more entertainment before the game than triumph in it. That was the Welsh half, anyway, of the near 80,000 who had walked up Wembley Way, looked at Sir Owen Williams's Twin Towers of this 1922 stadium, and settled in for their last home-and-away match in the family-friendly oval in north London. Max had delighted his fans: even reminding them that the roof of Cardiff's Millennium Stadium would roll back so that God 'could watch us play'. At Wembley She could just look straight down and smile as a century of Welsh clichés were greeted and applauded with great humour by Welsh supporters now well used to fondling their passions with distancing irony.

'Sing us your song' they gently mocked an English opposition as prophetically stuck on a one-line groove as their groaning team would prove to be two hours later: 'Swing Low Sweet Chariot' kept doing its circular tour until the wheels came off and the Welsh, gleeful at last, advised something painful about chariots and sphincters. But that was all to come. For now it was the London Welsh Male Choir and 'Cwm Rhondda' and 'Calon Lân' and, to thunderous applause, Tommy Woodward from Treforest in his reincarnation as Tom Jones from Pontypridd and Hollywood about to deliver, in person, Welsh rugby's unofficial hymn 'Delilah'. We had been betrayed so often, why not one more time? The rendering was a magnificent pastiche, a chorus of 'Ha! Ha! Has!' sent ricocheting back to a delighted Tom Jones in a mass *opera bouffe*.

The Royal Regiment of Wales, headed by Shenkyn the goat, strutted onto the pitch in front of the about-to-be-slaughtered Welsh XV while their white-shirted nemesis, Dallaglio's beef-on-the-bone team, all planed cheeks and rooted stance, waited. Then in the bright April sunshine, warm but with sudden hints of colder mistiness, the anthems. Lusty and confident as usual from England, fervent but nervy from Wales, the players looping their arms over each other's shoulders, the New Zealand contingent in the team, full-back Shane Howarth and flanker Brett Sinkinson, straining for the words of the Land of their Grandfathers. And the crowd, certainly those who had come from Wales that day, singing inside themselves the refrain of the Stereophonics' lead singer, Kelly Jones, who had been popping up on a trail on

BBC Wales TV to tell England 'We don't want to be your enemy', but also 'So long as we beat the English we don't care'. It was only half true but as Neil Jenkins kicked off it was a settlement much to be desired and, in the eyes of most good judges, an impossible dream. Yet, in reality, the songs had only just begun as the red caterpillar of the Welsh regiment side-stepped its way off the pitch by going under the posts.

When it was all over the crowd stayed and stayed until the Welsh heroes came out to join the mutual self-congratulation. A conversion of an improbable try in injury-time had brought Wales victory by a single point, 32–31, and the celebrations would not stop until laughter rictus set in. Not since Muhammad Ali had turned his rumble in the jungle with George Foreman into Rope-a-dope had escapology been refined into such a winning sporting tactic. At Wembley, on the streets and out-side the pubs, strangers hugged each other, Jacks embraced Turks and anyone wearing red-and-white colours was cheered. For hours the coaches and cars heading home honked at the revellers outside as the revellers inside leaned out of doors, windows and roof hatches. Ecstasy on the move and not a pill in sight. All over Wales on that early Sunday evening telephones rang and people rushed out to find their friends. In Cardiff the capital's usual Sunday-evening calm turned into a *bach*-on-ale night such as even worldly taxi drivers had never witnessed. And no trouble anywhere. Pedestrianized precincts filled. Pubs let tidal flows of happiness in and out of their doors. Vehicles stalled by the crowds were swept along in a riot of noise and joy which resembled a French general election or a Rio street carnival. Can it possibly mean so much?

The delivery of an expectation beyond any rational belief had, certainly, brought the wider desire to this peak of euphoria. To all intent and purpose, England had won the game they lost. Their dreadnought pack had rumbled and steamed in the loose (though significantly not in the tight where the Welsh front row gripped them for the whole game). They began sensationally when full-back Perry, exploiting missed Welsh tackles after a quickly taken penalty, had broken through, found England's right wing, Dan Luger, on a diagonal run and saw him thrust over at the Welsh posts with less than three minutes gone. The pattern was set. English forward bump and grind, and incisive though not always rewarded running from Catt and his centres, Jonny Wilkinson and the cheekily named 16-stone 6'6" giant Barrie-Jon Mather, were followed by penalty goals from Jenkins to keep Wales in touch. Just. For, with the scores at 10–9 to England on twenty minutes, Dallaglio, for the first but not the last time, tells Wilkinson to kick a penalty to find touch in the Welsh 22. England win the line-out, move and drive imperiously right, then left, to put their 19-year-old left wing, Hanley, in almost under the posts. Inexplicably the left-footed Wilkinson misses the conversion so the score remains at 15–9, but if he had taken the earlier penalty as a shot at goal and succeeded it would have been only 13–9 so Dallaglio's confident decision was, at this stage, justified.

Meanwhile, and until the very end, Gibbs was being nutcrackered by the English pincers in the centre, clean Welsh ball was dropped or turned over and England's fanned-out defensive line did not buckle (some thought a Welsh chip kick might have been useful but with the backs playing so flat they would have to turn quickly if it was returned: or, as in their irksome defeats that season at the hands of Scotland and Ireland, charged down with dire consequence). The only consolation was that Jenkins seemed incapable of missing goal from any point or distance on the field and the English propensity to be so up in defence as to be offside gave him the chances he took. The number 10, winning his sixty-fourth cap, had brought Wales to 15–15 with twenty-eight minutes gone, with a straight-on trajectory thump from just ten yards inside the English half. Again Dallaglio spurned two more penalty shots for Wilkinson, who had only missed with one kick after all and had slotted seven against the French at Twickenham only three weeks earlier, before letting the Newcastle youngster stroke one over from in front of the Welsh posts, 18–15. With the English score still first in the mind's eye, for it truly seemed like a home game for them, English voices neighed and bayed around the amphitheatre. In the stands the English coach, Clive Woodward, resplendent in what looked more like an admiral's headgear than a baseball cap, gazed out on victory across the horizon. The Welsh coach, Graham Henry, as inscrutable sartorially in regulation dress of blazer and tie as he was po-faced in expression, arched his eyebrows, more Mephistopheles than messianic – and thought. Half-time approached. His big-hitters, those pedigree Scarlets, the Quinnell brothers, Scott as blond and as bulky as Marlon Brando in *The Young Lions*, Craig as bulky and bald as Telly Savalas in the *Dirty Dozen*, were auditioning like mad but, despite being ably cued-in by the leaping Wyatt and the bullocking Charvis, neither they, nor anyone else, were getting the part they wanted to play. The lines were forgotten completely when Dawson's hanging downfield kick was bumped out of Gareth Thomas's grasp by the oncoming Howarth and seized by Richard Hill for a scrambled but effective flanker's try. Conversion followed and, surely, at 25–15 on half-time, England were moving out of range. Not so. Another huge penalty from Jenks on the stroke of time and Wales went in, battered but not yet beaten, only seven points adrift.

At the outset of Graham Henry's reign, Ray Williams, along with other rugby patriots, had wondered about the efficacy of appointing a New Zealander to coach Wales. After all, and no matter how special Henry's record with Auckland in the Super 12 had been, the very nature of Wales would suggest 'a completely different environment' than the one in which he had succeeded. Williams, however, had been both reflective and supportive.

> I can predict a culture shock for him when he comes to Wales. But the die has been cast and we need to give Graham Henry our fullest support. I was interested to learn that he had previously been a schoolteacher as had Clive Rowlands, Carwyn James and John Dawes, Wales' most successful coaches by a very wide margin.
>
> This is the profession which has been denigrated from time to time in the correspondence columns of the *Western Mail* with the statement that teachers did not make successful coaches at senior level. But coaching is about communication and motivation, hallmarks of the outstanding teacher . . .

How the Welsh coach needed those key hallmarks to work for him now. In the dressing-room he told his players they could play much better than that. It was time to start playing. Just as they had sensationally against France five weeks before, when Jenkins firecrackered the entire team with his runs from broken play and tries from Charvis, Ponty's Dafydd James ('There's always so much time playing outside Neil') and Craig Quinnell had bagged the first triumph in Paris since legendary 1975 and the first ever at Stade de France. This was the first time at Wembley against England. Another omen perhaps. Besides, England had been negative, lucky on the bounce of the ball, clumsy in executing a final thrust. They had to be moved wide, pegged back and stretched until their advancing line gaped a hole or two. He had told them after they had narrowly blown a close game against world champions, South Africa, on this same ground and in his first outing in charge of Wales, that he respected them as individuals and as players, but that, cold and pausing before they met Italy, and even with a wobbly win at Stradey Park against powerful Argentina behind them, he did not, yet, respect them as a team. After Italy, all parts firing together, he gave his crooked smile and offered them that too. Now, in the bowels of Wembley, all pre-match joy long dissipated, he told them, again, what to do. It was only the English whose respect they did not have now. Not yet anyway.

The light was becoming greyer as the afternoon advanced and yet, sporadically, more golden and luminous. In the tunnel, out of sight but not out of hearing, workmen began preparing the wooden podium on which Dallaglio would receive the glittering prize for England's record fifth Triple Crown win on the trot in their sixth consecutive win over Wales and their twelfth Grand Slam at the end of the Five Nations Championship forever. Did it mean so much? If the podium became a gallows it would. And two minutes into the second half Wales hinted mercilessly at what would indeed come. Howarth's massive hoof into the England half was knocked on by Neil Back, squinting from under his dove-grey helmet and, tetchily, a liability to his side all afternoon. This time Wales used the penalty to go for a try and, controlling the ball through successive scrimmages and breaks in midfield, they sent Jenkins right across the face of a closing English defence. Superbly, the Pontypridd pivot bulleted a huge pin-point cut-out pass to Howarth who strolled over the line. Jenkins, who converted from the touch-line, had had a split second to make the courageous decision. This was a rugby executive. He simply made it.

Everything about Neil Roger Jenkins looked at odds with what he was achieving. He did not look ice-cool: his shirt flapped loose on the side, his thinning ginger hair was plastered against his scalp, he took his gumshield out to snap and snarl, the perspiration ran down his face and he flicked the sweat from his ears. Wales were hanging on by a fingernail and he knew it. All thought of the cold revenge he had exacted on Thomas Castaignède for the drubbing he and Wales had received (51–0) against France the previous year was no comfort now to the man who, at full-back against England at Twickenham in that doleful 1998, had been part of a record 60–26 defeat at English hands. This was not then or there but it was backs-to-the-wall and Jenkins knew more than anyone about that.

It was as if, in the spirit of this remarkable footballer, somehow things were as defensive and awry as they were in the country itself. In the press conference after the stunning win against France the hacks had quizzed him about his, to them, unexpected dummies and runs. He visibly bridled. He had made breaks before, he told them. In the very first season of the Welsh National League, aged nineteen, he had hit the headlines at Stradey Park when, intercepting a pass and, as his autobiography modestly put it, 'showing a turn of speed' he had helped Pontypridd hold Llanelli to a 'highly improbable 10–10 draw'. Improbable, amongst other reasons, because Ponty had seen their second row Jim Scarlett sent off. It was following that dismissal that Jenkins had chosen to announce his arrival in senior rugby and to recall, in 1998, that the 'minutes which followed Jim's dismissal were probably the most significant in my career. We were looking down the barrel and Llanelli came at us with fresh purpose'. He became a Welsh international in that same season. No one felt the lows, and the occasional highs, of the 1990s more than the unassuming man who had stepped out at Wembley that day already Wales's record points scorer. He ended the game with 767 points scored in all internationals and as the second highest points scorer in international rugby of all time.

It was England who were coming at him, today, 'with fresh purpose'. In 1996, for his beloved Pontypridd, it had been Neath. The favourites, Ponty in their second Cup Final in two years and never a winner (defeated by Swansea 19–12 in 1995), had reeled under the western All Black onslaught to 22–9 down with the clock running out. An inspirational 39-year-old captain, the bearded prop Nigel Bezani, had refused to yield to this arm-wrestle and in the most thrilling Welsh Cup Final Pontypridd ran out winners at 29–22. Jenks had been partnered then, and through the decade, by his childhood friend Paul John, the son of Dennis, the club's inspiring guide since 1991. This was all about family. About connections. On the Sardis Road ground Jenkins kicked his kicks and made his runs, against a backdrop of a colliery winding house (defunct), the unfolding hills of the lower Rhondda (penetrated every twenty minutes by a punctuating train) and a river eponymously named Taff (clear enough now for trout). That was real heritage. Crowds flocked here to see French teams braved (Brive) and English champions (Bath) bested. If there was a symbolic team in Wales for 'the people's game' in the 1990s amongst the ruins of management and philistine commercialism, it was Pontypridd, champions themselves, at last, in 1997. And all the while their catalytic force was judged by outsiders to be a journeyman player and dropped or moved seven times as the Welsh fly-half, or in his case, more accurately, as the half outside. Only Graham Henry had had the immediate courage and insight to put him permanently on the inside straight for Wales.

Graham Henry would proudly talk, later, of the character and guts of his team. He knew that his chosen fly-half personified the relished characteristics. The game, however, was swinging away from the metronomic contribution Jenkins had made, the heartbeat that had, yet again, kept Wales alive. The pendulum moved again. Wilkinson hit over a penalty in direct line of the Welsh goal posts. 28–25. England tightened the noose. Only fifteen minutes into the second period and the Welsh lie offside so Jonny Wilkinson takes England to 31–25. Chariots oscillate close to the ground all over Wembley. The Welsh front row do an all change but it is the English, balls clutched and then fumbled, who storm on. In an allegedly dangerous passage of play that looks like Shrove Tuesday folk football in Derbyshire, Tim Rodber, the gifted and immense English second row, is upended and toppled over at a rolling mêlée. Penalty England. And out of reach, beyond three scores. Except that Dallaglio, with less than five minutes left, supremely and with self-assurance ahead of insurance, tells his young centre to find a touch in the Welsh left-hand-side 22. England attack. Wales, all tension and resolve, escape, clear from under their posts. Back towards the half-way line. Gallant, doughty Wales are sinking to defeat. Consolation prizes are being offered: Jenkins is named man-of-the-match.

Not yet. Not quite. In open play Rodber tackles Colin Charvis's face with his shoulder and fractures the Welshman's cheekbone. The ensuing penalty allows Jenkins to clear to touch upfield for one last effort. Full-time has been played but at a three-man line-out on the right-hand touch-line in the English 22 the bounding Wyatt takes a two-handed catch and throws to Howley who passes to Scott Quinnell standing out to break the line as Wales had attempted before. He shuttles sideways juggling the ball uneasily and so unsettling the drift English defence. And suddenly, coming in fast on a slanting run is Scott Gibbs.

If Jenkins is the beating heart of this team, Gibbs is its mind. The soul thing he will leave to the crowd. He, too, has been in the eye of the storm before. His trick is to pretend, to himself and to others, that it is all about the individual self – on and off the field of play – and that just being a professional is what matters. When in April 1994 he left Swansea for that other St Helens, and rugby league, he was shamefully called a 'rugby prostitute' by the chairman of the club which, at the end of the 1999 season, as another kind of rebel, he will captain to a Welsh Cup victory by a record score against 'loyal' Llanelli. Yet this loner was the clear leader of the Lions in South Africa in 1997. More redolent of this than his ferocious dumping of Os du Randt was his televised exhortation to his gathered team-mates in the crucial Second Test to raise their game, higher and yet higher. They did. Neil Jenkins with whom he had debuted for both the Welsh Youth and the Wales XV had kicked fifteen points, as many as South Africa managed altogether, in the Lions' 18–15 win.

Gibbs and Jenkins were neither a pair of builders nor a firm of solicitors. They were not even alike, physically or socially, except in several vital respects. They were born in the 1970s just as the Welsh world whose apex rugby had seemed to be was disappearing. They grew up on frustration not fulfilment. They had to make their own history if they were not to be the parasites of others' memories. Heritage meant nothing to them. The present was theirs to shape. Scott Gibbs toughened himself mentally against Welsh sentimentality and physically hardened himself in rugby league. He grew in every sense. In the modern era the close, popular appeal that Jenkins epitomized but only found in Pontypridd was the soul put at risk by moneyed, managed, so-called professional Welsh rugby; the heart of the game was none the less, only to be kept alive by a hard-headed understanding that the modern world had altered the stakes and the rest was propaganda. Gibbs could not wait for Welsh rugby to save itself, if ever, by restructuring root and branch. He did it for himself. But, thereby, he was doing it beyond himself, binding the bobble hats and the bourgeoisie in the only possible salvation. For if pits could close and communities shrivel so could clubs shrink and rugby die. How much would that mean? Well, in a populist sense, Wales itself. A National Assembly could be chosen (in 1997 by just 50 per cent of the Welsh population) and elected (in 1999 by rather less than 50 per cent), but if it could not fill the cultural space it inhabited by entering the Welsh imagination it would have no tenable hold on the Welsh future. Gibbs was a patriot beyond politics.

In a slight lull in play just before he scored he had eyed up his Lions colleague the fourteen-times English captain Lawrence Bruno Nero Dallaglio. The drummer from Pencoed sang out, loudly enough to have Lawrence scratch his head:

I feel good. I feel good tonight . . . I feel good.

Then we all did.

He took the ball from Quinnell on the burst to brush past a shell-shocked Rodber. The side-step, more baffling than the rubic cube he resembled, had just begun. Matt Dawson's ankle grab was walked out of; Matt Perry was bamboozled in mid-air by Gibbs's own special re-run of Walt Disney's *Fantasia*, as a balletic Welsh elephant; and the despairing Hanley was sent one way whilst Gibbs left by the other exit. He even saluted with a triumphantly raised fist as he galumphed his 15 stones over the line. 31–30. To England. The Welsh centre gave the bedraggled Jenkins the ball. 'I had no doubts . . . He'd kick those over in his sleep, left-footed, wouldn't he?' Gibbs said later. Unlike Jonny without-an-aitch Wilkinson, Neil without-an-aitch Jenkins was a right-footed kicker. So, as it had been an hour or so earlier for his counterpart, it was the wrong side of the pitch for him.

The ritual began. The sandcastle was made. The ball placed at an angle and the foot aligned. Then, five steps, one rather tentatively done as ever, back, before three taken, within an increasing and easy arc to his left side. The foot had been wiped on his calf. Imaginary mud is picked from the sole of the boot. The kicker bows to the ball. He stares at it and up, away to the posts, at it. Eyes down again, and up. It becomes shamanistic. The left hand swiped down the jersey, the right shaken loose, its fingers distended in a paroxysm, all the time the eyes moving from ball to posts, then the object imaginatively ushered in by the back-to-front sweep of an open palm. This eternity of preparation takes hardly any time at all before he runs and, as he says, 'boots it between the sticks'. 32–31. To Wales. We lead for the first and only time in the match. For the last time too. England are played out.

In the last couple of despairing scrums the vaunted English pack cannot reassert control. Garin Jenkins, with forty-two games Wales's most-capped hooker and now solidly propped by Peter Rogers and Ben Evans, was clear that their earlier shove had gone – 'At the end they were blowing through their arses'. Soon, some strategically placed chariots would prevent even that. Already Welsh wits were penning a new version of *Delilah* to the syllabically equivalent *Dallaglio*:

> I saw the light on the day that we played them at Wembley
> I saw the England Grand Slam slip out of their grasp
>
> Scotty ran past them
> Then as he went over I watched and went out of my mind
>
> My, my, my, Dallaglio (shove your chariots up your arse)
> Why, why, why, Dallaglio (shove your chariots up your arse)
> I could see that Jenks was so good for me
> But Henry's the main man, a god, I'm sure you'll agree . . .

Kicks have decided games before. None more so than John Taylor's in Murrayfield in 1971, 19–18 to Wales, when Neil Jenkins was still kicking in the womb. A decade of glory followed. It may be that Wembley 1999's famous kick will not bring the same, but it confirmed that the pulsating upset in Paris, followed by a runaway 60–21 victory in Italy, was no moment of madness. By June 1999 Wales had won six successive international matches for the first time since 1977–8. In so doing they finally exorcized the 35-year-old ghost of previous fruitless visits to the southern hemisphere by winning a Test series 2–0 in Argentina, where Neil Jenkins took his own total to more than 800 points. The reigning world champions, South Africa, posed, at the inauguration of a partially complete Millennium Stadium in late June, an even more formidable challenge than had the Pumas on the pampas, but it was one magnificently overcome in a first-ever Welsh victory over the Springboks (29–19). Further victories in August over Canada and France, once again at the receiving end of thirty-four points, made it eight consecutive wins as Wales went into the World Cup buoyed up on a swell tide of public and media expectation.

Pessimists – maybe they are realists – worry that behind the eye-catching front window of Graham Henry's senior squad, the interior cupboards are thinly stocked, the furnishings a trifle threadbare. But it is worth considering how in 1999, the false dawn of 1988 cannot be simply repeated. Not all has changed for the worse. Professional rugby league will not be a predator any more; rugby's lasting hold on Welsh affections, win or lose, is now amply testified; the ability of Welsh players, as individuals, to survive and prosper at the highest levels is not in doubt even if a larger doubt lingers.

And this is, principally, the chronic disunity in the game, a product of a sport's structure which once fitted and no longer does the social reality of a particular society and its aspirations. The social integument of Wales has changed. Its new institutions must reflect that deep change and in rugby terms too, aspirations, to be successful, will inevitably be subsumed by the larger reality and image of Wales. Graham Henry sees both the regional dream of Ray Williams and the traditions of great Welsh clubs secured in the concept of four or five 'super' clubs. It is, for sure, a way forward for Welsh rugby to claim once more a rightful place on the fields of praise, but only if Wales itself really means more than anything else. The alternative, for sure, is retreat from those fields forever.

# INDEX